D1422594

04138911

GARDEN DIY

GARDEN
DIY

Chris Maton · Mark Edwards · Richard Key · Toby Buckland

MURDOCH BOOKS

Contents

WATER FEATURES

Chris Maton and Mark Edwards

planning your water feature

your garden WATER FEATURE

A well designed water feature is likely to be the focal point of a garden. It therefore gives you the ideal opportunity to create a feature that revitalises your existing space or, if you are redesigning the whole garden, provides you with a stylish starting point to plan around. The following pages explain how to transform creative ideas into stunning water features.

You can enhance your garden with a beautiful, well designed pond.

Water features are added to gardens for all sorts of reasons. Even if you are very happy with your garden you can use a feature to highlight a particular area or to link two parts of your garden together.

Whatever reason you have for wanting to place a water feature in your garden, there are some simple points to consider that will help you decide which feature is most appropriate for your space. The process of elimination works well here. By looking at the site logically you can easily come up with a few suitable choices.

This book takes you through all the stages of planning, design and construction — removing the pitfalls commonly associated with the selection and practical inclusion of water in the garden.

Using this book

The information and projects covered in this book will inspire and challenge the conventional ideas surrounding water feature design and construction. Although natural features are included here, the majority of our gardens are just too small to incorporate this style with any conviction. This book therefore uses more realistic features that can be included in all our modern-day gardens.

The first section covers the basic information that you will need to plan and complete your project, from how to find the style that most suits you and your specific site through to practical knowledge of how to ensure that your feature is safe for children.

Correct construction is as essential as a suitable design as it will prevent unnecessary water leaks and allow the project to stand the test of time. All of the know-how you will need to do this is given. There is no such thing as a maintenance-free water feature and so this section also covers ways that you can keep your new feature looking good and working well throughout the seasons.

The main section of the book looks at 20 practical and inspirational features that represent distinct styles of construction for all the various types of gardens. Diverse subjects include fountains, springs and spouts, waterfalls and mini-projects for smaller gardens. The construction of these designs is clearly explained using step-by-step photography. Incorporated into these sections are practical techniques as well as some alternative material suggestions that may suit your style or preferences more closely. These should also inspire you to use your own creativity to tailor the basic project ideas to your own specific space.

Before you begin

Even before you start the practical part of the project, you will need to establish the type of skills you require to complete the feature. Water features are different from many other garden features as almost all of them require more than one skill. This does not mean that you shouldn't tackle a water feature yourself but you should look realistically at your repertoire. If you are in any doubt about the tasks ahead, contact your local tradespeople as they will be able to help with the parts that you feel less confident about. Always ensure that you get several quotes and build these into the overall project budget.

Take a look at the area around the site where you plan to build the feature, as there may be other areas that you need to plant and pave in order to create the cohesive design you are after. Occasionally, you may need an extra pair of hands to lift heavy objects – bear this in mind when you plan the project.

Budgetary requirements

It is surprising how the cost of garden projects can accumulate. Water features predominantly involve hard landscaping, which is the most expensive part of any garden in terms of both labour and materials. However, careful planning can prevent any nasty shocks. Materials and tool hire will absorb most of your budget and, if you need to bring in specialist labour, such as an electrician, you must make allowances for this.

It is vital to plan methodically, making lists of materials, labour requirements and any possible tool hire you may need. Then you can adjust costs where necessary. For example, look at the materials you have chosen to use as there may be cheaper options available; you could use reproduction stone instead of natural, or replace second-hand bricks with modern imitations. If you are installing a small feature, solar pumps will eliminate the need for an electrician and an excavated, lined pool with cleverly planted edges will be far more cost effective than one constructed from rendered blocks.

Finding unusual materials

Inspiration for water features is all around you. Take a look at books or magazines and visit garden shows to give you ideas. Specialist aquatic centres, for example, sell an ever-expanding range of products, but avoid the temptation to impulse buy as this often results in taking products home that will not actually suit the garden. There is a huge range of water features and associated materials available on the Internet too, and these are generally cheaper because the site does not have any shop overheads to pay.

You can stumble across amazing one-off items for reservoirs or water chutes by visiting your local salvage yard. By combining these older artifacts with much more contemporary materials, such as glass tiles, you can create a personalised water feature that specifically suits your taste and garden. Scrap metal yards are also useful places to look if you want to experiment with abstract materials. It may be a weird-looking spout that enlivens the look of your feature and helps it spring to life …

Materials should be chosen to reflect your budget.

Tiles can be used to great effect in water features.

designing YOUR FEATURE

Exciting and dynamic, water dramatically changes the mood and atmosphere of a garden; you should therefore take your time when choosing the style and position of your feature. Consider its shape, size and finished level and try to keep it simple – over-complicated designs tend to be at odds with a garden while a simple design blends in much more easily.

Style

The style of water feature you choose will depend on you – your likes and dislikes, passions and personal experiences relating to water. You may remember a beautiful rambling stream from a country visit or a stunning formal pool seen on a recent holiday. There are many ways to take these images and personalise the ideas behind them to create your own feature. Be bold and express yourself.

In general, the style of water features falls into two main categories: formal and informal. Perhaps the easier to achieve, formal features link more convincingly with the house and surrounding built features of a garden. This gives you opportunities to experiment with abstract materials

An informal pond in a natural setting.

and ideas, to create a strong architectural presence. Informal designs are better suited further away from the building, where planting and nature can interact without the dominance of the house.

Position

If you are redesigning your whole garden it is important to tackle the question of where to place the water feature early on. If you have an area in the garden that just needs a visual lift, some important questions need to be answered before you begin. The following factors are the kinds of things to consider when choosing the final position.

Trees and buildings

Are there large trees in your garden (or a neighbour's garden) that may shade your water feature during the day or have roots that could damage the foundations of your feature? Fallen leaves and poisonous berries will pollute the water and poison fish, so think about the species of plants that exist around the area and those you may want to introduce.

Most pools and ponds will need a minimum of half a day's sunlight for oxygenating plants to perform their job. If this is unlikely given the position, filters can be used (see pages 18-19)

Urban gardens are also affected by tall neighbouring buildings, which cast heavy shade over much of the garden, but fountains and moving water will help the oxygenating process in such

Moving water helps the oxygenating process.

a situation. Take a note of the shade position every couple of hours during a whole day by marking the shadows with canes, and then do a rough sketch of the garden to find potential sites based on the results.

Views

Make the most of what's on offer by positioning your feature to get the best views from the house and within the garden. Think about which room you view the garden from most or decide if you want to screen the feature from the house for a sense of mystery when you are in the garden.

If you would like to see the reflection of a tree or building on the water's surface from a particular viewing position then try laying a mirror on the ground in order to locate the reflection. It helps to position some canes or pots in the potential area and then to leave them in place for a few days. See how you feel about where the reflection appears and adjust or move the intended site if you are not entirely happy. Remember that once the feature has been constructed there is no going back, so take your time when choosing the site.

Existing site

Make a note of access holes, services and outside taps. If you are in any doubt about locating these, contact your service supplier for engineers to confirm the positions. They will also locate any cables and pipes that may interfere with excavations.

If you have a windy site it can make sitting in the area uncomfortable and also completely ruin delicate spray patterns and filmy waterfalls. If you have to place your feature in such a site then think about filtering the wind with planting or a creative screen or backdrop.

Decide which existing features you wish to keep as you may find that your preferred water feature clashes with some of them. This applies particularly to upright water feature designs, which look very contemporary. If you place one right next to a traditional pergola it will look at odds with it.

Compacted and rocky soil will make serious work of any large-scale

excavations needed for pools and ponds, so if your site is hard or rocky a wall fountain may be more appropriate. You should dig a 600mm (2ft) deep test hole to look at the natural water table. If the level is high, it may cause flexible liners to billow up. This can be overcome by placing heavy slabs on the area, but it is better to relocate the feature or choose another style as trying to control ground water levels can be costly and time-consuming.

To help you when you come to choose plants to complement the feature, make a note of the pH levels in the surrounding soil.

Think about the shortest route for an electricity supply from the house, garage or shed – do you need to chisel out huge amounts of concrete to get to the feature? Consult a qualified electrician for advice on such electrical matters.

Material choice

It cannot be emphasised enough how much your choice of materials will influence the look of your feature. When deciding on what to use look at the durability of the product and how it ages – natural stone, for example, wears more sympathetically than concrete. The cost will of course be an important influence on your final choice but try to buy at the top end of your budget as your feature will then look more professional and stand the test of time.

Also look to your site to give you ideas – materials such as brick walls and flagstones already in the garden will work well in your feature too. You can also look beyond your own garden boundaries to materials from the local environment.

Safety

Water seems to have a magnetic quality for children so safety is extremely important. There are some points to remember if the two are definitely going to meet.

Choose features that can be covered with a grid and a layer of cobbles, such as wall fountains, springs and cascades. If you decide to construct a raised pool then build the walls at least 600mm (2ft) high and overhang coping stones. If you really want an open water feature, make sure that the garden you create has a separated area with childproof locks.

A raised pool with a tiled, overhung edge.

As an extra precaution use a grid just under the water's surface, strong enough to support a child's weight.

Make pool edges as safe as possible by using heavy marginal planting to create a physical barrier. A shallow, gravel-edged feature is safe because of the gentle gradients to the edge.

Natural stone is prone to slime up, whereas concrete flags provide a much better grip and so are more appropriate. You should also check that edging stones or copings are well laid and mortared to prevent tipping.

planning AND ESTIMATING

By carefully planning your water feature you will ensure that you don't encounter any nasty surprises during its construction. Once the design and style of your feature have been chosen, you will need to break the project down and think seriously about all the practical implications: these range from ordering a specialist component to dealing with poor weather.

Estimating time

It is sensible to double the amount of time you think you will need for the planning and construction of your water feature as this gives a more realistic time period. Remember you must add all the ordering, visits to suppliers and general phone calls to your estimate.

You should also make allowances for unforeseen events such as machinery breakdowns or the odd downpour that floods your garden. There will be other factors beyond your control, such as how booked up a trades-person is (if you need specialist labour). Also bear in mind that it takes time to set things up in the morning and tidy the site at the end the day.

If you allow yourself extra time in the planning stages then you can relax and enjoy the job. This should also ensure that you finish on time (or even early), instead of rushing around getting worked up and frustrated.

Estimating tool and material requirements

Establishing the quantities of materials you need early on will give you a good idea of how much your feature will cost. Do this at the planning stage to avoid wasting time and money.

Make a thorough list of the materials needed and find out when your chosen supplier can deliver.

Delivery times range from a couple of days after ordering for general cement and sand, and up to four to six weeks for more specialist items that need to be made to your specifications. Suppliers are generally willing to help quantify materials. If you give them a sketch and some rough sizes they should be able to help you.

Concrete

Concrete is usually measured as a volume so, in order to calculate how much you want, you need to know what the area of the base is and then multiply that by the depth of concrete. Unless you are ordering a huge amount you can probably mix your own using pre-mixed bags of concrete from landscape supply yards. You can also mix your own concrete by using 1 part cement, 2 parts sharp sand and 4 parts blue metal. Mix them dry first and then add water.

Cement can be stored on a pallet in a shed or garage. Sand and metal can be bought in bags or bulk, and can be stored outside.

Bricks and blocks

These materials are measured by calculating the number needed per square metre (or yard), so establish the area of the wall you wish to build and multiply by the number of bricks or blocks per square metre. For example, for a single brick wall you will need 50 bricks per square metre. For a concrete block wall you will need 12½ blocks per square metre.

Bricks and blocks should always be safely stacked on pallets then covered with plastic until they are used.

Mortars

Used for rendering or brick laying and block laying, mortars are made up of cement, sand and water. An additive is often also used to help with the workability of the mortar.

Store sand on a flat surface, separated from stony ballast, as it can be annoying to keep fishing out stones from your rendering or bricklaying mix. Some sand can stain driveways so a plastic sheet underneath is advisable.

Mortar mixes

The following mixes are recommended.

Brick laying and block laying below ground: 1 part cement, 3 or 4 parts sand

Brick laying and block laying above ground: 1 part cement, 6 parts sand

Rendering walls: 1 part cement, 1 part lime, 4 parts sand

Rendering pools: 1 part cement, 1 part lime, 3 parts sand

Rigid and flexible liners

These cross-sections show two different ways to waterproof reservoirs. The right-hand one is a rigid construction and the left a flexible liner.

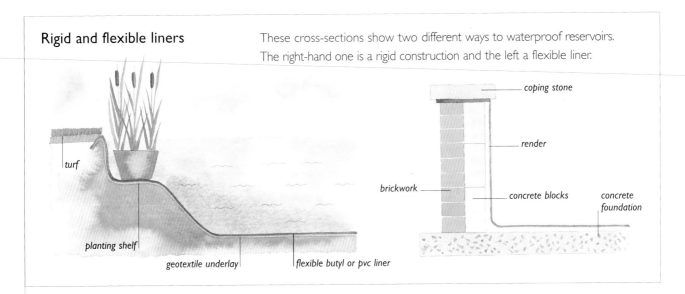

turf

planting shelf

geotextile underlay

flexible butyl or pvc liner

coping stone

render

brickwork

concrete blocks

concrete foundation

Pointing

This is the process of filling the joints in paving and brickwork to achieve a weatherproof, attractive appearance. Brick joints are pointed with a mix of 1 part cement to 4 or 5 parts building or soft washed sand, whereas paving mortar is slightly stronger. This has a ratio of 1:3 and is a dryish mix.

Timber

Try to order pressure-treated timber for any exterior use, though this may not be possible when you are using planed or one-off sizes, which will need treating with clear or coloured preservative at some stage. Order timber by the linear metre (or foot), and store it on a flat surface in a dry or covered storage area.

Specialist products

Some of the water features in this book have components that need to be ordered from more unusual suppliers such as stone merchants. These need ordering weeks in advance. Also, remember to take into account that one-off items from salvage yards may need cleaning before being used.

Tool hire

There will inevitably be some hire tools on your shopping list, and it is best to book them a few weeks in advance. When you collect a tool, make sure you pay close attention to the safety information.

Reservoirs

Every water feature has a reservoir of some description that the main body of water is held in and pumped from. There are many ways to create one but here are two basic techniques.

Rigid construction

Used for many formal pools, the strength and durability of this style of construction gives you a number of alternatives as it can be incorporated into raised pools, multiple cascades or a simple ground level reflective pool. The cost of construction is high because you may need specialist labour and building materials.

Flexible lined pools and ponds

Flexible liners are mainly used in naturalised ponds. They obviously cost much less than the rigid constructions do because there is no need for concrete, bricks and mortar.

Liners are available in different grades but it is worth spending as much as you can afford on a quality one as this will save you from costly repair bills later on. Less expensive materials tend to degrade and become brittle due to UV rays present in sunlight. Ask your local supplier's advice and ensure the item you buy has a 10–15 year guarantee.

Calculating liners and underlay

The size of the liner and underlay that you will need can be calculated by adding twice the depth of the pool to the length and to the width. You should then add a tolerance of 300mm (1ft) to these figures.

So, for a pool measuring 3.6 × 2.2m (12 × 7⅓ft) and 700mm (2⅓ft) deep, the calculation would be:

700mm (2⅓ft) × 2 = 1.4m (4⅔ft)
+ Length of 3.6m (12ft)
+ Tolerance of 300mm (1ft)
= 5.3m (17¾ft) length

700mm (2⅓ft) × 2 = 1.4m (4⅔ft)
+ Width of 2.2m (7⅓ft)
+ Tolerance of 300mm (1ft)
= 3.9m (13ft) width

setting out
AND MARKING LEVELS

Once you have picked your water feature and have quantified and estimated the project, you are ready to start the physical work. Some initial clearance of debris and overgrown foliage may be required to help you see the entire area, to establish surrounding levels and to set out the outline for your excavations – which is a vital part of the process.

Using the 3,4,5 method

There is a quick and easy method to create a perfect rectangle or square. Once you know it, you can mark out anything from a set of coping stones above a sunken pool right through to a football pitch – this is the 3, 4, 5 method.

1 You can carry out 90 per cent of all your setting out by creating a 90° angle. Start by making a base string line that is 1m (3ft) longer than the proposed excavation, which can then be referred to at any time. You can eventually use this line to mark the front of your water feature, so check it is facing the right way and that you are happy with the position. Fix a peg at each end of the line and pull the string tight between them.

2 The width of the excavation can be marked on the base line by driving in two extra pegs. Make up a large timber square with the length of the sides being multiples of 3, 4 and 5. Usually a square measuring 900, 1200 and 1500mm (3, 4 and 5ft) is adequate. The square should be placed on the base line at your excavation peg to give you your 90° offset. Now mark the excavation length along this line using string and a peg.

3 Repeat this process beside the other peg on the base line in order to form a parallel string line. You can then finish off the rectangle by fixing a taut line to the remaining side. Next, check that each side is correctly measured and that the diagonals are equal.

4 Spread a line of sand beneath the string lines so that you can remove all string before excavating. It is useful to extend the string outside the area so that you can drive in reference pegs. Afterwards, the string lines can be used to set out other heights or lengths.

Marking out a circle

You may need to mark out circles or segments of circles when setting out the feature. It is quite straightforward – just locate your centre point first.

1 Unless you have a scaled plan with your feature plotted on paper, you will need to establish where the pool is going on your site. Insert a cane in the centre of the area for the proposed pool and slip a tape over the end of the cane. Check that the radius will fit the plot. Adjust if needed.

2 Tie a screwdriver to the tape. Scribe the surface, using a sand line or spray paint for extra definition as necessary.

Irregular shapes

If you are constructing a wildlife or naturalistic pond, irregular and free-flowing shapes will blend in better than will hard geometric lines. These shapes are sometimes difficult to get right so it pays to take some time to achieve the best looking form for your site.

Once your area is cleared of all debris and obstructions, lay a hose or some canes placed at 1m (3ft) centres around the perimeter of your pond. Don't worry about getting it absolutely perfect at the moment. Have a walk around and see if the shape works for your plot and check that there is enough room around the margins for planting and for maintenance tasks. To do this, try to get a bird's eye view of the pond either from inside the house or up a ladder. This will also give you a better idea of the scale and position of the feature within its location. It will show up any tight curves that are difficult to build and anything that looks at odds in a natural environment. As a rule, try to keep curves soft and long.

Make any adjustments to the pond and doublecheck the shape – you can now lay a thin line of sand to join up the canes or replace the hose line.

Site clearance

Your project will undoubtedly involve a certain amount of clearance as existing rubble and vegetation will need to be removed from the site. If you plan to install a pool or feature in an existing patio, make sure that you carefully cut the stone work with a diamond-tipped masonry blade.

A large natural pond may require the use of an excavator, so you should check the site for access as you may need to cover some areas of the garden with boards in order to protect the soil when you bring the excavator in. Even if you do not have machinery on site, a lot of serious damage can be caused to the soil structure and surrounding areas simply by walking on it, especially in wet weather conditions. Therefore avoid digging in these particular conditions. Valuable topsoil should be stored for use at a later date once it is stripped.

Levels

The height of a water feature generally relates to its surrounding ground level. Therefore, once the feature has been set out, a datum or reference peg can be installed 500–1000mm (1¾–3ft) away from any excavations.

Using a lump hammer, knock the peg into the ground making sure it is upright and stable. The length of the peg will depend on the height of the feature. Once the peg is in position you will need to mark off against the peg the height of foundations, final paving or gravel finishes.

As you build your feature make sure you check against the datum peg to ensure the accuracy of your work.

Place a datum peg next to your excavations.

pumps AND FILTERS

You will find a vast selection of pumps filters and associated fittings for every imaginable type of water feature at most nurseries and aquarium and pond suppliers. Rather than spend hours looking through the sometimes mind-boggling product information, you should visit your supplier armed with specific information regarding your water feature.

Buying equipment

Choosing the right pumps and filters can be quite daunting if you have never done it before, as well as costly. Once you have decided on your feature, make a sketch of what you want and write down various facts about the feature. Then talk to your local supplier and they will advise on technical issues such as pump capacity and type. In order to help the supplier find you the right pump and fittings it is a good idea to ask yourself the following questions beforehand: what is the size of your pool or feature (i.e. the volume of water to be circulated)? What height do you want your water jet (fountain) to be? What is the difference in height between the pump and the outlet

A submersible pump for recirculating water.

(head of water)? Will the pump be working continuously or intermittently?

Introducing pumps

There are two types of pumps available, submersible and surface pumps. The efficiency and cheap running costs of submersibles means that 99 per cent of all water features use this type. Surface-mounted pumps are mainly used in swimming pools, major commercial water features and in situations where large volumes need to be circulated. They can be noisy and need to be placed in a dry, ventilated, purpose-made housing, which creates more work, expense and complicated pipework.

It is a good idea to buy a pump that has a flow adjuster built into it. Alternatively, you can connect a flow valve on an outlet hose close to the pump. This adjustable pump gives you the option of fine tuning the amount of water that is being moved, which is especially useful for wall features and fountains.

Filters

In natural and many minimalist designs the key to achieving a successful feature is the clarity of the water. One of the main causes of frustration with still water is its tendency to cloud over and stagnate. Bacteria, algae and

waste products do build up quickly and affect water quality.

There are many chemical products that clear the water for a few weeks, but the water will need re-dosing, which becomes expensive in the long term and is not a particularly pleasant task. Although seen as an unnecessary initial expense, a filter is therefore often more appropriate. Filtration can also be used to aid the natural oxygenating quality of plants, especially in the first couple of years when a pond is establishing its own in-built eco-system.

A filter works by slowly recycling the body of water. This can be carried out intermittently or continuously depending on the size and type of feature. The pump simply pumps

A bio-media filtration unit removes algae.

water within the pool to the top of a filter unit. The water then passes through fine layers of bio-media, which purify the water, and then returns to the pool via an outlet at the base of the unit. Gravity is used to return the water, so the filter will need to be placed at a minimum of 500mm (1³⁄₄ft) above the pool. Filtration units are not very attractive, so think about screening yours with plants or some other form of trellis or fencing.

If additional clarity is needed, for example in a reflection pool or koi pond, the use of a UV (ultraviolet) clarifier is recommended. This can be attached to the side of the filter. The water then passes into the UV unit where ultraviolet radiation makes algae clump together so it can be strained out by the filter.

Electricity

Unless you are using a solar pump, which is really only suitable for small features because of its low output, you will need to have electricity installed at some stage. This is a great opportunity to install a switched main (a power cable that travels around the whole of the garden), particularly if you are designing your garden from scratch. Not only does it make it easier to plan the route and dig trenches, it gives you the scope to introduce lighting and so add another dimension to the garden. Any cable in the ground should either be armoured or laid in conduit and be placed at least 600mm (2ft) down so that it is out of the reach of forks and spades. Cables laid under paving need ducting for protection and to allow you to replace them should you need to in the future.

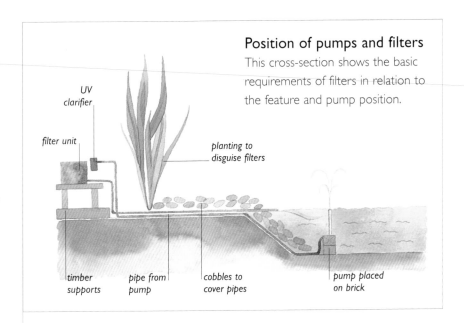

Position of pumps and filters
This cross-section shows the basic requirements of filters in relation to the feature and pump position.

UV clarifier

filter unit

planting to disguise filters

timber supports

pipe from pump

cobbles to cover pipes

pump placed on brick

If you are placing the water feature close to the house, the electrical feed can be run from the nearest socket indoors. If you do this, you will need a circuit breaker before it leaves the house in order to meet legal and safety requirements. Low voltage pumps are available for small features and fountains but you will need a transformer to reduce the power and make them safe for use outdoors. This should be placed next to the socket.

It is essential that all connections are carried out professionally because of the safety implications. Therefore you must employ a qualified electrician for this part of the project.

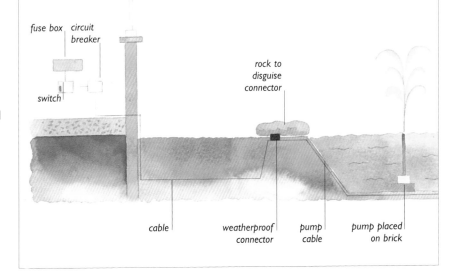

Installing cabling for a water feature
This cross-section explains how cabling is run from a house to a water feature. Always employ a qualified electrician to complete this part of the project.

fuse box   circuit breaker

switch

rock to disguise connector

cable

weatherproof connector

pump cable

pump placed on brick

planting and LIGHTING

Planting can make all the difference to your project, by enhancing it and creating connections to other parts of the garden. Water features also lend themselves beautifully to the subtle and sometimes magical effects that you can create with the right lighting. Both the features themselves and surrounding plants can be transformed into dramatic shapes at night.

Planting around water features

The water feature will be the focus of attention within the garden, so neighbouring plants should complement and enhance rather than dominate. A good rule of thumb is to keep things simple. When planting around any water feature use bold clumps and few species. This works far better than a confusing mixed bag of many varieties. Try to use a higher proportion of evergreen plants such as *Prunus lusitanica*, which will create a stable framework around the feature, especially during winter.

In small gardens, where the water feature is close to a boundary, allow an area for planting directly behind it. This will create a backdrop that will direct your view to the water feature rather than the boundary. Partially screening the front of water features with slender strap-like plants can create a feeling of mystery.

Planting in water

The balance and clarity of a natural pond relies greatly on a diverse range of plants. Plant categories for ponds are arranged by the conditions each type prefers.

Deep-water aquatics Plants such as lilies can be placed in aquatic baskets in deep, central parts of the pool. They have their roots at the bottom of the pool and their leaves float on the surface. They are ideal for reducing algae growth in the pond as they cut down the sunlight that algae needs to thrive. Aim to cover around half of the water's surface with such plants.

Waterlilies are deep-water aquatic plants.

Submerged plants Plants such as *Myriophyllum* spp. are also planted in deep areas and are most important for oxygenating and preventing water stagnation. They compete with algae for sunlight and nutrients and also helpfully exchange carbon dioxide for oxygen.

Marginal plants Plants such as some iris species are placed on shelves within aquatic baskets where their roots should stay wet and their foliage should be above the water line.

Planting styles

Your feature will dictate the style of planting you choose. Formal pools and fountains benefit from clipped evergreen planting, perhaps in the form of a surrounding hedge or topiary strategically placed to balance the geometry. If you are creating a minimalist, contemporary pool, use a single specimen or stick to a single species en masse to keep the style clean. Informal designs lend themselves to more herbaceous planting.

Reflections

Plants form intriguing compositions when mirrored on water. Single specimen planting looks dramatic if reflected on still clear pools. Grasses look really at home when planted in drifts around the edge.

The sun's reflection can actually create hostile conditions for plants as it kicks back sunlight onto the underside of delicate leaves, causing them to scorch and loose excessive amounts of water. If your feature is in a sunny spot, include grey- and silver-leafed planting as this can cope better with harsh reflected light.

Lighting techniques

Subtlety is everything in lighting – the football stadium technique, while great for stopping intruders, can be a bit much for the average garden. Whether you choose a single, well directed beam or dozens of randomly placed candles and tea lights, the result will be far more satisfying.

Pools and ponds

Still, dark water has the ability to duplicate any surrounding planting by reflection. In the same way, it can also amplify the size of background walls and other architectural features. The key here is to uplight the subject using discreetly positioned spotlights, keeping the angle of the beam low. This casts long shadows that provide depth and texture, as well as enhancing a plant's architectural structure. You can also place the light source directly behind a plant to silhouette it across the water's surface. Shining light straight onto still water, however, causes glare; it is better to downlight the pool.

When placing lighting under water remember that everything will be illuminated – including rocks, plants and pumps. If your water lacks clarity, your pool may resemble primeval soup. Underwater fittings can also become grimy, which reduces their

Lighting by water can be extremely effective.

effectiveness, so they do need regular cleaning. Position them on the perimeter facing the centre to make sure they are accessible for cleaning.

Fountains, springs and moving water

Jets and fountains can be lit in several ways. An upward-angled spotlight from the side catches the movement of water beautifully. Place the fitting within adjacent borders or behind strategically placed pots, as the idea is to see the effect rather than the fitting.

If you are after sheer drama, luminous effects can be achieved by placing lamps below fountains and behind waterfalls. The use of a tight beam shining upwards, placed just under the surface, creates the illusion of light clinging to the water. When using this technique, it helps to keep the background as dark as possible.

Practical considerations

When using lighting in and around a water feature there are many practical points that need addressing.

Cables and switches

Most lighting schemes can be run off the cable used for the pump. It is best to install five-cored cabling in the conduit as the pump and lighting can then be used independently, which is important if the lighting is to be tackled later on. It is a good idea to position switches inside the house as this is much more convenient in the winter, or when you want to see the feature lit in the evenings.

As with all external wiring, circuit breakers are needed and any cables in the ground need to be armoured and placed in a trench at least 600mm (2ft) below ground level. You must get a qualified electrician to do this.

What type of lighting?

Manufacturers have realised the huge market in outdoor lighting due to the increasing desire of people to use their garden at nighttime. They now produce an ever-increasing range.

Low voltage Operating through a transformer, these lights are excellent if you have a paved courtyard and need an alternative to chiselling out lots of thick concrete. However, if the lights are positioned too far away from the transformer, the voltage drop results in reduced performance; this means they best suit smaller gardens.

Mains If you want to have larger lighting schemes, or wish to view your feature from a distance, then use your mains supply to give you greater illuminating power. The extra capacity allows you to uplight trees and use multiple lights to create subtle effects.

Fibre-optics These lights also run off the mains. The light source comes from a bright projector lamp inside a box, which should be positioned discreetly outside the water feature. The light then travels along flexible single or multiple fibre-optic rods. Because the rods are flexible, you can bend and position the light source.

Products

Try to choose fittings that are dark and have a matt finish as these are easier to conceal and often less expensive. If there is no way of hiding the fitting, it best to use high-quality units made from brass, copper or brushed stainless steel.

Coloured lamps and bulbs, while initially attention grabbing, soon become tiresome. Plants and water absorb and reflect white light much better (depending on the surface), giving clean, simple, professional results.

good WORKING PRACTICE

The smooth running of a project involves very careful planning so that you have everything where you need it before you begin. It will also ensure that you and your family are safe while you construct your exciting project. And, once built, your water feature will need to be kept looking its best through regular maintenance.

Safety

Speak to anyone working in the landscaping industry and you will hear tales of chronic back problems and minor injuries. There are many ways you can prevent them from happening to you.

Before you start work, do a quick risk assessment of the day's work to open your eyes to potential hazards. Think about who is at risk, what jobs you are going to carry out and the tools that will be used. Finally assess how you can minimise any risks.

Poor lifting technique causes most back injuries. So when you are lifting a heavy object crouch down, lift using your legs and keep your back straight. Try to keep the object as close to your body as possible and avoid

Make sure you lift heavy objects properly.

twisting your back. Have a slow stretch before you start work and avoid jobs that involve lifting huge weights straight away – warm up first.

Make sure that you have protective clothing – steel-capped boots, overalls and strong gloves will be useful in most construction projects. Tie back long hair and always use goggles, ear muffs and breathing masks when cutting stone and metal.

When using any electrical equipment use a circuit breaker for your own and your property's protection. Unless solar powered, most water features require electrical work at some stage, so use a qualified electrician.

It is likely that your project will be the centre of attention in the garden while it is being constructed, especially if you have children, so keep an eye on all sharp tools and electrical equipment and lock such objects away at night. As you will have excavations and holes to start with, make sure that they are covered with strong boards each night, and cordon off the area.

Materials

You should try to store materials as near as you can to where you will use them when building your water feature. Also avoid handling materials

more than once as this takes time and increases the chances of damage. Always stack bricks, blocks and timber safely on flat areas and preferably cover them with plastic as they will then be clean and easy to use.

Ensure that materials are stacked on flat areas.

It is unlikely that you will need huge amounts of sand and aggregate so order them in 40kg (88lb) bags and try to store them off the ground. If you are using loose deliveries, tip them onto some ply sheeting or a hard-standing area, but cover the area with plastic first as some sands stain. Segregate different sands to keep the correct consistency when mixing mortars and concrete. Cement should be stored off the ground and covered with plastic, ideally in a shed or garage.

Working on site

Planning will make your day's work more productive and enjoyable. Try to build up a realistic work programme before you start, taking into account labour, material and tool requirements.

Remember that noise travels a long way outside and neighbours might not appreciate you drilling and hammering early on a Sunday morning. Plan noisy stages and jobs for later in the day.

As the work proceeds, stop for regular five minute sessions to have a tidy up. This will ensure you keep hazards out of the way. At the end of the day, have a good clean up. Make sure that you clean mixers and spades so that they are free of concrete, protect excavations and cover mortars and cements that might be damaged by rain or frosts.

Maintenance and repair

Once you have completed your water feature you need to keep it looking its best throughout the seasons.

Still water

The biggest problem with still water is the continual build up of algae, which thrives on sunlight and mineral salts

Make sure you remove any excess algae.

within the water. Cloudiness and green water can be removed in different ways. In planted pools and ponds, use oxygenating aquatics and floating lilies to provide shade (see page 20). Where plants interfere with the style of a reflective pool, filters and UV clarifiers can be used. Proprietary solutions and algaecides are effective when added to smaller pools, but will need to be reapplied regularly.

Moving water

Fountains, waterfalls and moving water provide less opportunity for algae growth, as the water is agitated and the reservoir is often cut off from direct sunlight. However, you will still need to clean the reservoirs of all harmful material occasionally. You should also replace the water, which can smell if left too long.

Other considerations

In winter in extremely cold regions, ice may cause damage to wildlife and pool structures, preventing the exchange of oxygen in the water and creating considerable pressure on the sides of walls. To combat this, place a couple of black plastic balls on the water's surface. These will absorb any heat emitted from the sun, melt the surrounding ice and also take up the expanding ice sheet.

Moving water is less likely to ice up but it still may be best to turn the feature off during extremely cold conditions. If you do, remove, clean and dry the pump to prevent damage.

Pumps, filters and lights

By regularly checking your pump cables, electrical connections and filters for damage or blockages, you will keep costly replacements to a

Remove and clean the pump regularly

minimum. Light fittings and lenses require cleaning once in a while as algae and slime are attracted by the heat of the fitting.

Surrounding materials

The surroundings also have their own maintenance requirements. For example, timber may need re-staining and metalwork may develop rust spots and flaky patches. Remove smudges from stainless steel by applying baby oil, or wipe with window cleaner.

After inspecting brickwork, you may need to re-point the occasional joint. If so, take care to match the joint colour. Stone flags around pool edges may become loose, so test them for stability and re-lay as necessary.

Tool maintenance

Spades, chisels and hammers that are well looked after will give you years of reliable use. Check the handles and shafts for splits and stability and lightly oil all metal surfaces before storing them in a dry place over winter. Also inspect cables and working parts regularly on electrical equipment and remember to take them to a tool hire shop annually for a service.

tools and EQUIPMENT

Always try to buy quality tools, as these will last a lifetime. The following tool lists are broken down into the three main sections that are mentioned in the projects: groundwork, building and wood-/metalwork. There are also details of power tools that you may buy or hire. The tools featured in the photographs are described in the text preceding the images.

Groundwork tools

Bow saw This large toothed saw is for cutting out large unwanted shrubs and small to medium trees.

Pinch bar/crow bar This is ideal for levering concrete and brickwork out.

First aid kit This kit needs to be checked before the start of any building work and then kept at hand in case of emergencies. It is useful to include emergency telephone numbers within the kit and make sure you are familiar with the general principles and procedures of first aid.

Fork A sturdy heavy-duty fork is used for breaking out hard ground. A planting fork would not be sufficient for groundwork.
Garden rake The rake is essential for moving and levelling beds as well as removing unwanted debris.
Hand loppers Loppers are used to cut the limbs of trees and shrubs that are too big for garden snips. Sharpen and oil the blades and joints regularly.

Hand rammer This tool is used for compacting small areas of roadbase by hand.

Mattock This looks similar to a pick axe. One of the sides has a spade-like head and is best used for digging out channels and trench work. The other is like the head of an axe and is great for removing unwanted roots.

Pick axe This tool is used for cracking through and breaking out old concrete and very hard ground.

Sledgehammer This has a large solid steel head attached to a long shaft handle, which is used for driving in and smashing up materials.

Spade This is the best tool for edging work in trenches and hole digging.

Tape measures The hand tape is essential for all construction measurements as well as triangulation work. Large reel tape measures are used for setting out reference points in the garden.

Treated timber pegs These short lengths of timber, which are normally 450mm (1½ft), are used for installing levels, marking and setting out.

Wheel barrow and shovel The wheel barrow is needed for carrying heavy loads. You should buy one with an inflated tyre as this will cope with the weight more easily. The shovel, with its large plate and sides, is ideal for loading loose material and is also helpful for spreading roadbase and mortar.

Building tools

Bolt cutters These are used to cut through reinforced road mesh and steel rods.

Bricklaying trowel This is used to lay and spread mortar.

Builder's square A wooden triangular frame used to set out corners.

Chisels and lump hammer Chisels are used for cutting and chopping out various stone or brick surfaces. Use them for removing concrete channels when installing ducting. The lump hammer has many uses such as breaking bricks and driving pegs in. The handle can also be used for tamping down paving stones.

Craft knife This is used for cutting butyl liners and protective underlay.
Levels You should ideally purchase two of these – a 1m (3ft) level and a smaller boat level for handy use.

Lines and pins Pins refer to the short metal pins onto which a string line can be attached at both ends. This is then used to show level, height and direction by being pushed into soil, or positioned along mortar joints in brickwork or at the ends of paving.
Plasterer's hawk and float The hawk is used to hold mortar next to the surface it is being applied to. The float is a levelling and smoothing tool used to apply mortar to walls.

Plastic sheets Sheets are used to cover up work in bad weather and will also protect it from on-site debris.
Pointing trowel and tool This trowel is for pointing paving and brickwork. The pointing tool is half rounded and is rubbed over mortar to give a particular finish.

Safety equipment This gear is a must and includes a breathing mask, eye protectors and ear guards. Make sure that you wear them whenever you are instructed or advised to. For example, you should always ensure that you protect your ears and eyes when cutting through materials such as stone.

Using these tools lists

To save long, repetitive lists of tools appearing at the end of each project, only the necessary categories of equipment (groundwork and metalwork for example) have been recorded. If one item from another section is also required to complete the project it is listed individually. (Hire tools are always given separately too.) Therefore you will need to refer back to this section as you are planning the projects that you wish to carry out in your garden.

Straightedge A straightedge can be made from hardwood or, more often, steel. It is used on its own to quickly check for consistent level or can be used alongside a level for more accurate results.
Tool belt This is very useful for carrying fixings, fittings and hand tools around as it frees up your hands.

Wood- and metalwork tools
Claw hammer A claw hammer is used to drive in and remove nails.
Hacksaw This saw is used for cutting copper and other metals, which is particularly useful when you are dealing with pipework.

Hand clamp Used to keep materials together when drilling or cutting – it is basically a second 'pair of hands'.

Panel saw This saw is needed for precision cutting, mitres and ripping timber down the grain.

Sandpaper This comes in different grades and is used for removing rough edges and splinters on timber.
Spanners and grips These are used to tighten bolts and nuts on posts and framework, as well as for holding and fastening plumbing work.
Tin snips and metal files The file is used to burr edges on metal and bamboo while the tin snips are for cutting sheet metals.

Try/combination square This set square is used to check and mark right angles on timber.
Wood chisel and mallet A chisel and rubber mallet are used together for cutting out joints, tidying corners and splitting bamboo.

Power tools

Cordless screwdriver This is ideal for outdoor use, as it has a rechargeable battery that does away with the need for a cumbersome lead while you are working outside. It makes fixing and undoing screws a painless job.
Jigsaw This type of saw can now be cordless as well as mains powered and is used for cutting sheet materials such as copper and steel and timber.
Power drill This is a drill that is specifically designed for masonry and timber, as well as concrete and blockwork. This heavy-duty drill can run off a generator or be plugged into the mains.

Tools to hire

Angle grinder This machine is in fact a petrol-driven stone cutter. When hiring it request that you are provided with a diamond blade. The instructions for attaching the blade will be given to you by the hire company.
Chainsaw For cutting sleepers the chainsaw is fantastic, but there are strict regulations if you wish to hire one – protective clothing must be worn at all times. Listen carefully to the guidelines and rules given to you.

Concrete mixer A mixer makes mixing concrete and mortar much easier than it would be by hand. A small stand mixer is ideal. These can be petrol or electric – the electric option is quieter and therefore much more neighbour-friendly.

pools and ponds

planning for pools and ponds

There are few gardens that are too small to benefit from a natural pond or formal pool. A simple birdbath, for example, can transform a small corner of a courtyard into an area of activity as birds queue to wash and drink on a hot summer afternoon. And any still pool, however small, will reflect its surroundings and capture the pure essence of water, captivating the viewer.

Function and style It is hard to put a finger on the benefits of a body of water in the garden. Nature and children are irresistibly drawn to it – just look at children playing in puddles after a downpour. Pools can be used to calm a busy, small urban garden or to reflect architecture and planting.

The distinct difference between styles of ponds and pools relates to the formality and informality of their shape, material selection and positioning. Ultimately, the style of the feature will depend on its surroundings and your personal taste. Buildings, materials and existing structures will often make the choice of style less difficult as you will want to use a sympathetic feature. Take a look at the garden's ground levels to pick up clues – a flat site will suit low-level simple pools whereas undulating surfaces provide you with the ideal opportunity to have fun with a small waterfall falling into a lagoon-style natural pond.

Design choices The key to designing the right pool is to consider the site and surrounding areas. Firstly, think about where you would like to position the water feature. The closer it is to the house, the more influence the building will have on its materials, shape and overall feel. This will usually mean that the controlled, clean lines of formal designs, which are dominated by materials and architecture, are the most suitable. The further away the pool is positioned from the building, the less control it has over the design. This gives you the opportunity to work more with curvilinear designs, and allows you to soften edges and introduce lush planting for a supportive role, providing shelter for wildlife.

Not all small gardens need formal water designs. If the site is long and narrow, simply screen off the last few

Contemporary pathway across a pool.

Spiky plants add interest.

Gravel edging creates texture.

Low planting softens a pool's edge.

To make the most of natural water areas, create an outdoor living area using decking to surround the water (top left). Enhance the fusion effect with strategically placed plants or steps (top right). On the other hand, if your goal is to create a sense of movement within the tranquillity of a pond, insert a vertical sculpture (above) that will add beauty and a three-dimensional effect to your water feature.

This modest pool incorporates striking cobbles, which have been laid on its floor, and it is also offset beautifully by the dense planting around its edge.

metres to create a place of mystery. Add a seat, small pool and pump and you have a place for contemplation.

The shape and contents of the site will strongly influence your choices. Unless you plan to alter the garden dramatically by ripping out most of its contents, you will need to work with what is already there. And unless trees totally dominate and oppress the site, you should try to keep the odd one in place, as trees add maturity to a garden. Pruning will improve the shape of a tree, which can then be uplit to create an exciting backdrop.

If reflection is your aim, take time to position the pool, checking with a mirror to view it from every angle. If the pool is to be formal, without planting, it is likely that you will need some form of filter to keep the clarity and reflective quality of the water. So, assess where the filter would be best placed and how it can be screened off.

A small, straight, rectangular site will be best left open with the pool located centrally. This is because any body of water will dominate this type of garden, so you might as well make it the star attraction. If, however, the garden is large and full, the feature will act as a calming foil. It is almost impossible to make a still body of water too big for a plot, so build as big as your budget and site will

> **Ultimately, the style of the feature will depend on its surroundings and your personal taste.**

allow. The larger the volume of water, the better chance it has of a natural ecology, which will keep it clean.

Curved and/or divided-up sites give the opportunity for intrigue and surprise as you can move people through different moods within the site. For example, it can be wonderful to come across a little oasis surrounded by ferns and mosses beneath a light-filtering tree.

When building a natural feature, the use of a liner to waterproof the excavations is now almost taken for granted. This is due to its ability to follow a curve and also because it saves money. Rock, cobbles, driftwood and timber edging work well to make the feature blend in with nature. If it is a natural pond that you are after, take a look at the real thing by visiting parks, lakes and lowland areas and take plenty of reference photographs.

Numerous materials and products are available to construct contemporary pools. A small metallic glazed pot will give your water feature a 'funky' style. In a gloomy courtyard, a stainless-steel-clad raised pool with mirror mosaics on the base will bring the garden to life.

The projects on the following pages give an idea of how pools and ponds can be included in a garden landscape, and provide various styles and materials that are suitable for use in most gardens.

The edges of a pool or pond are just as important as the feature itself. The right surroundings can soften the effect as well as enhance the overall design. Using planting, you can create a very 'natural' feel (above left). Harder materials such as brick (above right) provide a more definite, formal edging and can be offset with other materials. Here, brick is complemented by loose gravel and the effect is completed with a modern concrete bowl positioned right at the water's edge.

The tranquil reflection of planting.

Simple brick edging.

Modern timber, pebbles and block edging.

Waterlilies help oxygenate water.

traditional
BRICK POOL

A traditional pool is one of the most essential features in a formal garden. This beautiful stock brick pool, incorporating stone coping, is a classic design. It makes a statement about artisanship and character.

1 On a level piece of ground mark out the area for your pool using the 3, 4, 5 method (see page 16). Then dry lay the bricks, making sure that you include 10mm (1/2in) joints along the string lines to determine the size of the pool. This will mean you can avoid cutting any bricks when you construct the wall, saving both time and money. Now lay sand lines 100mm (4in) behind your dry brick edging.

2 Bang a peg into the area around the pool about 500mm (1 3/4ft) away from your pool edge. Knock it down to the finished ground level (this may be shingle, paving or whatever you choose). This peg is your datum level, which you will relate all other levels to. From this peg you will need to place another in the pool area 75mm (3in) lower down – this will be the height of your concrete base. This allows you to lay slabs up to the pool walls without the foundation concrete overlap getting in the way.

MATERIALS

Bricks

Reinforcement mesh

Cement, sand and blue metal

Wall ties

Concrete blocks

Coping stones

Conduit

Bitumen paint

Pumps and filter

Marginal plants

TOOLS

Groundwork tools

Building tools

Angle grinder

Soft brush

1 Lay sand lines approximately 100mm (4in) behind your dry brick edging to indicate where you should begin your excavations.

2 Once you have positioned your datum peg, you then need to add another level peg inside the pool, 75mm (3in) lower down.

KNOW YOUR MATERIALS

Bricks: Second-hand stocks have been used here, but these are only really suitable for areas with mild weather conditions. If your garden has heavy and prolonged frosts a different choice may be needed. Building and landscape supply yards are always good places to get advice from. As a rule, most bricks are fine for landscaping and can be bought new or second hand to suit your style.

Coping stones: Natural stone is widely available and will always look and weather better than concrete. However, many substitutes look remarkably similar and cost much less. Second-hand stone is also available.

Bang in a series of pegs to this lower level at 1m (3ft) intervals, which you will use to check the depth of your foundation (it should be 150mm/6in deep).

3 Now cut and lay the reinforcement mesh, which strengthens the slab and prevents cracking. It is often necessary to strengthen concrete foundations to prevent ground movement destabilising the structure. The mesh should be in the middle of the depth of the concrete slab for maximum strength, so place a series of house bricks under the mesh to keep it at the correct height. Mix your foundation concrete (see page 14) and pour it over the mesh into the pool base. Tip out the concrete from the wheelbarrow – don't shovel it in – until you have nearly reached up to the finished base height.

Tamp down the concrete using a float and then check it with a spirit level. The tamping action is important as it removes any bubbles. Tap down the level pegs 50mm (2in) and fill over them with concrete. Cover the base for about 48 hours to cure.

4 Build up the first corner of the brickwork using a 1:6 mortar mix to six courses high. Pay constant attention to the mortar joints, which should be 10mm (½in), and level the courses as you go. When you finish the corner, rub over the mortar joints with a small piece of garden hose to produce an attractive finish. Repeat this process with the other three corners. Using the 1.2m (4ft) spirit level raise the infill brickwork up to the finished height of the corners. Include two galvanised wall ties for bonding the inside block wall on top of the third course, at a minimum of 600mm (2ft) from the corners. Repeat this process along the other three sides. Finish the mortar and brush the brickwork. Clean any excess mortar on the inside of the wall then cover the pool and allow it to cure overnight.

5 Uncover the pool and begin the blockwork and planting shelf. Lay the first course of blockwork (using the same mortar mix) around the inside of all four sides. Make sure that the blocks are 10mm (½in) away from the brick skin and use a spirit level to lay them flush with the top of the

3 Once the reinforcing mesh is in place, you should tip the concrete mix into the area and then tamp it down.

4 Start the brickwork by laying one corner only, which should be six courses high. Make sure you use a 1:6 mortar mix.

5 As you are laying the blockwork you can also lay some blocks flat in order to build up your planting shelf.

third course of the outside brick wall. Then fill the void between the blocks and brickwork with leftover mortar. Lay the final course of blocks to the finished level with the top of the brickwork and fill the joint between the walls with mortar. Smooth with the back of a trowel. The planting shelf can also be laid at this time – simply build two courses of blocks laid flat to give depth to the shelf. Cover the pool and let it cure overnight.

6   The coping stones can now be laid. They need to overlap 50mm (2in) either side of the pool wall. The stones should be about 300–350mm (1–1¹/₆ft) wide. It is useful to dry lay them first, so start at a corner and lay one stone. Then lay the others around the edge, leaving a 10–20mm (¹/₂–³/₄in) pointing joint. You will probably need to cut a stone down to fit the final gap on each side using an angle grinder. Now decide where the pump cable will exit the pool and place a 10mm (¹/₂in) conduit along the wall.

   Lay the corner stones using a 1:4 mortar mix, checking the level, then add the other stones. Use a straightedge to line up the overlapping edge then run a pointing trowel along the bed joint to clean off any excess mortar. Point the joints the following day with a dryish 1:3 mortar mix and brush off the stones with a soft brush.

7   The inside of the pool can be rendered using a sand and cement mix to improve its strength and reduce the chance of leaks. Apply the render at a thickness of around 10mm (¹/₂in). After 48 hours paint two coats of bitumen paint over it.

8   Now fit the pump. To prevent silt and debris clogging it up, place it on bricks or a concrete block. Attach an extension pipe to the pump so it is 50mm (2in) above the coping stones. Ensure the pump cable is vertical and attach it to the brickwork. It can then run into ducting laid under the surrounding area and on to the mains supply.

   Fill the pool up and check the height of your fountain by adjusting the pump flow rate. Then add your chosen marginal plants to the pool (see page 20).

6 Lay the coping stones on the wall, making sure that you leave space for pointing joints. A piece of copper pipe laid in the space can help.

7 After the render has been allowed to dry, paint over its surface with two coats of waterproofing liquid.

8 Pull the cable tight and then attach it to the brickwork. It can then run into the ducting to reach the mains supply.

wet and
DRY POOL

The wet and dry pool is a piece of contemporary art. Its angular shell, made from steel, houses a still, calm body of water that is dramatically reflective. This design needs no decoration – it should just stand alone.

MATERIALS

Mirror

Roadbase

Sand

Steel pool and centre unit

Metal paint

Sandstone

Sharp sand

Cement

Pump and filters

Silicone sealant

Hoses and fittings

TOOLS

Groundwork tools

Building tools

Workbench

Angle grinder

Sealant gun

1 This feature will need to be kept perfectly level even when it is full to the brim. It will also weigh a substantial amount so it is important to provide a sturdy base. Check the position and orientation of the feature before you excavate. As it is a reflection pool, you will need to make sure that the subject you wish to reflect will be seen from the preferred viewing angle. You can check this by using a mirror laid on the ground. When you are happy with its final position, mark out your proposed base to the exact size of the pool using the 3, 4, 5 method (see page 16).

2 Now excavate the base down to a depth of 100mm (4in) below ground level, ensuring that the sides are clean and upright. To produce a level base, simply hammer in timber pegs 25mm (1in) down from the surrounding ground. Place them slightly in from each corner and check that they are level using a spirit level.

1 Use the 3, 4, 5 method to mark out the proposed base and then follow along the string with sand to create sand lines.

2 Excavate the hole and then hammer in timber pegs to produce a level guide for your base. You should use a spirit level to check them.

KNOW YOUR MATERIALS

UV unit and filter: The pool should be positioned so that the inlet and outlet holes and pipework point away from the main direction the pool will be viewed from. The edge of a border or the foreground of a planted boundary would be the ideal environments for the pool. The UV unit and filter need to be placed above the pool, in a position that provides a measurement of at least 450mm (1¼ft) between the outlet hole in the pool and the outlet at the bottom of the filter unit. Remember when positioning these that you will need regular access for maintenance, so when you come to disguise the equipment make sure you allow room for access.

3 Fill the hole up to ground level with roadbase. When the roadbase has been compacted it will allow room for a thin layer of sand, which is needed to create a level platform for the pool to sit on. To compact it, use a hand rammer and work from one side across the whole square, ramming the roadbase down into the base. When you have finished the area, go over it once more in the opposite direction, ensuring any holes are filled and bumps taken out (roughly check it with a spirit level).

4 You now need to paint both parts of the pool (main pool and centre unit) with black metal paint. Make sure they are free from dust and water, then place them on a workbench – it is important to be comfortable when painting these (it will take a couple of hours). Paint the inside and outside of both pool units and leave them to dry (protected with plastic sheeting) for 24 hours.

5 Once the pool units are dry the stones that make up the central feature of the pool can be laid in the smaller of the two steel units. It is likely that the stones will need cutting to fit exactly, so use an angle grinder.

Mark down from the top of the unit the depth of the stones minus 20mm ($^3/_4$in) – this is the height the infill material will be, allowing for compaction. Fill the unit up to this line with a dryish 1:6 cement and sharp sand mix. Using a rubber mallet, tap each stone down until it is level with the top of the unit. Repeat this process until they are all in place. It is a good idea, if you are building this alone, to work with the centre unit in a wheelbarrow. The unit will be very heavy when completed so if it is already in a barrow you only have to lift it once into the pool.

6 The pool needs to sit very level in its final position, so a thin screed is laid over the compacted roadbase. Spread a layer of river sand over the top of the roadbase to a depth of 25mm (1in). Then, with the use of the spirit level and float, flatten the sand to produce the base for the pool. Ask for help to lift the pool into position, making

3 Once you have filled up the area with roadbase you need to compact it down. Do this by using a hand rammer.

4 Place both parts of the pool on a workbench and then paint both the insides and outsides with black metal paint.

5 Place the stones in position in the smaller unit and tap them down so that they are level with the top using a rubber mallet.

sure that the holes for the pipes are facing the least viewed area of the garden. Gently lower it into place, ensuring that you do not drop one side quicker than the other. Check if any adjustments are needed by placing a spirit level across the top of the pool from side to side. Then lift the small steel unit with the stones into the steel pool. Position the stone unit into place by eye then check it is centralised by measuring between the unit and all the pool sides.

7 Now fit the pump, positioning it on the opposite side to the inlet hole in the side of the pool. This will ensure that the whole body of water is cleaned, not just around the inlet hole. Lay the cable for the pump neatly around the inside edge of the pool and then pass it through the pre-drilled hole next to the inlet and seal around the cable using clear silicone sealant. When you choose the position for the feature, it is important to take into account how you will disguise the filter and UV system. They need to be on a secure base (e.g. a timber platform)

and it is important that they are kept higher than the pool as gravity feeds the water back into the pool.

Once the filter and UV clarifier are in place, measure the distance of hose from the pump to the UV unit, and cut and fit it using a jubilee clip (remember that this needs to pass through the pre-cut hole next to the power cable hole). Next measure and cut a pipe for the return journey from the filter and fix this to the side of the pool, fitting a filter cone over the end. Make sure you leave enough for the pipe to protrude into the pool. Now connect the pump, UV and filter following the manufacturer's recommendations (see also page 19 for general guidelines on safely installing pumps).

8 Finally, you can fill the pool with water. It is best to doublecheck the levels of the unit one last time before you do this, as it will be almost impossible to move the pool when it is filled with water. Once the pool is full the pump can be switched on and the connections and joints checked for leaks.

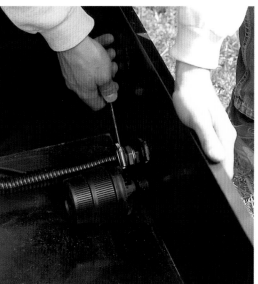

6 Carefully lift and position the central stone unit into its final resting place inside the steel pool. Then check that it is centred.

7 Now connect all the pipework for the filters and install the pump. The pump should be on the opposite side to the inlet hole.

8 Once you have done one last check to see that the unit is level, fill it up with water using a garden hose.

spiral POOL

The spiral pool has the calm serenity of a natural body of water. Its interest lies in the pattern that you create within the pool, whether it is a formal geometric design or following a more natural style – the choice is yours.

MATERIALS

Steel pin or bamboo cane

Sand

Geotextile underlay

Butyl liner

Pump and filter

Hoses and fittings

Reinforcement mesh

Membrane

Chicken wire

Broken slate

White cobbles

Conduit

TOOLS

Groundwork tools

Building tools

Gloves

1   Choose the area in the garden for your pool – you will need at least a 3 x 3m (10 x 10ft) plot of relatively flat soil. Take a steel pin or bamboo cane and push it into the centre of the plot. Then, using a string line that is marked with the correct radius or a builder's tape placed over the cane or pin, rotate it around the central cane laying sand as you go at a radius of 1.2m (4ft). Lay the sand around the circle until it is complete; this will give the markings for a pool with a diameter of 2.4m (8ft). Hammer in and level a series of pegs around the circumference to give you a reference after you have finished your excavations.

2   Now remove the cane and begin the excavations. The idea is to create a shallow pan that gently slopes to a depth of 400mm (1¼ft). Once the main pan has been dug out, a central sump hole measuring 600mm (2ft) wide and 400mm (1¼ft) deep will need to be excavated. This

1 Rotate your tape once you have measured the correct radius and, as you do so, lay sand to create an entire circle.

2 After you have excavated the main pool, dig out the central sump hole. This will eventually contain the pump.

KNOW YOUR MATERIALS

Slate: Check with your local tile shop or landscape supplier regarding availability of slate. Many suppliers keep broken slate in crates on site and you can go and pick the pieces you want. Put them into small boxes that are easy to handle. If you need a large quantity of slate, remember to order it in advance in order to ensure that you have all the materials you will need before beginning construction of your pool.

Stone: During the quarrying process all stone will naturally attract a layer of dust and dirt. Therefore it is important to wash all pebbles and cobbles thoroughly prior to placing them in or around your water feature.

hole will contain the pump that will slowly move the water to a filter system, which is needed to keep the water clear.

Start the main excavation from the edges and gradually grade it down to the centre. Keep standing back to check the evenness of your work and, when you are happy with the overall shape of the pool, check the surrounding edges are level with the pegs. You will need to excavate the central sump hole, paying attention to the sides to keep them upright with the walls intact.

3 Before you lay the protective geotextile underlay, remove any large stones or sharp objects from the pool. Spread the underlay over the whole area and, starting in the sump hole, carefully fold the material into the hole. Then work your way out to the edge of the pool, keeping folds to an absolute minimum.

4 Now place the butyl liner over the pool and fold it into the sump hole. The liner needs to be 3.5 x 3.5m (11½ x

11½ft). Start by laying the liner over one side of the pool. You should remove your footwear so you do not rip or puncture the liner. Next, fold the liner into the sump hole. Do not worry about any resulting small folds as the liner will be covered with the slate. Continue to fit the liner over the rest of the pool until it is complete.

5 Place the pump into the sump hole in the middle of the pool. Then attach the hose to the pump outlet, fastening it with a jubilee clip. Now the hose and power cable need to be positioned flat against the liner so that the broken slate can disguise them. The hose will need a flow adjuster to control the quantity of water (see page 19). This needs to be situated at the edge of the pool for access, but can be disguised later with plants or stones.

You now need to place a grille over the sump hole. Using bolt cutters, cut a grille measuring 1m² (3ft²) out of a sheet of reinforcement mesh before positioning it. Also cut four lengths of membrane about 1.1m (3¼ft) in length – these will be the cushioning for the grille over the sump

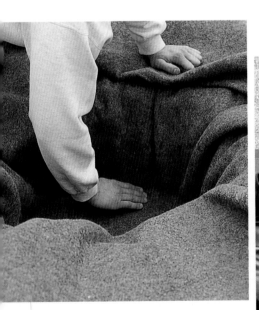

3 *The protective geotextile underlay can be laid in place once you have removed any large stones and debris.*

4 *Carefully lay the liner over the hole. Remove your shoes when you do this to reduce the risk of tearing the liner.*

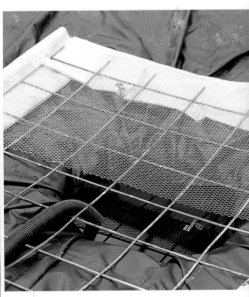

5 *Once the grille is in place you can add a layer of chicken wire over the top, which is needed for the slate to sit on.*

hole. Place the membrane on the liner so that it will lay under the sharp edges of the grille, then place the grille carefully over the sump hole. Finally a layer of expanded metal or chicken wire is needed to allow the slate to lie over the top without the stones falling through.

6 Next cover the whole pool area with a membrane. This will protect the liner from the sharp slate and will also provide a barrier to prevent the pump being clogged up with silt and sediment. Wearing gloves, wash and then lay the slate over the pool at a depth of 50mm (2in), trying to keep it as even and flat as possible. When it is completely covered, take a step back so that you can make sure there is no membrane showing through.

7 You can now fill the pool with water. The level that you fill the pool up to will depend on the height of the cobbles that you have laid. As long as these are covered then the water level is adequate. Now connect the pump, ensuring that all cabling is ducted in rigid plastic conduit 450–600mm (1½–2ft) below ground level until it reaches the switch box. Turn the pump on and adjust the filtration unit so that the flow back into the pool does not disturb the view of the pool.

Using washed white cobbles, the pattern can now be laid out on the bottom of the pool. Start from a central point with a large cobble and then lay a continuous line of stones, unravelling the shape until you have completed your spiral. When you have laid them all out, stand back and decide where you feel you need to alter the shape or width of the cobble lines. Try to use stones of similar size for this and lay them as flat as possible.

Alternative materials

In this feature broken slate and white cobbles were used to provide a stunning contrast of colours and give depth to the otherwise shallow pool. There are other materials that could be used to line the pool such as crushed glass or coloured aggregate. The pattern that you decide on can echo themes that already exist in your garden.

6 Once the membrane is in position, lay the washed slate over the whole pool, wearing gloves to protect your hands.

7 Create your spiral pattern for the bottom of the pool. Work from the centre outwards, checking the pattern as you go.

Alternative materials: There are many other materials you could use to line your pool, such as glass or coloured aggregate.

natural
POND

The natural pond is the most commonly built feature in domestic gardens and it is easy to see why. In this manic world the pond can be our connection with nature, wildlife and the moments of calm we enjoy in our gardens.

1 Choose the area where you want the pond to be positioned and mark the shape on the ground using sand. Drive a reference peg into the ground just outside the sand line – this will indicate all of your levels. Drive in pegs every 1m (3ft) or so around the remainder of the sand line down to just above ground level. Check these are the same height by using your spirit level and, if needed, a straightedge. On the outside of the sand line (i.e. not the pond area) remove the turf or soil to a depth of 50mm (2in) and a width of 300mm (1ft). If you want to put the turf back as a natural edge to the pond at the end then lay it out in the garden and keep it well watered.

2 Excavate down within the sand line to a depth of 250mm (10in) from ground level, using pegs to check that you have excavated to the correct depth. Rake over the surface and remove any large stones or debris from the

MATERIALS

Sand

Geotextile underlay

Butyl liner

Bricks and slab

Pumps and accessories

TOOLS

Groundwork tools

Building tools

1 Drive in a reference peg every 1m (3ft) along the sand line and use your spirit level to check that they are at the same height.

2 Once you have excavated the deep part of the pond, rake over the bottom in order to ensure that no large stones are left in.

KNOW YOUR MATERIALS

Environment: If nature is to be encouraged then hundreds of koi carp and plastic flamingos are not ideal features. A natural pond needs to be about creating an environment for wildlife. The water should have the right planting and leave room for nature.

Edging: This can change the feel of the pond and its function. A wildlife pond may need no hard edging at all. If you back the lawn up to the water's edge, and mix this with surrounding planting, you can create the feel of a natural environment for wildlife. A stone or slate edging will, alternatively, create a definite frame for the pond. This provides a focus on the planting within the pond.

site. Now mark out the deep area of the pond. You will need to leave a marginal shelf around the edge of the top of the pond for planting. Measure in from the sides of the pool 300mm (1ft) then lay a sand line as before to mark out the shape to be excavated for the deep part of the pond. Excavate the inside of the sand line down to a depth of 400mm (1¼ft), then rake the bottom over to check for sharp or large stones.

Due to the pressure of the water being greatest at the bottom of the pond, you will need to make a 50mm (2in) layer of either sifted soil or river sand to help cushion the liner, which will ensure that it doesn't get punctured.

3 Next, lay the geotextile underlay over the pond and work it into the edges and contours of the pond. Push the underlay into its position firmly. As you do this, try not to lean or stand on the planting shelves. When the underlay is in place, trim the edges off using a craft knife or scissors. Make sure you leave a small overlap going over onto the edge of the surrounding soil.

4 Roll the liner out over the top of the pond. Push the liner roughly into the shape of the pond and use bricks to hold the edges of the liner in place temporarily. When the liner is ready for filling with water the pump can be positioned on two bricks, which have a small slab on top of them, in the deep part of the pond. Then position the power cable along the inside of the pond where you wish it to pass under the edging. The water needs to be passed through the pump to stop it from stagnating. Once the pond has been planted up, the plants will take care of the oxygenation and also provide shade.

5 Fill the pond up slowly with water. The liner will spread into the contours of the pond with the increasing weight of the water. As the pond fills up you will need to fold or pleat the larger parts of the liner into place. Remember to adjust the bricks on the edges as the liner becomes taut.

6 Once the pond is nearly full you can check the edges for level using the water line as a guide. Simply adjust the soil

3 Place the geotextile underlay over the pool and then, taking care not to lean on the planting shelves, work it into the edges.

4 Once the underlay has been positioned and cut, you can then roll the liner out over the top of the pond.

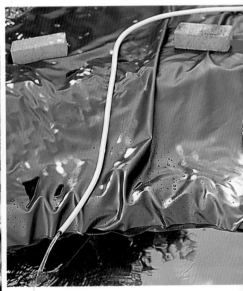

5 Begin to fill the pond with water. The liner will naturally spread into the corners of the pond but you will need to adjust the bricks.

evels behind the liner to provide a consistent level edge. You will then need to excavate a trench 150mm (6in) deep around the pond into which you can tuck the liner. This also produces an edge that can be planted up to, which looks pleasing to the eye.

With the edges completed, trim the liner more accurately using a sharp knife or scissors. Then backfill the trench and gently firm the soil down with your heel. Rake this over to produce a medium tilth for plants or turf.

7 The power cable from the pump needs to be at a safe depth of 450mm (1½ft) to protect it from tools and animals etc. So, from the conduit exiting the pool, run the rest of the cable in the same protective tubing until it reaches the connection point.

8 Now that the edges are tidy you can plant or turf right up to the pool. If you choose to turf, it is preferable to use the grass that was stripped out when you cleared the site. This is because it will blend in far better than new grass

would as it will be in keeping with its surroundings. Once you have laid all your turf, firm it in using the back of a spade and then water it thoroughly until it becomes established. It is often best to let the grass grow longer around natural ponds as this softens edges and provides extra protection and habitat for wildlife.

Now a recirculating pump can be connected and switched on. The power connection from the pump needs to be carried out by a qualified electrician.

If after a few weeks your water turns green use a pump with a simple oxygenating tube attachment. This will help your pond in the first few seasons while the plants become established.

Alternative materials

You may prefer to use a hard edging, such as stone or slate, rather than turf. This provides a safe edge for inquisitive children. For this reason, it is important to bed the stone correctly on a minimum of 75mm (3in) ratio of 1:4 cement and sharp sand or river sand.

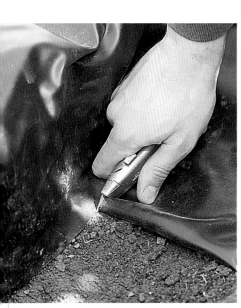

6 When the pond is full and the liner has become taut, you should trim the edges. Check the height of the liner using the water.

7 Power cables always need to be protected so run your cable in conduit underneath the paving and on to the connection point.

8 If you decide to dress the edge of the pond with lawn, you can re-lay the turf that you removed when excavating the pond area.

streams and rills

planning for streams and rills

A natural stream will always fascinate and inspire, providing hours of calm meditation as you follow the path the water takes over and around rocks, boulders and planting. In contrast, rills are formal features that demonstrate control and precision. Rills developed from the need to tame nature and direct this valuable, natural resource to irrigate pastures. In a garden setting, this style of feature allows you to create modern design with real impact.

Function and style Put simply, the difference between a stream and a rill lies in the overall style – a stream is natural while a rill is artificial. Both can be defined as watercourses, as they are a means of channelling or moving a body of water from an outlet to a reservoir or ornamental pool. The key to creating an authentic, 'natural' stream is the ability to emulate nature. Attention must be paid to the way water unpredictably gushes and then suddenly dissipates – this effect is often difficult to achieve in modern-day garden plots. It can also be hard to escape from the domination of the house, so natural streams are more appropriate in larger gardens where they can be placed far from the house, or where there is some sort of physical barrier such as a screen. This will allow you to create a naturalistic environment.

Formality and geometry are characteristics associated with rills and small channels. These water features tend to be straight and fairly narrow – mainly due to the difficulty and expense of constructing curved and sinuous shapes through terraces or paving. The straighter shapes are also far more in keeping with more modern architecture, giving an ideal opportunity to bring water close to a house. You can create cohesion by linking the materials of the rill with those used for the house or the existing components of a patio. For example, stone or brick can be used to form the edges of the feature. Alternatively, if your property lacks a strong period style try using more contemporary materials such as steel, glass, concrete and mosaics.

Design choices Your site will, to a certain extent, dictate the type of feature that is most suitable and it will also give you clues to the design and choice of materials that should be used. A sloping area, for example, provides

A naturally shaped rill.

Core-ten steel slabs with a steel-sided rill.

A formal rill edged with stone.

A winding rill leads to a pond.

Whether built or natural, a passageway of water can be highlighted or softened using planting. When creating a 'natural', meandering stream, you can add to the effect with informal, dense and overhanging plants (top left). And placing a walkway over the top adds yet another dimension. You may choose to create a traditional bridge (above) or a more adventurous 'stepping stone' using pieces of timber (top right) – either way you will be able to enjoy the view from above.

This shallow pool empties into an angular rill. The strong shapes used in the design are softened by surrounding gravel and planting.

the ideal opportunity to introduce an exciting series of falls that add noise and animation to the water's journey (see pages 74-7). In natural stream design the rapid change of level of a small waterfall is often followed by stillness as the body of water re-groups to continue its passage. This can easily be achieved by excavating a mini-pool directly beneath the fall to increase the volume of water and absorb the kinetic energy of the turbulent flow. It is often this stop-and-start characteristic of a stream that gives a sense of natural movement. Without it, the stream could become a rather one-dimensional, single run of water.

Arching and overhanging trees and shrubs provide a vertical dimension, linking the horizontal elements of the water with its surroundings. A bridge, on the other hand, is a wonderful way of experiencing the feature in a more intimate manner, as it allows you to see a totally different, close-up view of your creation. Stepping stones are another great way to interact with the water – children will love moving across a stream in this way.

Look to nature and study the way it creates its streams. Pay attention to the way rocks have been moved into the middle of a stream. This indicates the power of water and should be a useful guide to where you should position your

The key to creating an authentic 'natural' stream is the ability to emulate nature.

final boulders. Nature, over time, also grades sand, gravel and rock so avoid using a lot of the same-sized material.

The strong geometry of a rill can be difficult to introduce successfully into the garden. The dominance of a straight line naturally draws attention and creates strong directional movement, leading the eye to its end. You can take advantage of this by terminating the rill with a focal point, such as an elegant water jet in the centre of a low-level pool. You may want to dissect an area of your garden by using the rill or link a relaxing seating terrace through to a wilder area. With all this in mind, take your time when positioning the feature. Mark out the rill with sand then look at the overall balance of the area and check that you can still use the connecting areas as you want to.

A rill, by its very nature, is the middle section of a water feature – the beginning, or outlet, can be as simple as a stone covering a hose or an elaborate series of spouts feeding the channel. The channel itself can be transformed by decorating the bottom with shells, pebbles, glass etc. The destination, or reservoir, should suit the overall style.

The following projects incorporate all these design principles and provide you with details of construction techniques to enable you to create the perfect stream or rill for your garden.

In a large garden, you can create a very natural-looking stream that reflects the ground contours and blends in with the natural environment (above left). However, a stream or rill does not need to take up so much space. A small, self-contained feature that includes a reservoir and watercourse to emulate the flow of a river can be just as effective (above right). This even adds an abstract art dimension to the garden and will probably become a talking point among visitors.

A timber walkway over a stream.

Slate covers the bottom of this stream.

Dramatic planting beside a stream.

Cobbles line this straight rill.

copper RILL

Nestled among the natural textured sleepers runs this inviting and colourful copper rill. The elements of water and metal combine here to reflect the light and provide a focal point.

MATERIALS

Timber sleepers

75 × 50mm (3 × 2in) and
15 × 25mm (6 × 1in) pressure-treated timber

100mm (4in) galvanised nails

Sand

Concrete blocks

Cement

Membrane

Gravel or wire loops

Pump and fittings

Hose and fittings

Timber preservative

75mm (3in) zinc-coated screws

Copper sheet

10mm (½in) copper pins

Silicone sealant

TOOLS

Building tools

Gloves

Tin snips

Power tools

Felt tip pen

Silicone sealant gun

1 This feature should be a minimum of seven sleepers wide – about 1.75m (5¾ft). First decide how wide your deck needs to be in relation to the overall area you are installing. Measure the width of a sleeper and multiply it until you get as close as possible to the required site width. Now construct the outside frame using 75 × 50mm (3 × 2in) treated timber. It should be constructed smaller than the final deck size so that the sleepers will overlap the frame by 50mm (2in) on each side. Check the frame is square by using a builder's square and nail it together using 100mm (4in) galvanised nails. Then fix intermediate timbers at 1.2m (4ft) intervals. Lay the frame in its proposed site and mark the position of all the timbers using sand. Then put it aside.

2 The foundation blocks should be laid on 75–100mm (3–4in) of 1:3 sharp sand and cement. Work from the

1 Once you have decided how big your framework needs to be, construct it and fix it together using galvanised nails.

2 Once the corner foundation blocks are in place, sit your frame on top of them to check that the corners align correctly.

KNOW YOUR MATERIALS

Copper: Although copper can look a little new and glittery, verdigris quickly forms on it to calm down the reflection and give character to the metal. Copper has a unique quality when it is used alongside such natural and earthy materials as wood and water because the effect is always rich and satisfying. Some alternative materials can create a modern, clean and refreshing look. Stainless steel can expand light in a shady garden, reflecting the purity of running water. Copper has the advantage of being relatively easy to bend and work with while stainless steel is a little more resilient, needing a specialist fabricator to produce the shapes and bends.

corner of the frame and level around using a straightedge and a spirit level. Once the corner blocks are in position, carefully sit the frame on the blocks and adjust them if necessary so that they sit flush with the outside corners. The intermediate blocks can be laid at 1.2m (4ft) intervals along the outside frame and internal timbers. Check their position after they are laid by placing the made-up frame over the blocks again. Leave the blocks to set overnight.

3 Fit a membrane underneath your framework and pin it down with wire loops or spread a 50mm (2in) layer of gravel over the area. Having covered the soil, set your sleepers in their final position and check the overlap of the frame on each side. Measure the opening for the rill and adjust each end to form a parallel channel, then mark the frame underneath for reference when fixing. Next, fix the sleepers using 100mm (4in) galvanised nails.

4 Whether you are using an existing pump in the reservoir or are connecting a new one, the hose will carry the water up to the outlet at the top of the rill. Make sure your connections to the pump from the hose are tight using a jubilee clip. Then, in order to feed the hose under the deck area, ensure that the hose has ample length at each end, about 1m (3ft). If you are using a lined pool, cut a small hole just under the frame timber and push the pipe hose through this, to lay the hose under the rill opening. Positioning the hose here will allow you easy access to it in the future.

5 Now attach a timber fascia to the frame directly under the sleepers. This covers the hose entry point and also hides the liner upstand. When filled, the water line should be 25–50mm (1–2in) from the bottom of this timber, which makes an attractive water edge and a good indicator of when the pool may need topping up. Prior to fixing, paint the 150 x 25mm (6 x 1in) treated timber with black timber preservative and allow it to dry for 12 hours. Screw the boards to the frame using 75mm (3in) zinc-coated screws as high up to the sleeper as you can.

3 Once you have put a membrane over the ground, put the sleepers in place and fix them with galvanised nails.

4 Feed the hose that takes water to the outlet at the top of the rill under the deck area, ensuring there is ample length at either end.

5 Paint the timber fascia with black preservative before attaching it directly under the sleepers using zinc-coated screws.

6 Now start to form the copper rill. Measure the width of the opening and add the two sides to the measurement – this will give your copper strip width. When deciding the length allow 150mm (6in) for the chute at the front and 150mm (6in) extra if you need more than one length of copper. This will provide an overlap for fixing two sheets together (to fix, apply silicone sealant over the surface and lay one sheet over the previous one, working up the rill).

   Wearing gloves, mark the width of the sheet – the rill opening plus two upstands of 110mm (4½in). Then, using a high-quality pair of tin snips or a jigsaw fitted with a metal blade, cut along the lengths. Once this has been done, the upstands can be bent into shape. Mark the height of the sleeper, around 100mm (4¼in), at each end of the sheet and line up these marks with the edge of a piece of timber. Slowly bend the copper along its length to form a right angle. Repeat the process on the other side.

7 At one end of the rill measure back along 150mm (6in) and mark it with a felt tip pen. Then mark down 40mm (1½in) from the top of the upstand with a set square. With sharp tin snips, cut down the 40mm (1½in) you have marked, then bend this over at a right angle to the rill side. Next, measure out 30mm (1¼in) from the top edge of the bend and mark along the entire flap, leaving a 10mm (½in) right angle. Cut along the pen mark with your tin snips. Repeat this on the other side to create your water chute. Put the chute into position and nail it securely in place using small 10mm (⅓in) copper pins.

8 The outlet at the top of the rill needs to be constructed from one piece of copper sheet. Using a metal drill bit, drill an 18mm (¾in) hole for the tank connector to attach to. Then bend the copper over a piece of timber. The outlet should fit tightly into place, held by the sides of the fixed rill and four copper nails. Seal between the outlet and rill sides with silicone sealant. Finally, attach the hose to the tank connector with a jubilee clip, turn the water on and make any necessary adjustments to the flow.

6 Once you have cut the copper to the required width, bend it along a length of timber to form a right angle for the rill.

7 Once the rill has been put in its final position in between two sleepers it can be nailed into place with copper pins.

8 Now connect the flexible hose to the tank connector using a jubilee clip. Ensure that all the connections are tight.

meandering RILL

This feature is a clever fusion of two classic forms, combining the organic shapes of the natural stream with the precision of the straight rill. The gently curving shape is reminiscent of water's natural path while the steel edge and brilliant crushed glass are thoroughly urban.

MATERIALS

Sand

Geotextile underlay

Butyl liner

Sharp sand

Blue metal

Cement

150mm (6in) wide steel edging, 1mm (¹/₃₀in) thick

Hoses and fittings

Two 40kg (88lb) bags of crushed glass

25mm (1in) plastic pipe

Two 25mm (1in) plastic bends

Pump and fittings

Granite bridge

TOOLS

Groundwork tools

Building tools

Bucket

1 This feature needs to be built at one end of an existing pool or pond, which will act as the reservoir. If you need to build a new one see page 15 for advice on construction. The rill needs to be a minimum of 5m (16ft) long, and 150mm (6in) in width. Your reservoir must be able to accommodate the amount of water needed along the meandering rill, so the longer you make the rill, the larger the amount of water you will need. With sand, mark out the passage of your rill and then dig it out, using your spirit level to make sure that its base has a gradual slope towards the existing reservoir.

2 Cut 1m (3ft) lengths of the geotextile underlay. Work out the width you need by adding the base width of the rill, the sides and an extra 200mm (8in) to allow for trimming to the necessary shape. Then lay the cut pieces into place, making sure you push them into the corners of the rill.

1 Once you have cleared the whole site and marked out your rill, begin to dig the area out using a spade.

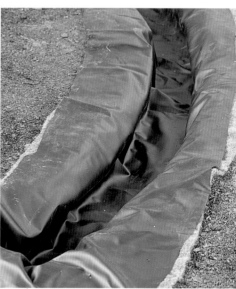

2 Once the underlay and liner are in place, and have been folded where necessary, cut the edges, leaving a 150mm (6in) overlap.

KNOW YOUR MATERIALS

Rill base: The inside of the rill is a base of sharp sand and cement. The steel sides will reflect the water's motion, and create a contemporary feel. The steel could be replaced with copper, galvanised steel or plastic. The base of the rill could also be dressed with crushed glass or flat pebbles to give a very different look.. This rill is also set in a woodland surround as the ground is covered in natural fall from surrounding trees and shrubs. Such a rill can actually be positioned anywhere – for example in a patio leading to a pool or with a cascade trailing into your rill. There are no restrictions – the only factors that may need consideration are safety, gradient and reservoir size.

Lay the liner out over the rill and push into place, folding where necessary. Then cut the liner to fit around the edges of the rill, leaving a 150mm (6in) overlap on each side to allow for adjustment. At the edge of the reservoir, overlap the liner into the reservoir by another 150mm (6in) as this will guarantee the safe return of the water from the rill to the existing reservoir. With the underlay and liner in shape, the base of the rill can be covered in 50mm (2in) of 3:1 sharp sand and cement mix. With your level, make sure that the fall towards the reservoir is still the same on top of the sand and cement as it was on top of the liner. Use your float to create a good finish.

3 Take the lengths of 150mm (6in) wide steel and place them roughly into position inside the rill and then bend them into shape. When you are happy that all the steel sides are their correct shapes remove them and label them so you know which position to put them back into. Store the steel safely until you are ready to set it into the sand and cement. Be sure to keep the steel sheets on their edges while they are being stored. Once they have been bent into shape they should stay as you want them. However, due to their thickness, if the sheets are laid flat they will lose their shape.

4 Take the steel strips and, starting from the outlet end of the rill, place them onto the mortar mix. Overlap the edges of the steel in the direction of the reservoir. With a rubber mallet or the handle of your hammer tamp the steel into place. The top of the steel should be 25mm (1in) above ground level. Check it is all level then leave the sharp sand and cement mix to cure for 48 hours.

5 Place the pump into the reservoir inside a bucket – this will stop the pump from sucking in debris from the reservoir. Connect the hose to the outlet on the pump and secure it with a jubilee clip. Take the crushed glass and spread it around along the concrete surface of the rill. Be sure to give it an even covering – around 10–15mm ($\frac{1}{2}$–$\frac{2}{3}$in) should be enough to disguise the mortar floor.

3 Once you have placed the steel strips inside the rill and have bent them into their correct shapes, remove and label them.

4 Place the steel strips onto the mortar mix and then, using a rubber mallet, tamp the steel down, checking both sides are level.

5 You can now disguise the mortar bed by placing crushed glass along the rill's floor. A covering of 10–15mm ($\frac{1}{2}$–$\frac{2}{3}$in) is enough.

6 | The outlet needs to be fixed into place at the beginning of the rill. Cut two 100mm (4in) lengths of 25mm (1in) plastic pipe, then fit both pipes into a 90°, 25mm (1in) plastic bend. Cut and fix the flexible hose from the pump in your reservoir to reach the outlet end of the rill. Fit this to one end of the plastic pipe with a jubilee clip.

Cut a 150mm (6in) length off one of the steel strips to form an end to the outlet of the rill. Fit this the same way you did the sides. Fit another 90°, 25mm (1in) plastic bend to the other end of the plastic pipe. This will angle the water down into the rill and cut back on splashing.

Position the hose and the pipes so that the end of the 90° bend rests on top of the steel end that you have fitted. With this in place, concrete the area and check the pipe is central to the rill. Cover the concrete and leave it to cure for 48 hours.

7 | Neatly position the hose from the pump to the outlet along one side of the rill. The pipe needs to be below the level of the mulch and against the steel. Fill the reservoir up with water. Turn on the power to the pump and observe the water flow. The flow rate may need adjusting so fiddle with the flow rate adjuster on your pump to increase or decrease the rate at which the water moves. The material covering the bottom of the rill will be washed away constantly if the pressure of the outlet is too high, so this is a good indication that adjustment is needed.

8 | You can now disguise the outlet by covering it with the granite bridge. This bridge will need to be positioned so that it disguises the pipework completely. The granite bridge will not need to be bedded on a mortar base, as it is added purely for aesthetic reasons and will therefore not be used as a real bridge. Depending on the material that surrounds the rill area the backfilling can be soil or forest mulch. Whichever you use, the steel needs to be a fraction higher than the surrounding area to protect it from debris. Tidy up the area and check that you are happy with the feature.

6 *Before the cement cures, check that the pipework is in its correct position, so that it is aimed into the centre of the rill.*

7 *The hose that runs from the pump to the outlet needs to be positioned neatly along one side of the rill, below the level of the mulch.*

8 *Once the granite bridge is in place you can add the surrounding material. Here, mulch has been used.*

raised steel
RILL

This cool volume of shimmering water links beautifully with modern interiors. Where two outdoor areas of a contrasting design or style meet, use this rill to divide them – for example, to separate a more formal space from a 'wilder' area.

MATERIALS

75 × 50mm (3 × 2in) treated timber

100mm (4in), 75mm (3in) and 35mm (1½in) zinc-plated screws

12mm (½in) and 9mm (⅓in) external marine ply

Geotextile underlay

Butyl liner

30mm (1¼in) galvanised clout nails

3 adjustable submersible pumps

Associated nozzles and extension pipes

Prefabricated stainless steel sheets

Clear external silicone sealant

Masking tape

Three bricks

TOOLS

Woodwork tools

Building tools

Staple gun

Drill

Sealant gun

Damp rag

1   The beauty of this feature is that it can be almost completely built before being put into its final position. A basic framework of treated 75 × 50mm (3 × 2in) timber makes up the structure of the rill, which is then clad with external ply. Construct the two long sides of the rill so that they are 1.8m (6ft) long and 600mm (2ft) in height. Check the corners are 90° using a combination square, then fix the timbers using 75mm (3in) and 100mm (4in) zinc-plated screws. You will need to attach a central support timber to add extra stability. Now connect the two main sides with a 400mm (1¼ft) long timber top and bottom so the overall width of the ends is 500mm (1¾ft). The base of the feature will also need a support timber.

2   Once the frame has been screwed together, check each corner for square. All internal and external sides of the frame then need to be clad with marine ply, including

1 Make up the basic framework of the rill using central support timbers and fixing everything with zinc-plated screws.

2 The internal and external sides of the frame are then clad with marine ply. Attach the outside ply using screws again.

KNOW YOUR MATERIALS

Stainless steel: This is a versatile material, usually associated with modern interiors, but it is increasingly being used outside for its clean, contemporary, hard-wearing qualities. It can be ordered in different grades and surface finishes. Although it is slightly more expensive, you should choose a marine grade, as the standard grade will develop tiny oxidised rust marks. The steel used in this feature has a brushed finish that is more suitable for exterior use as it prevents the extreme sunlight glare that is associated with the usual polished surface. It also has the added bonus of not marking as easily. To help maintain its reflective and cool appearance, regularly apply baby oil.

the base. Use 12mm (½in) thick for the external and 9mm (⅓in) for internal cladding. Attach the ply using 35mm (1½in) zinc-plated screws. Decide which end of the rill your cable will exit and leave the internal ply unscrewed to ensure ease of access for the cabling later.

3 Before you install the liner, check over the surface of the internal ply for splinters or screwheads that may pierce the liner. Geotextile underlay is also laid between the liner and internal ply for protection. Measure and cut the length and width of the underlay and liner (see page 15), adding an extra 500mm (1¾ft) to each to allow for corner folds. Then fold the underlay into each corner and staple or nail using 30mm (1¼in) galvanised clouts, so it is about 40mm (1½in) below the top of the rill. Trim the top of the underlay with a sharp blade and repeat the process for the liner. Try to ensure the liner is tucked into the corners snugly and is sitting flush on the floor of the rill or the weight of the water will pull down the liner and tear the fixing. Don't attach the materials where your cables exit.

4 Three separate pumps are used here. The pumps should each have a built-in flow valve or a flow adjuster positioned close to the pump within the nozzle extension, to adjust the volume and height of individual jets. A jet nozzle is then attached to the extension pipe.

   The pump will sit on a brick at the bottom of the rill, so this needs to be taken into account when cutting the length of the nozzle extension – the water line will be just above the stainless steel lip and the nozzle should sit about 30mm (1¼in) above this.

5 Place each pump close to its final position, laying the cables along the floor of the rill. Group the cables together using cable ties. Give each pump an extra 50cm (1¼ft) of cable in case of adjustments. Using a timber fly bit, drill a hole through the top and bottom of the frame and feed the pump cables through. Re-fix the sheet and attach the underlay and liner back in position. The cables will need to be connected by a qualified electrician to a weather-proof junction box that carries the live armoured cable.

3 Once the underlay is in position to protect the liner from the wood, tuck the liner in on top of it and staple to fix it.

4 Three pumps have been used to create the fountains. They have extension pipes that need to be cut to the right length.

5 Once you have drilled your holes through the timber frame, feed the pump cables through them.

6 The stainless steel panels can be lifted into position to check that they fit together correctly. Pay particular attention to the corners as they will be the most visible part of the rill. When you are happy, remove one of the long panels and apply a 6mm (¼in) bead of clear exterior silicone sealant in a zigzag pattern across the face of the ply. Carefully lift the panel over the top edge of the rill and lower into its final position, checking the corners are flush with the side panels and that the liner is covered. Gently slap the length of the sheet with your palm to ensure the silicone grabs hold of the steel and repeat the process on the opposite side. Then fix the steel to the remaining side panels and make sure that you leave the silicone to dry out overnight.

7 It is important to seal and waterproof all the joints with silicone sealant so that water cannot penetrate the wooden framework. Gently pull 50mm (2in) of the protective plastic away from each joint and fix masking tape to both sides to prevent smearing silicone over the steel. Apply the clear silicone along each joint, ensuring the compound goes right into the joints. Squeeze in more sealant than you need and clean any excess off with a damp rag. Once the silicone is dry the feature is ready for its final location.

8 The rill needs to be placed on a flat level surface, ideally on a patio. You will need some help to lift the feature to its final position, taking care not to twist the structure as this would break the seals. Once it is in position, check the level along its length and from front to back, adjusting where necessary using timber wedges or slate packed under the base. Place the pumps on one brick each, laid on some underlay to protect the liner.

You can now remove the plastic protection film to reveal the stainless steel. Fill the rill with water so that it finishes 40mm (1½in) down from the top of the steel lip and adjust your nozzle extension pipes so they sit just below the water line. Turn the pumps on and fine tune the flow adjusters until you are happy with the water jet.

6 Be sure to apply an evenly spaced coat of silicone sealant to the ply panel – the zigzag pattern will allow it to firmly grip onto the steel.

7 Stick the masking tape along the edge of the steel where you will be applying sealant. Now fill the small void between the steel sheets.

8 Adjust the height of the fountains with the pump flow adjusters. Do this while the water is flowing.

natural STREAM

Although carefully constructed, this stream really does look as if it has formed naturally, with the water flowing haphazardly across the stones. The stream's sound, movement and size make it an exciting and impressive garden feature.

1 Mark out the area in which the feature will be built – this should be 1m (3ft) wide and at least 3m (10ft) long. You will also need an existing reservoir, or a new one can be built (see page 15). Clear the ground, removing any stones and rocks – pile these at the outlet end of the site. Now create a shallow pan-like shape for the stream. It does not need to be any deeper than 100mm (4in) in the centre and should have gently sloped sides. Its total width should be around 350mm (1⅙ft).

To create the shape of your outlet, stack broken paving slabs or cheap bricks in a pile to create a height of about 400mm (1¼ft). Then cover it with soil that you removed from the stream. Compact this and flatten the top of the pile to give room for the outlet stones.

2 Take the stones that you have for the stream and, with a hose and brush, give them a good scrub and leave them to

MATERIALS

Old paving slabs or cheap bricks

Hand picked, variously sized rocks

Geotextile underlay

Butyl liner

Sand

Cement

Pump and fittings

Hose and fittings

Conduit

10–50mm (½–2in) pebbles and 50–125mm (2–5in) cobbles

Small piece of timber

TOOLS

Groundwork tools

Building tools

Stiff hand brush

Bucket

1 Once you have cleared the ground, excavate a shallow, pan-like shape for the stream, giving it a gentle slope on either side.

2 Cut and fit the geotextile underlay into the stream shape and then do the same with the butyl liner, leaving extra liner at each side.

KNOW YOUR MATERIALS

Rock and stone: The whole ethos behind creating a natural stream is to try to capture some of the exquisite beauty provided by nature. Each stream will be unique; it is only the theory and construction that are provided here. However, if you really want inspiration, go and look at some natural streams. Observe the journey or passage of the water and see how the rock and loose stone seem to guide the water's path – although in reality it was the water that created their position. It is up to you how authentic and true you want your built version to be to the real thing. There is no right or wrong, just your own perception, so be creative.

dry. With the shape for the stream created, the liner that holds the water can be laid. First cut the underlay to the size of the stream's pan shape, leaving an extra 300mm (1ft) each side. Spread the underlay across the stream and push it firmly into place. Cut out the liner in the same way, this time leaving a little more at either side than you did with the underlay. Drape the liner over the stream and work it gently into the shape.

3 Take the clean, dry stones and lay them around the outlet. First take the flattest stones and lay them in a stair-like formation up the middle of the pile, facing down the stream. These can be wedged into place using smaller stones, as can all the other rock work. Now choose the larger stones that will provide the sides to guide the water as it passes down the stream. Lay these around 150mm (6in) apart at the top, widening to around 250mm (10in) at the end of the outlet. With these in place, create the base layer of the stone mound that will conceal the outlet. The stones need to be cemented to guarantee the water's route. Mix a strong 1:3 cement and sand mortar and point between the stones you have laid. Cover the stream and let the cement cure for 24 hours. During this time, the naturalised stones that mark the water's edge can be placed along the stream.

4 Attach the hose outlet before placing the pump into a bucket. Put the bucket into your existing reservoir and run the pipe up to the stream's outlet. The pipe itself should be disguised if at all possible. This could be achieved by concealing it underneath the rock, or perhaps by burying it inside a protective conduit pipe. The pipe needs to be positioned on top of the layer of stones that are laid on the mound. Position the pipe so it protrudes fractionally over the top of the first stone on the 'stairs' that you laid. Then check that the pipe cannot be seen from the front of the feature and that it will flow into the channel provided by the large side rocks. Lay a bed of mortar and press the pipe into place. Now lay the final layer of rocks on top and around the outlet to finish off the mound.

3 *After you have laid the stones that will be the base layer for the stream, point between them and then leave to dry.*

4 *Once you have laid the pipe in place, lay a final layer of rocks on top of, and around, the outlet to finish it off.*

5 *You should create a natural flow for the stream by mortaring along the bottom of it with a strong sand and cement mix.*

5   A natural flow needs to be created, so mix up a strong sand and cement mix, a little wetter than last time, and shovel this out onto the liner in the shape of the stream. Begin at the top where the outlet stones stop. Start to smooth and spread the mortar into a bowl or pan shape down the stream. You should make sure that this mortar is laid about 20mm ($^3/_4$in) deep. As you do this, be careful not to get any on the stones along the stream's edge as it would be difficult to remove.

6   When you are completely happy with the shape of the stream, take the smallest pebbles and cover the cement and sand mix that you have just laid. Make sure that you have given it a generous covering before tamping the pebbles down. Then take a small piece of timber and gently tamp the pebbles into the mortar. Avoid bringing the mortar through the pebbles to the top by overtamping. Also ensure that the pebbles creep up around the edges of the stream out into the surrounding garden.

7   The cobbles can now be arranged in and around the stream. The best way to try and avoid 'over kill' as you do this is to work up in size. First randomly lay some of the smallest cobbles and then increase the size until the large cobbles are added. With all the cobbles in place you can then review the area and add or subtract any as necessary. As you do this remember that you are trying to create a natural stream. The bed of such a stream would be made up of small cobbles with some larger breaking the surface here and there. The edges should vary in size, leaving large stones prominent at the water's edge.

8   Now turn on the power at the pump. The water will flow out of the pipe outlet and among the stone with some force. This will probably seem very fast to start with, but remember that even the quietest of streams move at some speed. Finally, adjust the stones and rocks along and in the water to improve the look and passage of the finished natural stream.

6 Once the mortar mix is in place, cover over it with the smallest pebbles and then tamp these into place with a small piece of timber.

7 Randomly place the pebbles into position, ensuring the smallest ones are laid first and working up to the largest ones.

8 Once the water is flowing down the stream, adjust the stones and rocks to improve the water's passage.

waterfalls and cascades

planning for waterfalls and cascades

One of the most inspirational and dramatic conclusions to a stream or rill (see pages 52-5) is a waterfall. It can also be used mid-course to add extra interest. Such water management provides high drama, sound and movement in the garden. If, however, you substantially reduce the scale of a waterfall and increase the number of falls along the watercourse, you will have a series of gentle cascades that help direct the flow of the water.

Function and style Waterfalls and cascades provide an ideal way to introduce water into a terraced or sloping garden. In such positions the water in a stream or rill would gather too much momentum and cause the erosion of banks and water loss. In much the same way as a stepped ramp works, waterfalls reduce the angle of a stream. This gives you areas of tranquillity between the energy of the cascades and an overall balance is created.

Ponds and pools benefit enormously from the introduction of a waterfall. The power of falling water breathes life into the lower catchment pool, which is vital if you wish to introduce fish and encourage wildlife. It also clarifies the water, reducing algae and stagnation.

Our modern-day urban lifestyles may reward us in many ways but traffic and neighbourhood noise can wear down the spirit. However, the resonance of a mini waterfall or tumbling cascades, no matter how small, can revitalise a garden and mask unwanted sounds remarkably well.

Few gardens have the capacity for huge rock-built waterfalls. The sheer logistics of humping around giant rocks and boulders, coupled with the expense involved and construction skills needed, means that this style is rarely undertaken. More realistic solutions are achievable, however. If you want a wall of water you can use traditional materials such as natural sandstone. This would suit a rural environment but, if you replace the natural stone with rendered blocks, reflective steel sheets or even marble and glass, the same style can be used to achieve the ultimate contemporary feature for an urban garden.

Design choices A waterfall will be imposing within any garden design so you may want to use it as a focal point that can be seen from the house. The tantalising

The dramatic effect of moving water.

A cascade created by using containers.

Water trickles from a steel container.

A natural stone waterfall.

Waterfalls and cascades work particularly well in a tiered garden, where the various levels provide a natural fall for the water. Whether your feature is part of a magnificent modern ensemble of geometric shapes, dense planting and synthetic materials (top left and right) or simply glides gracefully over the top of a more laid-back brick pool surrounded by simple planting, the movement of water will add another exciting dimension.

Waterfalls and cascades do not have to be huge – a simple trickle of water into a pool beneath works extremely well, especially when surrounded by planting.

movement of water will draw the eye and lead the viewer towards the action, inviting further inspection. People want to stop and take a closer look, so it may be useful to provide seating. Cascades offer a completely different experience. They are usually placed along a watercourse so it is best to have a path beside the stream or rill to enable people to enjoy the feature up close.

On a smaller scale, a cascade can literally be made of three or four pans or bowls – the water just overflows from one into another. This gives you the opportunity to bring water close to your house and means that you don't have to rule out this type of feature if you have a small garden. Almost any style and combination of containers can be used, and planting arching grasses to act as a backdrop to the movement of water will enhance such an intimate design.

The catchment pool or reservoir for a waterfall or cascade should be in keeping with the overall style of the feature. It is often best to keep it low key, as it is not the primary focal point of the design. A sunken pool at ground level works well, but make sure that you have a pool large enough to take the impact of the falling water. Although there is inevitably some water loss it is surprising

> **The tantalising movement of water will draw the eye and lead the viewer towards the action.**

how quickly a pool can empty. By simply adjusting the flow rate on the pump or placing angled stones under the fall to absorb some of the energy you should be able to control the water level.

Most people's senses seem to work overtime when confronted by a waterfall, as these features are wonderfully tactile. In view of this, try to design pathways or standing areas that entice the onlooker to reach out and play with the curtain of water. Natural sunlight shimmers on the surface of a sheet of water so carefully position the angle of the fall to catch the best of the sun's rays. At night, by simply placing an underwater spotlight just beneath the water surface directly under the fall, you can illuminate the natural qualities of the moving water. This technique is perhaps suited to formal and modern styles of cascades where the repetition along a geometric rill can look astonishing from a distance when lit up.

Although you can plan meticulously, accidental changes often achieve the best results. This style of water feature truly provides some of the most exciting ways to play around with water. The following features incorporate some of these ideas and will inspire you to experiment with waterfalls and cascades in your own garden.

A large, rushing waterfall creates an exciting, dramatic effect when used in a large garden (above left). However, waterfalls and cascades can also be much more ordered and tame. For example, the geometric design shown here (above right) incorporates a series of pools and cascades to provide a formal yet calm focal point to the garden. This is surrounded by planting to soften the overall effect.

Water falls onto decorative shells.

A clinging wall of water.

Cascading metal waterfall.

Free-flowing water and steel.

contemporary WATERFALL

This feature is a wonderful use of space – any garden with a wall, patio or border will spring to life with this waterfall. The sound and presence of the fall make it ideal for the contemporary garden.

MATERIALS

High-density concrete blocks

Aerated concrete blocks such as Hebel blocks

Cement, sand and blue metal

Wall ties

Steel waterfall outlet

Render

Exterior plaster bead

Galvanised nails

Exterior masonry paint

Coping stones

Sharp sand

Bitumen paint

Hoses and fittings

Pump and fittings

Conduit

TOOLS

Groundwork tools

Building tools

Metalwork tools

Block saw or old panel saw

Angle grinder

Paintbrush

1 For this feature, you will need a clear, level area that is a minimum of 2.5 x 2.5m (8¼ x 8¼ft). First, mark out the shape of the foundation using sand lines – the back wall is 1.8m (6ft) wide and the pool measures 900 x 1100mm (3 x 3½ft). These are minimum dimensions – if you want the wall to be higher, you will need to increase the thickness of the blocks. Check the corners of the excavations for square before digging using the 3, 4, 5 method (see page 16). Allow an extra 100mm (4in) width all around the blockwork for your foundations. Dig out the reservoir to the required depth and lay the concrete foundation. This should be covered and left for 48 hours.

2 The rear wall can now be built using two courses of concrete blocks below ground level and four courses of Hebel blocks above. Concrete blocks are most durable underground but Hebel blocks allow the shape of the

1 Once you have dug out the reservoir to the required depth, lay the concrete foundation in place.

2 Next, build the rear wall by using concrete blocks below ground level and Hebel blocks above these.

KNOW YOUR MATERIALS

Render: The render applied to the surface of the wall and the inside of the pool performs two important functions. First, it bonds the whole structure together, and second, it provides a resilient surface to the exposed wall. It guarantees the surface will not crack or deteriorate whatever the weather conditions. The base of the pool has had a chamfer haunched around its edge – this is to strengthen the corners of the pool and guarantee the render gives a waterproof edge to the area that is under the most pressure. To make sure the render sticks to the walls or the base of your structure, apply a bonding agent such as Cemstik or Bondcrete to the surface before you render.

waterfall outlet to be cut out with greater ease. Use a 1:4 mortar mix below ground and a 1:6 mix above or a tile glue suitable for external use.

On top of the first course of concrete blocks, lay three wall ties to bond in the pool blockwork. Then lay four more courses of blockwork, leaving the middle block out of the last course because this requires a hole to be cut for the outlet. The pool construction can now be completed using a 1:4 mortar mix. With a hammer and chisel, cut a small section out of the top of a block on the last course – this will give you room to place your conduit pipes to take the pump hose and cable later on.

3 Now, using the steel outlet as a template, draw the section to be removed – check that this section will be central to the pool when it is re-positioned in the wall. Measure the width and length, allowing for an extra 10mm (½in) around both sides and the base for a mortar joint. When the top of the outlet is installed, it should finish flush with the top of the block. Using a block saw or

old panel saw, cut down the two sidelines then carefully chisel out the section. The block can now be built back into the wall and the final course laid on top and levelled. With a pointing trowel, clean off any excess mortar.

4 To fit the outlet, first make up a small amount of 1:6 mortar mix and spread an even 10mm (½in) layer over the bottom of the outlet void. Then place the steel outlet into the hole and use a small level to make sure that the outlet is tilting slightly towards the pool and is perfectly horizontal across its width. This is important as it will give you an even film of water. Now continue to point around the outlet, filling all the spaces and finishing the mortar smooth to the blockwork on the front and the back.

5 Once the main construction of the walls and pool has been finished, covered and left to dry out for a couple of days, the render coat can be applied. To ensure the rendering on the wall has protected, neat edges you will need to fix external plaster bead to them. Measure the

3 *Measure the area that needs to be cut out for the outlet and then saw and chisel the block. Check the outlet sits flush.*

4 *Once the outlet is slotted into its final position, point all around it and smooth the mortar on the back and front.*

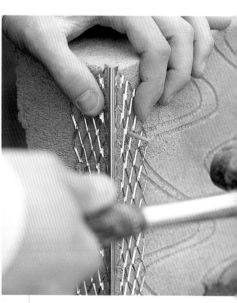

5 *You need to fix external plaster bead to the edges to ensure that the rendered wall will have neat edges.*

edges of your wall and then, with tin snips, cut the lengths of beading. Fix them with galvanised nails, levelling the front and back top beads then fixing the side sections and upright. Pay special attention to how the corners meet.

6   Mix the rendering mortar of 1 part cement, 1 part lime and 3 parts sand. Then, dampening the wall as you go, render the back wall as well as the pool's inside walls and base to an even thickness of 10mm (½in). This is done to give the corners of the pool extra strength. Build up a chamfer where the base meets the walls. Allow the render to dry for a minimum of 48 hours and then paint the main wall with exterior masonry paint.

7   Lay the coping stones around the pool, bedding them on a 1:3 cement and sharp sand mix (see page 14). They may need cutting down to size with an angle grinder. The joints can be pointed with a dryish 1:3 mortar mix. Make it similar to the stones in colour by making up some test samples and adding mortar dyes, letting them dry out until

you have the right colour. Cover and allow the stones and pointing to dry thoroughly for 48 hours. Then apply two coats of bitumen paint to the inside of the pool and allow them to dry.

8   Measure the length of hose needed (from the pump, through the conduit then flat against the wall and onto the back of the waterfall outlet). Add another 300mm (1ft) tolerance and feed the resulting length through the conduit into the pool. Slide the hose over the copper pipe fixed to the back of the outlet and fasten using a jubilee clip. Screw clips to the wall that will secure the hose as it travels down the rear of the wall. Position the pump onto a block or a few bricks to stop sediment from the bottom of the pool getting into it. Attach the hose to the pump outlet with a jubilee clip and draw the power cable through the conduit to the power source. Fill the pool to the underside of the coping stones then turn the power on. Decide if the pump flow valve needs opening or closing to maintain the correct flow of water from the outlet.

6 Once you have mixed up the rendering mortar, you should dampen the back wall and add the render to it.

7 Lay the coping stones around the outside of the pool, bedding them down on a sharp sand and cement mix.

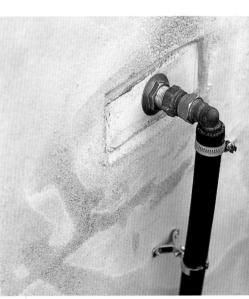

8 With the pump in place, you can connect the hose to the pump's outlet and secure it with a jubilee clip.

steel and STONE WATERFALL

This piece of structural simplicity is a perfect partner for a stunning sculpture. The purity of the forms combine irresistibly with the gentle sound of water, creating a soothing, tranquil environment.

MATERIALS

Road pin or bamboo cane

Ten 150 × 50mm (6 × 2in) pressure-treated timber posts

Prefabricated steel rill

Timber battening

Screws

Cement, sand and blue metal

Timber treatment

Copper sheeting

25mm (1in) copper pins

Flagstone

Bricks

Sand

15mm. ($^2/_3$in) copper pipe

Conduit

Hoses and fittings

90 litre (20 gallon) granite bowl

Pump and fittings

Quick-setting concrete

Bitumen paint

TOOLS

Groundwork tools

Brushes

Building tools

Metalwork tools

Power tools

1 You will need an area 3m² (10ft²). Push a road pin or bamboo cane into the centre of the site. Place the end of your measuring tape over the cane and mark a circular shape at 500mm (1³/₄ft) along the tape using sand. This is the most important shape as it represents the position of the basin. Now repeat this process to create semicircles at 800mm (2¹/₂ft) and 1.2m (4ft) along the tape to give the shape of the excavation. The footing needs to be dug out to a depth of 500mm (1³/₄ft). Remember to keep the sides of the excavation upright and at the correct width.

2 With the footing dug out, the rill can be fitted. Take two pieces of timber that are about 1.5m (5ft) long. Lay them on top of each other, then measure 300mm (1ft) from one end and screw them together. This will give you the cradle support for the front of the rill. Ask for help to position the rill at the central point of the excavation then

1 Once you have measured and marked a sand circle at 500mm (1³/₄ft), mark semicircles at 800mm and 1.2m (2¹/₂ and 4ft).

2 Position the rill in the footing and support it with the cradle. Adjust the upright and level with a spirit level to give a small fall.

KNOW YOUR MATERIALS

Granite bowl: The bowl in this feature is made from solid granite, and was handmade in China and imported. There was a ten week waiting period for the delivery of this basin. We felt this was worth the wait, but if you need to finish your project more quickly there are other alternatives. Half an oak barrel or a glazed bowl could be used to catch the water from the rill. You can use whatever you want as long as the capacity is similar to that of the bowl. You can also change the style dramatically by treating the upright timbers with clear preservative for a more natural look. Alternatively, use mild steel instead of the copper sheet covering the rill post.

support the front of it with your cradle. Adjust the upright and level with a spirit level, ensuring that there is a very slight fall towards the basin.

3 The timber uprights can now be fitted at either side of the rill. Position these in the bottom of the footing to the side of the rill. Keep the heights of all the posts the same – check this with your level. Next, fix a length of timber between the two posts to give support. Now repeat this, erecting all the timbers on both sides of the rill leaving an equal distance between them. You may find that the posts will not create a complete semicircle; this is fine as the aim is a backdrop – you do not need to encase the bowl completely. Mix the concrete (see page 14) and pour it around the base of posts and rill. Leave it to cure for 48 hours. After 24 hours paint all the posts with timber treatment.

4 The upright post of the rill can be seen clearly through the space between the two posts, so hide it by fixing the copper sheeting into place. Measure between the two posts at the rear of the feature, the height from 50mm (2in) above ground level to the top of the posts and the rill. Mark all these measurements onto your copper sheet and cut the shape out with tin snips or a jigsaw with a metal blade. Then fix the copper to the back of the timber using 25mm (1in) copper pins spaced 100mm (4in) apart.

5 Within the circle for the basin excavate down 175mm (7in) from ground level and fill 100mm (4in) of this with concrete – this is the footing for the bowl. Level it off and allow it to dry overnight. When the base is dry, mark around the flagstone onto the dry concrete base. Remove the slab and lay bricks on the inside of this line. Keep them level and ensure the good faces are pointing out. Cover the bricks and let them dry overnight. Measure the lengths of copper pipe needed for between the inside of the basin and the rear of the rill. Also measure between the base of the copper sheet and 150mm (6in) short of

3 Fit the timber uprights either side of the rill and attach a length of timber in between them in order to provide extra support.

4 Hide the part of the rill that shows through the timber uprights by attaching copper sheeting using copper pins.

5 Take the flexible hose, which runs from the copper piping, and fix it to the rill outlet using a jubilee clip.

the rill outlet as well as the upstand that leads into the basin. All these need to be measured with the 90° elbow joints taken into consideration, and any pipe travelling across the open ground will need ducting in rigid plastic conduit. Cut and fix all the pipework, securing it with a bracket at the base of the rill. Attach a small section of flexible hose between the copper pipe at the bottom of the rill post and the tank connector at the back of the rill. Fix the hose into place with jubilee clips.

6   Take the flagstone and drill a hole in the centre large enough for the copper pipe to pass through. Place the flagstone over the copper pipe and onto the brick edge – the flagstone is laid dry in case you need to access the pipework in the future. Check for level and then make any necessary adjustments.

7   Place the bowl over the top of the pipe and onto the flagstone. It will be extremely heavy so ask for help when placing it in position. The pump can now be fitted, but bear in mind that all the connections should be carried out by a qualified electrician. Feed the power cable through a pre-drilled hole at the base of the bowl side and duct it out to the connection point. Place the pump onto a section of slab to keep it off the bowl floor as this will stop sediment from clogging up the pump. Fill the hole in the bottom of the bowl with quick-setting concrete. Fill around all sides of the cable and pipe and finish level with the inside. Fill around the power cable with silicone and then apply two coats of bitumen paint around the pipe to seal the hole.

8   You can now make final adjustments to the pump flow rate and check that all the joints are watertight. Dress the remainder of the site by laying paving or gravel or simply by planting evergreen structural plants.

Alternative materials

This feature is very versatile. The upright timber could be replaced by existing trelliswork or the rill could start from within a banked area or a rock garden.

6 Drill a hole in the centre of the flagstone and place it over the copper pipe. Check for level and make any necessary adjustments.

7 Fill the void in the bottom of the bowl with quick-setting concrete. Ensure that you give it a smooth finish as bitumen paint will be applied on top of it.

8 With the water running, adjust the pump flow rate to suit the speed and rate at which the rill discharges into the granite bowl.

bamboo CASCADE

The passage of water through this clever bamboo cascade will intrigue and delight, while the gentle movement of water adds a zen-like calm to any environment.

MATERIALS

Reclaimed galvanised reservoir

Sand

Bamboo cascade

Oriental bamboo outlet

Garden cane

600mm (23½in) long, 25mm (1in) wide galvanised pole

Membrane

Butyl liner

Pump and fittings

Block

Hoses and fittings

Conduit

Angle iron

Chicken wire

Fuse wire or electrical ties

25–40mm (1–1½in) crushed slate

100–250mm (4–10in) slate paddle stones

Glazed bowl

TOOLS

Groundwork tools

Building tools

Angle grinder

Metalwork tools

1 Decide on the position for your feature and work out where the reservoir will need to be. Put the reservoir on that spot and mark around it using sand. Allow 100mm (4in) extra all the way round for ease of fitting. Excavate the hole, keeping the sides upright and the bottom level. Make sure that when the reservoir is in its final position its lip sits 50mm (2in) above ground level. When it is in place, fill around it with excavated soil and compact it in.

2 Roughly lay out the bamboo feature on the ground to decide on the position for the bamboo outlet. Mark its location on the floor with a garden cane and then remove the feature.

    Next, take the 600mm (2ft) long, 25mm (1in) wide galvanised pole and drive it into the ground over the top of the garden cane using a hammer. Make sure that you

1 Once you have excavated the hole for the reservoir and put it in place, fill the surrounding area with soil, compacting it in.

2 Drive the galvanised pole into the ground with a hammer. Keep 450mm (1½ft) of the pole above ground level.

KNOW YOUR MATERIALS

Bamboo: This is a very popular material for water features but it does need some preparation before it can be used. Within bamboo there are natural internal nodal membranes that need to be removed because they would stop the flow of the water if left in place. They can in fact be taken out very easily by simply pushing a broom handle down the pole. You may also find it surprising that the fleshy inside and the hard exterior of bamboo are not actually waterproof. You therefore need to give the bamboo a generous coat of yacht varnish in order to ensure that you retain the water on its passage through or along the poles.

keep the pole upright and also leave 450mm (1 1/2ft) of the pole above ground level in order to support the bamboo pole outlet later on.

3 Cut and lay membrane on the ground under and around the feature. This will prevent weeds from growing underneath the slate. Measure the amount of butyl liner needed to cover the area beneath the bamboo structure and then around the reservoir. Cut and fit this over the membrane. The hole can then be cut in the liner that will enable the water from the feature to return to the reservoir. (Use a craft knife to do this.)

4 Place the pump into the bottom of the reservoir on top of a block as this will prevent the pump picking up all the sediment from the floor of the reservoir. Lay the power cable into one of the corners of the reservoir and out onto the liner. Attach the flexible hose to the outlet inside the upright bamboo pole with a jubilee clip. The hose will travel down the pipe and out at ground level to the reservoir. Using a jubilee clip again, fasten the hose to the outlet on the pump. The power cable should then run through plastic conduit from the edge of the reservoir to the power source, where it needs to be connected by a qualified electrician.

5 Place the bamboo outlet over the top of the galvanised steel pole, making sure that it points towards the reservoir. Next, fit the angle iron supports over the top of the reservoir. These need to be cut using an angle grinder that has been fitted with a metal cutting blade. File down the ends of the angle iron to prevent puncturing the liner.

Once they have been cut to size, lay the lengths of metal over the top of the reservoir and cushion the edges of the metal against the liner with membrane or extra liner. A small grille will be needed on top of the angle iron to prevent the slate falling through. This can be cut from chicken wire using tin snips and then be laid onto the grille. You may need to secure the two of them together – if so, use fuse wire or electrical ties.

3 Once you have laid the membrane and liner in place, cut a hole in the liner that will allow the water to return to the reservoir.

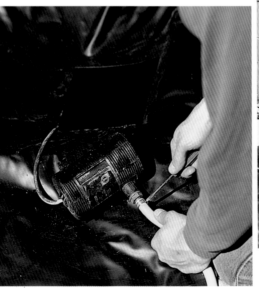

4 Fix the hose to the pump using a jubilee clip. This will ensure that water is taken to the outlet.

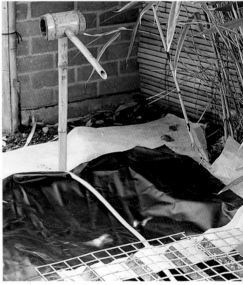

5 Once it has been cut, lay the grille on top of the reservoir. Use membrane to cushion the liner against the hard edges.

6 | Now lay the slate over the entire area and make sure that the liner is completely disguised. Lay the smaller sized slate over the area first and build up to the large slate stones, which should be placed individually. Now position the cascade. It is important to have this safely on level ground, so arrange the slate underneath to suit it, keeping the area as level as possible. (The feature has an integral gradient so you do not need to create a ground level fall.)

7 | Fill the reservoir up with water and, when it is full, turn on the power to the pump. The water will be flowing through the system at a particular speed so you can now adjust it to flow sensibly into the cascade and reservoir. The flow-adjusting valve, within the pipework or on the pump, will give you this control. You may also need to make small adjustments to the outlet on the upright pole or to the angle of the cascade over the grille – try to carry out each of these changes while the water is still flowing.

8 | Ensure that you cover generously where the hose and conduit travel across the top of the liner with the slate. Position the bowl in front of the spout so that the water flows into the bowl before overflowing into the reservoir. Tilting the bowl towards the reservoir will help to do this. Make any final adjustments to the slate or the feature to complete the cascade.

Alternative surroundings

The dressing of the bamboo cascade can be as simple or involved as you make it. Obviously the oriental theme is already in place, but the association with the Japanese garden always warrants some careful thought. You may not want to create a temple garden in your outdoor space, but with a few carefully chosen accessories you can still conjure up an Eastern atmosphere that will sit well with a contemporary or classic setting. It is worth bearing in mind that if you choose to sit the cascade on a patio, you will need to use different materials from those you would select if it were to be sited in a border.

6 Cover the entire area with slate, starting with smaller stones and working up to the largest. Try to keep the area as flat as possible.

7 Turn the water on and check the flow along the feature, adjusting the angle of the cascade over the grille if necessary.

8 Finally, position the bowl in front of the spout. You will probably need to tilt it towards the reservoir.

granite CASCADE

The light granite in this feature is striking against most backgrounds, while the tiered effect creates shadows and interest – as does the dramatic movement of the cascading water. This cascade works well surrounded by water and marginal plants.

MATERIALS

Geotextile underlay

Butyl liner

Cement

Sand

Bricks

38mm (1½in) plastic waste pipe, 2m (6½ft) long

Granite wheels (4 large, 3 small)

38mm (1½in) plastic bend

Silicone sealant

Pump, flexible hose and fittings

Bucket

Pebbles (various sizes)

Steel sheeting

8mm (⅓in) nuts and 100mm (4in) long 8mm (⅓in) bolts

150mm (6in) length of wire

Fishing weight

TOOLS

Groundwork tools

Building tools

Metalwork tools

Pencil

Mastic gun

Felt tip pen

Power tools

1 Choose your site, which needs to be close to an existing body of water or reservoir. The area need be no bigger than 1 x 1m (3 x 3ft), but must be cleared of all debris and left with a smooth gradient towards the reservoir. Cut a piece of geotextile underlay to the size of the area you are building on and lay it into position. Then do the same for the butyl liner, but make it fractionally larger than the underlay. Be sure to drape the liner into the reservoir to ensure the water returns there after flowing down the cascade.

2 The cascade will be placed centrally on the liner. Mix up a small amount of 1:3 cement and sand on which to lay the foundation bricks. Lay a bed of mortar under each brick to form three sides of a square, with the open end pointing away from the reservoir. The bricks should be laid level, so use a spirit level to check this. It is important to

1 Cut and lay both the underlay and liner, making sure that you drape the liner into the reservoir so the water will return there.

2 Lay the foundation bricks onto a 1:3 mortar mix and then ensure that they are level by placing a spirit level on top of them.

KNOW YOUR MATERIALS

Outlet cap: The outlet cap disperses the water from the pipe evenly over the granite wheels' edges. The construction of the cap looks very difficult but is in fact straightforward. The fishing weight inside the tube acts as a restraint to the pressure of the water, so for a more powerful flow a larger weight would be used. There is nowhere for the water to go apart from the sides under the small gap provided by the cap, so this gives good control from a very simple design. The circle is steel, which will rust but won't harm the water or feature. The cap can be made from other sheet metals, but if you decide to use stainless steel it is best to get it cut by a metal smith.

get this right as the stability of the whole feature relies on the foundation bricks. Clean up the area once the bricks are laid, cover them and leave to cure for 24 hours.

3 Construct the pipework for the cascade by using a 2m (6½ft) length of 38mm (1½ft) plastic waste pipe. There are seven granite wheels and seven mortar joints that are needed to secure them together, so calculate the total combined measurement of the granite and the joints, which will give you the measurement for the first cut. You need to take 10mm (½in) off this measurement to recess the pipe at the top of the finished cascade. Cut the pipe with a hacksaw and connect one end of it to a 90° plastic waste bend. The other pipe needs to fit in the other end of the 90° bend and protrude over the granite base stone by 75mm (3in).

Next, lay a 10mm (½in) layer of mortar on top of the foundation bricks. Place the pipework into position, making sure that the larger pipe that passes through the granite is roughly in the middle of the bricks. Now slide one of the larger granite wheels down over the pipe through the hole provided. With the wheel in place take a rubber mallet and level, and tap the wheel onto the mortar. Repeat this process until you are happy with the level of the base stone.

4 With the base stone in position you can complete the cascade by adding the other granite wheels. On top of the base stone you need to lay a 10mm (½in) mortar bed, but remember that the size of the next wheel is smaller. To prevent laying mortar where it is not wanted, place the smaller wheel on top of the base granite stone dry, and mark the width of the smaller granite wheel onto the base stone with a pencil. Remove the smaller wheel and apply the mortar inside the markings. Then slide it back on, repeating the method for securing it into place.

5 Repeat this process until you finish the stack with one of the large granite wheels at the top. Your last stone should be around 10mm (½in) above the pipe. There will be a gap around the pipe of around 3mm (⅛in), which will

3 Slide the first granite wheel down over the pipe, tapping it into the mortar using a rubber mallet. Then check it is level.

4 Once you have marked the area on the base stone that needs to be covered in mortar, put the mortar on, followed by the next stone.

5 The final stone sits above the pipe. There is a gap around this pipe that should be filled with silicone sealant.

need sealing. Take a tube of silicone sealant in a mastic gun and carefully fill the void. Smooth on the sealant with a wet finger, then cover and leave to dry for 24 hours.

6 The pump should now be positioned in the reservoir to provide the water for the cascade. Place the pump into a bucket, as this will cut down on the weed and debris from the existing body of water that is sucked up. The flexible pipe from the pump will need to be connected to the waste pipe that comes out from under the foundation bricks. The pipe should be hidden, so plan a route through planting or, as here, lie it flat against the liner so that it can be covered in stone later. With a jubilee clip, connect the end of the flexible pipe to the pipe at the bottom of the cascade. Tighten it well and lay the hose flat against the ground.

7 Next, cover both the waste and flexible pipes with small pebbles. Lay these out over the entire area of the liner. Lay them in increasing size, not only to cover the pipes but also to naturalise the area. Lay some in the water and the surrounding planting too to cover the butyl liner.

8 The outlet will now be dry, so you can make the steel cap. Mark a 100mm (4in) diameter circle on a piece of steel sheeting with a felt tip pen. Lay this onto a thin sheet of plywood and, wearing goggles, cut the shape out using a jigsaw with a metal blade in it. Then mark the centre of the circle and drill an 8mm (⅓in) hole in the steel. Take a 100mm (4in) long 8mm (⅓in) eyelet bolt and pass it through the hole in the steel. Screw an 8mm (⅓in) nut onto the end of the bolt – this will stop the bolt passing back through the drilled hole in the circular steel. The large fishing weight needs to be attached to a 150mm (6in) length of wire, the other end of which is fixed to the eyelet on the bolt. When you are happy that this is secure, lower the weight into the pipe and the steel circle will rest on top of the final wheel. Turn on the power to the pump and observe the water as it cascades over the edge of the granite from under the cap. Adjust the flow if necessary.

6 Tighten up the jubilee clip that connects the end of the flexible pipe to the pipe at the bottom of the cascade. Lie the pipe flat against the ground.

7 Cover all the pipes and the liner with pebbles. Lay them in increasing size in order to naturalise the whole area.

8 Attach the large fishing weight to one end of the wire. The other end of the wire should then be fixed to the eyelet bolt.

fountains, springs & spouts

planning for fountains, springs & spouts

Fountains, springs and spouts collectively form the largest proportion of the water features that are commercially available for gardens today. There is a huge diversity of features – from a simple overflowing urn to a formal classical fountain. You can let inspiration run riot with the technology available and the diversity of modern-day materials, which will allow you to create exactly the type of feature that you want.

Function and style Fountains are extremely diverse in style and function, ranging from basic bubble features to huge, multi-jet systems that are operated using computer-control mechanisms. Formal fountains are associated with high jets of water with varying spray patterns. They are ideal as centrepieces in small courtyards and, if you have the luxury of a long garden, make excellent focal points at the end of a vista. However, before you try to recreate Versailles in your back garden, there is a golden rule to follow when deciding the height of the jet – it should not exceed the radius of the basin or you will lose most of the water over the side. In windy sites you may have to reduce this further or use another style of feature.

You can be really creative with informal fountains as there is a huge choice – from contemporary stainless steel or glass to handmade folded concrete. Glass, copper and ceramic work very well with water and can be an amazing source of inspiration.

Nature has a simple way of filtering and cleansing ground water and then delivering it back to the surface through a natural spring. The bubbling effect of a feature created in a garden brings the same life and movement. If you place such a feature further away from the house, this provides an ideal opportunity to create some mystery around it.

Wall-mounted spouts, on the other hand, can be placed in an area of less than 0.5m² ($1^3/_4$ft²), which means that they are the perfect choice for smaller gardens. The great thing about such features is the sheer number of products that are available on the market – traditional animal and human masks are easily obtainable but you can use anything – such as junk from a metal yard or a moulded plaster shell – to create your own unique spout.

Bubble fountain among cobbles.

Amorphous fountain.

A stone spout.

Bamboo spout guiding water into a metal

Fountains are extremely versatile water features. Whether they be formal or informal, the sound of moving water means they are very pleasing in both large and small gardens. Do not be afraid to experiment with unusual materials. The tiered fountain shown here (top left) is made up of metallic-finished plastic pillows. If you have a small space, a bubble fountain can be a good feature (top right). Alternatively, use circular ceramic discs to create an elegant tiered fountain (above).

In a larger space, water can be jetted in many different directions using a system of spouts. Here the water is creating arches over a big pond.

The water will need to be collected in a reservoir of some kind. This could either be a pot overflowing into a hidden chamber containing the pump or a container placed in the ground that collects the water directly. There is so much choice of style that you will easily be able to find something suitable for your own particular garden.

Design choices   These features have perhaps the widest range of tricks and effects to design with, so consider the following carefully before deciding on which type to have. Do you, for example, want to create a mysterious, intriguing feature that can't be seen straight away? If you place a fountain or spring behind a division along a pathway, the sound will draw people closer as it is hard to resist. Partially screening a feature with tall plants will also make everyone want to peer into the feature.

You don't have to have a lot of space to make a mysterious feature, however. Surprise can also be created by using a grotesque wall mask that is covered in mosses, with just a little trickle of water that enters a mossed-up stone trough. To give the stone an aged appearance, simply paint on yoghurt or liquid fertiliser. If you keep it moist then algae and lichens will start to appear.

> *Partially screening a feature with tall plants will make everyone want to peer into the feature.*

Does your garden have a lot of surrounding noise, such as that of traffic or from other houses? If so, then you may want to use a fountain or spring to mask it. The trick here is not to overfill your own space with noise or you could end up shouting at your family or guests in order to be heard. To avoid this, fill a bucket with water and trickle a hose into it from 500mm (1¾ft) to see how much noise it creates.

Moving water features can easily be combined with other features. For example, a natural spring could flow into a rock-filled pan that then overflows into a stone rill that takes the water on a journey to another part of the garden. It can then be collected in a chamber and be pumped back directly to the spring.

Moving water also gives you the chance to create some stunning effects at night, so you should decide whether this is something you want to experiment with. A direct light placed high up and then shone on a fountain pool will throw a free light show onto a wall or temporary canvas. Alternatively, the ability of a single jet to hold onto light when it is lit from beneath using an underground source will never cease to amaze the viewer.

The projects constructed on the following pages provide you with all the inspiration and basic techniques that you need to create your own distinct moving water feature.

This evocative geyser (above left) will create an atmospheric feature in a larger garden. Alternatively you could use a sculptural spout (above right) to create a focal point within a pool. The water cascades down this centrepiece to provide an eyecatching element. These features have both been used to add interest to existing bodies of water.

A ceramic sphere with bubble fountain.

Sand-blasted, tubular glass fountains.

Oriental bamboo spout.

Domed fountain spray.

medusa head
WALL FOUNTAIN

There is nothing so enchanting as discovering water trickling from a mysterious animated mask surrounded by lush planting in a secret part of the garden. This type of feature is ideally suited to smaller gardens where there is little floor area for a feature.

MATERIALS

Sand

75 × 75mm (3 × 3in) post

Sleepers

Cement, sand and blue metal

Battens

Concrete slab

Reservoir tank 900 × 600m (2³⁄₄ × 2ft)

Conduit

Coping stones

Oak timber plank, minimum 2.4m (8ft) in height

Galvanised coach screws

Wall mask

10mm (¹⁄₂in) soft copper pipe

15mm (²⁄₃in) copper pipe

Pump, hose and fittings

Brick or block

10–15mm (¹⁄₂–²⁄₃in) elbow adapter

15mm (²⁄₃in) elbow

TOOLS

Groundwork tools

Drill

Woodwork tools

Building tools

1 Measure and locate the pool position and size with a sand line. Then mark out and position the post support and front sleeper. This should be placed approximately 1m (3ft) from the centre of the pool. Excavate the post and sleeper hole so that about a quarter of the height of the post will be below ground level; that is, with 1.8m (6ft) above ground level there should be 600mm (2ft) below. Excavate an equal measurement – approximately 100mm (4in) – around the post or sleeper. Now position the post and sleeper in the hole and concrete to 100mm (4in) below ground level. It may help to use battens to hold the post as you do this.

2 Allow the post concrete to cure overnight, then mark out and excavate the reservoir, allowing space for a slab to be bedded on sand at the bottom of the hole (approximately 75mm/3in). This slab should be levelled both ways so that

1 Once you have excavated space for the post and sleeper and put them in place, concrete around them.

2 The reservoir lip should sit 75–100mm (3–4in) above the surrounding soil. Once this is levelled, position the ducting pipe.

KNOW YOUR MATERIALS

The mask: The head is made of granite and lead was used to create the serpents. These materials have the advantage of looking aged even though they are new. There are, however, many other traditional heads and masks available that are made of reconstituted stone or concrete. They do tend to look a bit harsh when new, so it helps to paint the surfaces with a yoghurt to encourage premature ageing.

Oak upright: The weathered oak plank used here has been specifically chosen to add interest due to its contorted and twisted character. You can pick up all sorts of amazing one-offs by visiting your local salvage yard.

the reservoir will also sit level. The height of the reservoir lip should finish 75–100mm (3–4in) above the surrounding soil height in order to allow for the base material under the coping stones, which should finish flush with the top of the reservoir. Once the reservoir is placed and levelled, the conduit for the pump hose and the electrics can be positioned. Drill holes as high up the reservoir as possible as this will dictate the final water level. Now the base material of concrete can be laid around the reservoir. A general concrete mix is suitable as a base for the stones to be laid over (see page 14).

3   After the concrete has cured overnight the coping stones can be laid. These should overhang the inside edge of the reservoir by 35–50mm (1½–2in) to conceal the top and the water line. Some of the coping stones might need cutting, so do this before laying them on the mortar. Once you are happy with the positioning of the stones they can be laid with a strong bricklaying mortar mix (see page 14). Finally the stones should be pointed with a dryish mix.

4   Now the oak timber can be fixed to the post with galvanised coach screws. Try to fix one behind where the mask will be and another as low as possible so that the screws cannot be seen when the project is finished. Hold the fountain head in place and mark the position of the fixing and pipe holes on the timber. The hole through the post can then be drilled and the mask fixed into position.

5   Having secured the mask, feed a 10mm (½in) soft copper pipe through the post, oak plank and mask so that it protrudes by 10mm (½in). The pipe can then be cut at a 45° angle with a hacksaw and pushed back into its final position. This angle needs to be cut for two reasons: firstly, the pipe slightly protrudes from Medusa's head so cutting it at an angle will make it look less obtrusive. Secondly, the water will pour out of an angled cut on a pipe much better than it would from a flat-ended pipe.

Next, cut the end behind the post for connection to the upright 15mm (⅔in) copper pipe – this will be done later.

3 Once you have made any cuts and checked their positions, lay the coping stones onto mortar so that they overhang the reservoir.

4 Now fix the oak timber to the post using galvanised coach screws. Try to place the screws where the mask can cover them.

5 Once the mask is in place, feed a 10mm (¼in) soft copper pipe through the post, oak and mask so that it protrudes out the back.

6   The pump can now be placed in the reservoir pool. Sit the pump on a brick or block to prevent any silt or grit entering the mechanics of the pump. Thread the hose and pump wire through the pre-drilled holes in the pool wall and into the ducting at the back of the post. Check that you lay the hose and cable as close to the pool wall as possible. Although the hose seems bulky and intrusive, you will not see it against the black reservoir, which will be filled with water.

7   Fix a length of 15mm (²/₃in) copper pipe to the back of the post. This connects the spout tube to the hose from the pump. You will need a 10–15mm (¹/₂–²/₃in) elbow at the top of the pipe and a standard 15mm (²/₃in) elbow at the base. You can now do the final connections at the base of the post. The hose is attached to the copper upright using a jubilee clip. A flexible hose is ideal, as it is easy to pass through the ducting and onto the copper pipe. The pump cable can be connected to an external junction or switch by a qualified electrician.

8   Fill the pool up to just under the pipe holes and then turn on the pump. Try to adjust the water jet so that it falls in the middle of the pool. You can do this with small adjustments to the pump flow valve.

Alternative materials

Although this mask is fixed to a weathered piece of oak plank, most gardens have a wall, garage or boundary of some description that can be used instead. These alternatives are just as effective – as long as you can get to the other side to do the pipework, they are ideal structures. If you are after a 'softer' approach, a post can be fixed within some hedging or taller planting (*Miscanthus*) to create a more subtle effect as it will suggest the head is actually peering out. Planting around the reservoir at the base of the feature so that the water disappears into a planted hole will further highlight the effect. Alternatively, you could use a narrower edging on the pool, dig in organic matter around the reservoir and then plant it up with ivy or vines to climb around the mask.

6 *Make sure that you place the pump in the reservoir on a brick or block to prevent any silt or grit getting into its mechanism.*

7 *The connections at the bottom of the post can now be finished. Flexible hosing should be used and fixed to the pipe with a jubilee clip.*

8 *With the water running, adjust the speed and distance of the water by turning the flow-adjusting valve on the pump.*

glass cube FEATURE

This glass cube feature is ideal for a garden that has no room for a big water feature. It uses the bare minimum of space, but its impact and style compete with the most elaborate of waterfalls.

MATERIALS

75 x 75mm (3 x 3in) posts

75 x 18mm (3in x 1¾in) pressure-treated timber

Cement, sand and blue metal

Zinc-plated screws

Wood preservative

Glass cubes

Vessel for reservoir

Bolts

Rubber washers

15mm (⅔in) and 10mm (½in) copper pipe and elbows

Porphyry flagstone slab

Sharp sand

Bricks

Pump and fittings

Hoses and fittings

Bitumen paint

Conversion and size-reducing joiners or adaptors

TOOLS

Groundwork tools

Building tools

Pencil

Power tools

Metalwork tools

Brushes

1 You will need a 2 x 1m (6½ x 3ft) area for the feature. Excavate two 600mm (2ft) deep holes. They should be 1.1m (3¼ft) apart centre to centre, making the holes 300mm (1ft) square. Now centre the 75mm (3in) posts in the holes and check that they are exactly 1.2m (4ft) apart (outside to outside). This will be easier if you use battens to support them. Use a 5m (15ft) tape to check that they are an equal distance apart top and bottom. Now mix up your concrete (see page 14) and shovel it into both holes, tamping it down as you go. Ensure that the posts are upright again and support them with lengths of timber. Leave the concrete for 48 hours to cure.

2 Using a set square, mark your horizontal slats and cut them using a jigsaw or quality panel saw. Starting at 1.8m (6ft) above ground level, fix the first slat using zinc-plated screws and check for level. Then measure down 15mm

1 Concrete your posts and check that they are still upright before supporting them with lengths of timber.

2 Once you have cut the timbers to the same length, fix them to the posts with screws, ensuring the spacing is consistent throughout.

KNOW YOUR MATERIALS

Glass cubes: When working with glass cubes it is best to keep them away from the building work until they are ready to be fitted to your surface so that they remain clean. When fixing each cube, it is important to use rubber washers in order to cushion the glass against the surface you are fixing it to. If the cubes are to be fixed to a brick or block wall, be sure to coat the wall with sealant, as this will prevent the excess water from the cubes and vessel causing the wall to deteriorate. Practically anything can be used as the reservoir (vessel) – this depends on your taste, garden and budget. Visit a salvage yard or scrap metal dealer to see what is available.

(^{2}/$_3$in) and fix the second slat and repeat the process until you are 150mm (6in) above ground level, checking as you go that the slats are level. Then coat the trellis with wood preservative and allow it to dry for 12 hours.

3 | To attach the glass cubes to the trelliswork you will need to know how high up the trellis your vessel sits – this will give you an approximate height for your bottom cube. Simply measure the height of your vessel and add the height of the base slab that it will sit on. Transfer the final measurement to the trellis from ground level. Mark a pencil line exactly in the centre of the panel. Your bottom cube should be positioned around 150–200mm (6–8in) above the top of the vessel. Using a pencil, extend the centre line up the entire panel (checking for upright using a level) – this will help when positioning the cubes. The top cube is placed three or four slats below the top of the panel and the middle cube should be an equal distance between the top and bottom. You should aim for a gap of 200–250mm (8–10in) between cubes.

Now mark and drill the bolt holes for each cube. Drill from the front to prevent unsightly splinters. Bolt the cubes onto the trellis using rubber washers in front of and behind the glass, which will prevent the bolts coming into direct contact with the glass. Do not overtighten the bolts.

4 | The slab that the vessel sits on has a void beneath it for pipework. It is created by laying four bricks on a 50mm (2in) sharp sand and cement (1:3) bed. The sides of the bricks should be flush with the edge of the slab so check the centralised position of the 450mm^2 (1^1/$_2$ft^2) slab first. The tops of the bricks should be at ground level.

Using 15mm (^{2}/$_3$in) copper pipe and elbow joints, install the pipe that will travel down the back of the trellis. It should start 75mm (3in) below the spout and pass through the void. From there a 150mm (6in) upstand travels through the vessel's base to connect onto the pump.

5 | The slab will need a 25mm (1in) hole drilled through its centre to allow the pipe and pump cable to pass through.

3 When you are bolting the cubes to the trelliswork use a rubber washer between the glass and bolt to protect the glass.

4 Once the bricks that will create the void are in place, install the pipework that will connect to the pump.

5 Pull the pump's power cable through the bottom of the pot until the pump is positioned at the bottom of the vessel.

Lower the slab carefully over the pipe upstand and check its position and level. Also check that the hole in the vessel is 25mm (1in) in diameter, then pull the pump power cable through it and through the hole in the stone until the pump is positioned at the bottom of the vessel on a brick. Place the vessel over the top of the upstanding copper pipe and onto the flagstone. Fill the hole in the bottom of the vessel with cement until the cement is level with the inside of the pot. Paint the inside of the vessel around the pipework and power cable with two coats of a bitumen sealant and leave to dry for 24 hours. Connect the pump to the copper upstand using a short length of 18mm (³/₄in) flexible hose and jubilee clips.

6   At the top of the pipe that runs vertically up the rear of the trellis, fit the 15mm (²/₃in) side of the conversion joint. Measure the length of 10mm (¹/₂in) soft copper pipe that you need to run from this joint, through the point that is marked on the timber and down to 75mm (3in) above the first glass cube. Drill a hole at the point on the

timber using a 10mm (¹/₂in) drill bit. At one end of the 10mm (¹/₂in) pipe cut an angle using a hacksaw in order to make it look more ornamental. Carefully bending the soft copper pipe, pass it through the hole until it is over the top of the first cube. Then fit the connecting end into the size-reducing joint. Adjust the spout so it is in the right position over the cube.

7   Fill the vessel up with water and turn the power onto the pump. The height of the water in the vessel is important to the success of the feature. This is because the water falling into the vessel is meant to be seen and heard. This is achieved by filling the vessel up fully, to within 50mm (2in) of the top.

8   Observe the flow of water through the cubes and then decide whether any adjustment is needed. If the fall of the water into the vessel is too erratic, turn the flow rate adjuster on the pump down. If there is hardly any water flowing through the cubes, turn the flow up.

6 Once the copper pipe has been bent and passed through the timber, fit it into the size-reducing joiner.

7 Fill the vessel with clean water. You should see the level of water in the vessel at all times, so fill it up until it is 50mm (2in) from the top.

8 With the water running through the cubes, adjust the flow valve on the pump to change the overall speed of the water.

volcanic SPRING

Springs and geysers appear to erupt from the depths of the earth, giving a garden a wonderful feeling of excitement. This feature is a white water spring; the battered rock and close pillars of water provide real atmosphere.

1   As a guide you will need around 2m² (6½ft²). Mark out a 1m (3ft) diameter circle in the middle of the area using a peg driven into the ground and then attach a loose string around the peg. Measure along the string 500mm (1¾ft) from the peg, then mark the string at this point with a felt tip pen. Holding the string in one hand, travel around the peg in a circular motion, laying sand on the ground at the point of the mark. Continue until you have a circle marked on the ground, then remove the peg and start to excavate inside the sand line. When you are digging the hole, concentrate on keeping the inside edges of the hole vertical. The depth of the hole should be around 800mm (2½ft) as a large volume of water flows through this feature and therefore it needs a reasonably large reservoir.

2   The hole now needs to be screened with 50mm (2in) depth of sand. This is to protect the pool liner from any

MATERIALS

Sand

Pool liner

Pump, spouts and fittings

Bricks

Conduit

Steel rods

Membrane

Reinforcement mesh

Chicken wire

Grotto rock

TOOLS

Felt tip pen

Groundwork tools

Building tools

Metalwork tools

1 Excavate the hole to a depth of about 800mm (2½ft). As you do this, ensure that you keep the sides as vertical as possible.

2 Start laying the liner from the bottom of the pool, carefully folding it as you go. It is best to do this with your shoes off, to prevent ripping.

KNOW YOUR MATERIALS

Geysers: The key to an effective geyser is the nozzle fittings that are placed on the end of each pipe. A mechanism inside disrupts the flow so that air is added to the jet of water, thereby creating the geyser's distinctive bubbling white water. Your choice of geyser will be influenced by how much noise and movement you wish the spring to create in your garden. When planning this feature think about the position. In order to give a powerful impression of excitement and surprise, you may choose to plant around the spring with grasses to give a 'lost world' look to the feature. But for a modern interpretation the volcanic spring could stand alone, within a seating area.

objects in the soil that could tear or puncture it, so you could use a geotextile underlay instead. You will need to create a collection area surrounding the main reservoir to allow the excess water to drain back into the reservoir. Create this with sand too. This area needs to be roughly circular in shape, sloping down towards the reservoir. It should have a heaped lip to prevent water flowing further outwards than intended. When you have compacted and spread out the sand you can lay the liner. Calculate the size of the liner required (see page 15). Removing your footwear, start laying the liner from the bottom of the pool and work up, carefully folding and overlapping around the circular pool out onto the collection area. Leave the liner untrimmed until the reservoir is filled.

3   The pump work for this feature can be achieved in several ways – the submersible pump here has three heads that are attached via ready-made arms. There are individual flow adjustments on each of the heads, which gives you the flexibility to change the individual heights of

each geyser. An alternative method involves using three separate smaller pumps with a flow adjuster attached to each riser pipe. Remember that all pumps should sit on bricks within the reservoir to prevent debris from damaging the internal workings. Once the pump cable leaves the water feature, feed it through the conduit until it reaches the junction box, where it can be connected to the mains supply by a professional.

4   Cut four lengths of the reinforcing steel rod to completely bridge the reservoir and overlap by around 300mm (1ft) either side of the pool. Lay these at equal intervals across the pool surface – the rods may be sharp, so lay a geotextile underlay or membrane underneath to prevent damage to the liner. Measure the size of your reservoir pool and transfer this measurement to the sheet of mesh. Cut it out at this size and place it over the steel rods.

Cut a final layer of expanded metal mesh to size (you can use chicken wire) and lay it over the reinforcement mesh as before. All of the mesh work up until now has

3 The submersible pump used in this project has three heads that are attached with ready-made arms.

4 Once the reinforcement mesh is in place, put a layer of chicken wire over it. You will need to cut around the fountain heads.

5 Now that all the meshwork is completed, fill the pool up by using a hose and directing it through the mesh.

been large enough to arrange around the fountain heads, but you will need to cut holes into the expanded metal grille to allow the heads to come through. The weight of the stones will hold the mesh down so don't worry if it doesn't lie completely flat at first.

5 After all the mesh work is in, the pool can be filled up. The quickest way is to use a hose. You need to fill it up to about 100mm (4in) from the top to provide an ample amount of water for this feature. Now turn on the pump to see how the springs work together. Take a few steps back and make a note of which springs need to be raised or lowered. Turn the pump off before making any changes.

6 Now position your rock. In this case Grotto rock was used because of its character. The spouts that are sticking out through the grille need to be disguised. Begin to place the rocks on top of the grille around the spouts. At first, position the rocks directly next to, and a little higher than, the spouts so that the spouts are completely hidden. Then spread the rest of the stone out to cover the entire grille, checking the overall appearance and making sure that no grille or liner shows through.

7 Water will naturally evaporate from the pool and the hotter the weather the more water you'll loose. Therefore you should keep an eye on the water level every so often by removing one of the stones and having a look. If necessary, top it up with a watering can or a bucket until it is 100mm (4in) from the top once again.

8 With everything in place, and the water flowing, make the final adjustments to the positioning of the rocks.

Alternative materials

There are so many different stones and rocks for you to choose from that it is important that you go and see the selection available. The best place to go is your local natural stone supplier – they will be more than happy to show you their wide range.

6 Start laying your rocks around the spouts and then work outwards to cover the entire grille, making sure nothing shows through.

7 Your reservoir will need topping up with clean water every so often. Bring the level up to around 100mm (4in) from the top.

8 Final adjustments to the formation and positioning of the rocks can now be carried out while the geysers are in full flow.

contemporary WATER BASIN

This piece gives you the opportunity to place a stunning, modern water feature anywhere in the garden. As a patio feature, for example, this sculpture is a wonderful design statement.

MATERIALS

150 x 25mm (6 x 1in) planed timber

Screws

Sand

Roadbase

Cement, sand and blue metal

Concrete sealant

Tile adhesive

Tiles

Grout

Basin, with pump, hose and their fittings already in place

Chicken wire

Membrane

Pebbles

75–100mm (3–4in) cobbles

TOOLS

Groundwork tools

Building tools

Brushes

Metalwork tools

Bucket

1 The shuttering for the plinth of the basin is made first. Using 150 x 25mm (6 x 1in) planed timber make up a 700mm² (2¹/₃ft²) frame that is screwed together externally at each corner. Lay this on your proposed site and check it for square. Now mark out around the timber with some sand – keep the line about 50mm (2in) away from the edge of the frame. Remove the frame and dig out inside the sand marks to a depth of 100mm (4in). Then fill the hole to ground level with roadbase. Compact this with a hand rammer and check for level. Lift the frame into place and check the corners with the square. Take eight pegs (two for each side) and drive them down the side of the framework about 150mm (6in) in from each corner.

2 Check that the base is perfectly square before concreting. Also make sure that the pegs are below the height of the frame before the concrete is placed – this ensures you are

1 Once you have excavated the hole and filled it with roadbase, lay the frame back over and drive pegs around it to aid stability.

2 Fill inside the frame with concrete and level it off by dragging your spirit level across it, sliding the level left to right as you go.

KNOW YOUR MATERIALS

Surrounds: It is important to consider the way in which you surround the plinth of this feature with regard to maintenance and aesthetics. Here, the feature is surrounded with several different surfaces. Two sides of the feature have an exposed aggregate patio along them, one has a planted border and the lawn cuts into the other. The bulky timber edging provides a strong edge to the entire area. The simplicity of the basin is in stunning contrast to the striking tiled base. The same effect is achieved by using a simple surround of pebbles within the timber frame. Because this is positioned at the bottom of the tiles, the contrast is striking.

able to strike off the concrete easily. The volume of concrete needed can be worked out with a simple calculation (see page 14). A general concrete mix is adequate for this task, as it will be wet enough to work into the corners of the frame. Mix the concrete on a board near the base, then shovel it in making sure that any voids are filled, concentrating on the corners as you go. When you are happy there is enough in the frame, begin to level it. Take your spirit level and place it on the top of one of the sides of timber then, standing over the base, drag the level towards you sliding it left to right as you go. Remove the excess concrete and begin again – keep this process up until the concrete is level with the timber over the entire base. Be careful to replace any holes and remove bumps. A few gentle taps with a hammer on each side will encourage the water and cement to come to the surface, which will make tiling easier. Take care not to overtamp the concrete as this segregates the aggregate and weakens the slab. Leave this covered to cure for 48 hours before tiling.

3 Your base should now be dry enough for you to remove the framework. You will need to unscrew the fixings and release the sides gently. Do not panic if there is the odd divot or hole – you can take care of this with tile adhesive. Give the base a quick brush over with a soft hand brush before sealing the concrete. The sealant needs to be painted over the whole base. Be generous, as the sealant hardens the concrete and stops the adhesive drying out too quickly, giving you time to position and fix the tiles. Cover and leave the base to dry for 24 hours.

4 In a small bucket, prepare your exterior tile adhesive to form a mix with the consistency of wallpaper paste. Clean up around the base to prevent debris getting mixed up with the adhesive. Before you apply the adhesive to the top of the base, dry lay the tiles to check their position. Allow for an overhang around the edge, which will help the top and sides meet up neatly. When you are satisfied, remove the tiles and apply the tile adhesive. Using your trowel, spread the adhesive over the top of the plinth

3 Brush the base over and then seal the concrete by painting a sealant onto it. Leave this to dry for 24 hours.

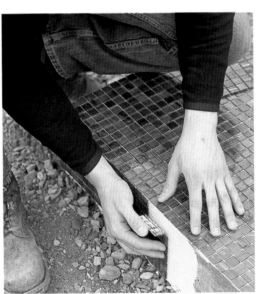

4 Apply your exterior adhesive and then lay the tiles on top of it, applying even pressure in order to ensure that they are bedded properly.

5 Once all the tiles are in place, spread grout over them using a rubber float to make sure that all the joints have been filled.

evenly. Then, with the toothed edge of the float, drag across the surface to create an even layer of adhesive. Lay the tiles on the top of the plinth, applying even pressure to bed them correctly. Check the overhang is even and remove any excess adhesive. Once the top has been tiled leave it for 24 hours, then tile the remaining four sides, paying special attention to the neatness of the top and side joint. Cover the base and allow 48 hours for it to dry.

5 Mix the grout up ready for spreading then apply an even layer of grout over the tiles, starting on the top. Work it in with a rubber float and make sure that all the joints are filled, especially the edges. Remove the excess grout with the float and repeat the process on the sides, finally wiping over the whole plinth with a damp sponge. Cover the plinth up and allow it to dry for 24 hours before polishing the tiled surface with a clean dry cloth.

6 Now the basin can be placed onto the plinth. Ask for help as it is heavy. Place the basin onto the plinth, keeping it centred. Take care not to disturb the tiles or chip the sculpture when positioning the basin.

7 Take a piece of chicken wire and cut a square section out that is large enough to cover the void for the pump. Using tin snips, cut a small hole for the fountain hose to come through, then cover it with a membrane to stop debris collecting in the sump hole.

8 Wash a bucketful of pebbles in water and spread them around the fountain hose, covering the membrane but ensuring the spout is uncovered. Turn the power on to the pump and see if it needs any minor adjustments. You may need to move the pebbles around to suit the water movement.

Now dress around the tiled base with 75–100mm (3–4in) pebbles. These should be cleaned first before being placed. For the best results pile the large pebbles several layers deep and arranged so that the base of the tiles are not visible.

6 Lift the basin onto the plinth. This is heavy work so ask for help. Take care not to disturb any of the tiles as you do this.

7 Take a piece of chicken wire and cut out a square piece to size, so that it will fit over the void for the pump.

8 Wash the pebbles and place them over the wire mesh. Be sure to cover over the membrane while creating a natural pattern.

small water features

planning for small water features

When it comes to water feature design, powerful falls and complicated water channels can sometimes be over the top and unnecessary. Reducing the scale of your feature gives you flexibility over style, positioning and budget – enabling you to use innovative materials to create one-off designs. Inspirational finds in junkyards or garden shows will convince you that small features are often the most suitable for today's modern lifestyle.

Function and style Small water features are perfect for those with smaller gardens who still want to enjoy having water nearby. For example, a tiny pebble fountain can easily be placed on a balcony or small patio. Or a little bird bath could be used to attract wildlife.

If you have children then a smaller design is by far the safest. This does not mean that you have to compromise on what you would want as smaller features can still visually stimulate and give pleasure to all ages.

One of the best aspects of small water features is the fact that they are so easy to install and maintain. Indeed they can often be bought as ready-made kits that need few or no tools to be put together.

Design choices Large water features may be spectacular but because of their size can be limiting. Naturally, by reducing the proportions, a small feature has less impact on its surroundings. This actually provides you with the opportunity to experiment with a wider range of exciting products such as innovative designs using ceramics, glass or reflective metal.

One of the beauties of a small feature is its ability to fill dead corners of the garden where a seat or pot would not quite work. This is a common design problem and can be confidently overcome by using a mini water feature.

One of the main things you must decide is whether or not you want to have movement within the feature. There is certainly plenty of choice if you do. Interconnecting containers come in a variety of shapes and sizes that allow water to trickle down from one into another. Alternatively, you may prefer to create one simple focal point by using a small water-filled pot on a plinth or a sphere that has water cascading down it.

A concrete bowl.

Moving water sphere.

Small designs can be humorous.

Water droplets clinging to reflective cylinde

Small water features can be as simple or complicated as you want them to be. If you decide to incorporate movement within the design you may decide to allow the water to simply flow from one container or another (top left). Or you may prefer a more intricate design that results in a series of cascades (top right). A small, still feature, on the other hand, can welcome wildlife, especially if you use a natural-looking design (above).

pebble CASCADE

This pebble cascade provides a well-designed and crafted vertical stack, which is so versatile that it will suit any surroundings – from a contemporary patio setting to a lush border.

MATERIALS

Ceramic reservoir bowl,
450mm (1½ft) diameter

Beech cover comprising:
1m (3ft) of 100 × 18mm (4 × ¾in)
planed beech
450mm (1½ft) of 150 × 18mm
(6 × ¾in) planed beech
1m (3ft) of 50 × 18mm (2 × ¾in)
planed beech

15mm (²⁄₃in) copper pipe

15mm (²⁄₃in) copper water tank
connector

Submersible pump with flow adjuster,
cable and small hose

Eight 75–100mm (3–4in) glazed
ceramic pebbles

10 rubber washers,
18mm (¾in) diameter

TOOLS

Brushes

Sponges

1   First, decide on your position for the pebble cascade as this will affect the route for the electrical supply. Lay out the ceramic reservoir bowl and the beech slatted cover with the copper pipe holding the ceramic pebbles. You should also have a mini-pump with a cable and a small hose – connect that to the copper pipe at the base of the cover. It can be secured with a jubilee clip if necessary.

2   Make sure the reservoir bowl is stable and on firm ground. Check that the ground is level. Fill the bowl with clean water and carefully place the cover over the reservoir. Check that the cable is not trapped under the hood. Next, place the remaining ceramic pebbles on top of the existing pebbles. It is important to place the supplied rubber washers between each stone to stop water running inside the stack and losing the effect.

1 Connect the small hose to the copper pipe that will hold the pebbles at the base of the cover.

2 Once the cover is secured stack the pebbles, remembering to insert a rubber washer between each one.

KNOW YOUR MATERIALS

Pebbles: These beautifully crafted ceramic pebbles give a delicate effect when they are subtly balanced on top of each other. Although they look precarious, the copper pipe that carries the water through the centre gives the stack great stability.

Timber: The timber-slatted base is made from planed beech, which has been varnished. In order to prevent excessive water loss the timber beading strips have been fixed to the top of the base. There are also additional timber beads placed on the underside to help position the stack over the bowl.

spherical FOUNTAIN

This project allows you to use a small body of water in a creative and effective way. Its reflective glaze and subtle sound make it perfect for any seating area.

1 Firstly, you need to decide on the position of the fountain. Physically move the sphere around the garden to find the best site. As you do this, ensure an easy route can be provided for the supply of power to the feature.

Clear around the area and dig out the hole in which the 'top hat' reservoir will sit. Be sure to keep the reservoir clean and free from soil, as the water for the fountain will be stored in it. Fit the reservoir firmly into place and use a spirit level to check across the top for a good level surface, which you will place the sphere onto later.

2 With your watering can, fill up the reservoir with clean water and place the mini-pump into the centre of the plastic bowl. Feed the hose from the bottom of the sphere through the hole provided in the lid of the reservoir. Position them both next to the reservoir and attach the hose to the outlet on top of the mini-pump.

MATERIALS

UPVC reservoir

Submersible mini-pump

Glazed spherical fountain, 400mm (1¼ft) diameter with an 18mm (¾in) hole in the top

450mm (1½ft) hose

2 x 40kg (88lb) bags of 30–100mm (1¼–4in) mixed pebbles

TOOLS

Groundwork tools

Building tools

Watering can

Bucket

Sponge

1 Once you have decided where you want the feature, clear a space for the reservoir and then position it.

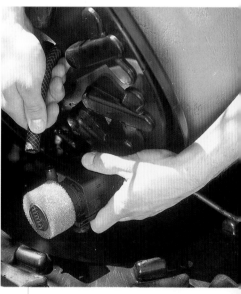

2 Next, connect the adjustable pump to the hose that comes from the top of the spherical fountain. Secure it with a jubilee clip.

KNOW YOUR MATERIALS

Glazed sphere: The vibrant glazed spherical fountain works because of its simplicity. The top of the fountain is a concave pool that fills with water and overflows, rippling down the side of the vessel. Extra emphasis is added by the ripple-effect glaze. The reservoir is made of durable UPVC and is ideally suited to small, light features that need a minimum volume of water to operate. The inside of the pool provides a good opportunity for you to be creative. There is a wide range of materials that could be used – crushed glass, stainless steel shards, white marble pebbles or rusty washers would all give a different and very effective finish.

3 With the hose attached to the pump, carefully place the lid and the sphere into their correct positions on top of the reservoir. Test the flow by turning on the pump. The basin in the top of the sphere will be permanently filled with water and the pump will create the fountain, which in turn will cause the water to overflow down the glazed sides of the sphere. The water should fall over the edge of the sphere equally all the way around because you levelled the surface in step 1.

Take a bucket and sponge and clean the pebbles before laying them around the base of the sphere. It is important to do this as any dirt or grime on the stones will be washed off into the reservoir and then re-circulated over the feature, causing unnecessary cleaning. Position the pebbles to disguise the top hat reservoir and complete the overall look of the feature. Check that all cables are covered with pebbles.

3 *To cover the plastic reservoir use a range of 30–100mm (1¹/₄–4in) pebbles. These will look stunning when wet.*

ceramic POOL

This uncomplicated, organic-look ceramic pool is a highly successful stand-alone feature. It will fit well in a wide range of garden themes, from 'natural' right through to 'contemporary'.

1 Find the right position for your feature in the garden by moving it around and taking note of the best location. It is often a good idea to put it in very different settings and leave it in each one for a while before deciding whether or not you can get the full benefit of the feature in that location. Be imaginative with your placing as this particular type of feature can live almost anywhere. When it has a spot in the garden, create a clear space in which the bowl can be positioned and levelled. Be sure that the power to the pump will have a reasonably easy route. It is best if the cables are hidden as the appearance of the pool will be tarnished if the source of its energy is exposed.

2 Take the mini-pump and position it in the centre of the pool. The point at which the cable leaves the side of the pump needs to be opposite the small hole for the cable

MATERIALS

400mm (18in) diameter glazed ceramic reservoir

A mini-pump with flow adjuster

125mm (5in) diameter ceramic dome with an 18mm ($^3/_4$in) central hole in the top

5kg (11lb) of 18–25mm ($^3/_4$–1in) white marble pebbles

TOOLS

Watering can

Bucket

Sponge

Soft hand brush

1 Clear around your chosen area, position your reservoir and then check for level using a small level.

2 Place the mini-pump in the centre of the bowl and feed the cable through the side of the reservoir bowl.

KNOW YOUR MATERIALS

Glazed ceramic bowl: The ceramic pool is one of the simplest ways to introduce water to any patio, border or balcony. The particular glaze finish that was used here contains hues of greens and blues with some subtle rusty markings. This enables it to be positioned almost anywhere in the garden, whether on a timber deck or nestled among planting. The power cable needs to be considered. This is extremely important if you are positioning the feature in a border. If the cable needs to travel a distance, or is buried, a protective conduit or tubing should be used. Employ a qualified electrician to install your pump for you.

3 Once the pump is centrally positioned place the pump cover over the pump. Turn the pump on and make any final adjustments.

in the top of the pool's rim. Leave the cable without a plug for now and feed it through the hole in the rim of the pool. Continue to feed it along until it lies neatly in the bottom of the pool. Then fill the pool up with clean water from your watering can until the pump is covered.

3　Take the ceramic dome provided and place it over the top of the pump. Ensure that the cable passes under the section cut out of the dome's base to ensure a neat finish. The outlet from the pump for the bubble fountain should be lined up directly beneath the hole provided in the top of the dome. Turn on the power and check that the fountain is passing through the hole in the dome with ease. If all is well, top up the water in the pool to just beneath the hole in the rim. Wash and place small white marble pebbles inside the pool, evenly spaced for best effect. Then dress around the bottom of the feature.

tiered CASCADE

An exciting movement of water from vessel to vessel, each one placed at a different height, provides interest and sound. The way in which the vessels are arranged can easily be adapted to suit individual tastes and gardens.

1 Decide where your feature is to be positioned and then put the base bowl in place. The largest bowl, which acts as a reservoir, needs to be at the lowest point so that the others can be arranged at sufficient heights for the feature to work. Feed the cable for the mini-pump through the hole provided in the rim of the base bowl. You also need to feed the hose that will carry water from the pump to the jug through this hole. Next, the glazed dome needs to be placed in the base bowl over the pump to disguise and protect it.

2 Now arrange the stands and other bowls, ensuring that the water will flow smoothly from one to the next without spilling, but also without the bowls being so close together that they look cramped. The distance of the stand and jug (which is the source) from the base bowl will be determined by the size of the bowls.

MATERIALS

Ceramic reservoir bowl

Mini-pump and hoses

125mm (5in) diameter ceramic, dome-shaped pump cover

225mm (9in) diameter ceramic stand

150mm (6in) diameter ceramic stand

300mm (1ft) ceramic pan with lip

250mm (10in) ceramic pan with lip

Ceramic jug with inlet hole for hose

TOOLS

None needed

1 Once you have positioned the base bowl and fed the hose through the hole provided, cover the pump with the dome.

2 Now arrange the other bowls and stands, making sure that the water flows smoothly and everything is stable.

KNOW YOUR MATERIALS

Frostproof ceramic bowls: This particular cascade is made of frostproof ceramic, which is a necessity in extremely cold climates. However, not all ceramic material is frostproof so make sure that you check with the supplier before you buy. If there is any doubt, empty the feature and dry out the pump during spells of cold weather.

Slab base: One of the problems with this type of feature is the lack of stability due to the number of components. If you have uneven ground, lay one or two slabs just under ground level to give a stable base for your feature. The slabs can then be covered with decorative bark or gravel.

3 Fill the reservoir bowl with clean tap water up to the brim and then turn the power on and adjust the direction of the flow.

3 Finally, fill the large bowl with clean water until the pump is covered. Turn on the power to the pump and observe the water's passage. Move and adjust the flow where necessary in order to give the best movement of water. When you are happy with the feature, dress around the base of the stands and bottom bowl to complete the setting for this cascade.

Alternative positioning

The positioning of this feature will really depend on the look that is to be achieved. A country setting would naturally lend itself to this particular feature, mainly because of the material and the fact that a jug is incorporated. However, there is room for this design in a modern and contemporary setting too. You could change the arrangement to a formal line of equally spaced bowls, perhaps contrasted against a dark slate patio.

SURFACES

Richard Key

planning your garden surfaces

your GARDEN LANDSCAPE

A good sound design is essential in achieving a well-balanced and harmonious garden with all elements in proportion. It is important to consider the layout of the whole garden especially if it is a fairly small plot and every part of it will be visible at any one time. This book will show you how to plan and execute your ideas to create the perfect garden landscape.

A well-planned garden results in harmony between all its elements.

Once you have decided that you want to make changes to your garden space, you need to determine how your plans for any new constructions can be incorporated into the existing garden. Their shape, size and finished level are all important considerations so that they blend in with what is already there.

A clear outline plan should be developed at this early stage because without one it is all too easy to fall into the trap of piecemeal construction. This book will lead you through each of the stages of garden planning and construction, providing you with helpful advice and explanations so that you can create a well-balanced, easy-to-maintain garden to suit your own requirements. Use it to ensure success in your garden.

Using this book

All the important stages of planning, constructing and maintaining your garden surfaces are covered by this highly informative book. This first section describes the basics of building up a good garden design, from listing all your requirements to surveying the plot and then putting your ideas down on paper.

Time spent on thorough design work will ensure that the overall appearance is good and in harmony with the surroundings, that everything is in proportion and that the whole space works. Invariably, if it looks right on paper then it will look right on the ground. Planning does not stop when the design is drawn up as you will need to plan the construction time and materials carefully as well. You

cannot just go straight out and build a patio, for example, without planning how long it will take and exactly what materials are needed in order to construct it.

The other main ingredient in the creation of successful garden surfaces is a sound knowledge of construction techniques, not only so the paving looks good but also so that it is safe and will be long lasting. The section on techniques runs through all the practical stages from the marking out of the site through to the final sweeping clean of, for example, the finished patio.

The book then describes 20 practical and inspirational projects that illustrate different styles of construction for all types of garden surfaces. The subjects covered by these projects include pathways, edgings, steps and patios.

The details of how to complete each project are given using clear step-by-step photography and accompanying text. Any alternative materials or methods that can be employed are also indicated in order to provide you with further ideas on how to tailor a specific project to your own garden space.

All-important advice on how to maintain your new garden surfaces, as well as the tools you will need to create them, is given at the end.

Before you begin

To aid you with the planning stage, there are several checklists that need to be drawn up that will help you to assess all your requirements for the garden. This may cover more than you need for your particular construction projects but it is as well to look at the wider picture to ensure that everything will fit together. You need, for example, to think about what you will use the space for, what existing features you wish to keep and any budget restraints you may have. From the lists that you draw up, you will then be able to pull out the information relevant for your construction projects.

Your basic requirements

It is important to spend time looking at your garden while thinking about what you want to be able to do in the space. You should also work out what landscaping needs to be done and what existing construction needs to be worked into your new design. The following two lists show the sorts of things you should be looking out for when you draw up your initial plans.

Front garden

• Is there clear access to the front door or do you need to create a new pathway?
• Is there an incline and, if so, are steps or a slope preferable?
• Is parking space required and how much space is needed?
• What existing features do you wish to keep?
• Is there space to use the front garden for other purposes (for a large front plot, also consider the requirements that are listed here for the rear garden).

Rear garden

• What do all the members of the family require from the garden: do you need to satisfy an enthusiastic gardener, want to use the garden for relaxation and entertaining or to provide play areas for children?
• Where are the most suitable places for seating, given the direction of the sun and other features such as boundaries and trees?
• How many people should the sitting areas be planned for and how much space will be needed?
• Which areas of the garden need to be accessed for gardening, playing, hanging the washing or storage and will these be best served with paths, lawns or steps?
• What are the best positions for these thoroughfares, both functionally and visually?
• Are edges or mowing strips required in the garden at all?
• What existing features do you wish to keep?

Budgetary requirements

In addition to this information you will also have to consider your budget for the construction work. If you are doing all the work yourself you will only need to plan the cost of materials and tool hire.

Choose the best surface material you can afford, but compromises can be made to fit in with your budget without spoiling the job; for instance, you could choose a good imitation of natural stone instead of the real thing. You could also spread construction projects over a couple of years, which would also cut the immediate cost. As long as you plan carefully, it can be helpful to construct your garden over different years and seasons.

You may also consider using a professional garden designer who will be trained in maximising the potential of your garden and so save you a lot of time and possible heartache. Many countries have a society of garden designers, which will have produced a list of designers who will be able to help you with planning, establishing budgets and will also be able to recommend contractors if you need help with construction work.

Existing site conditions

There is one final check list to produce before embarking on your site survey and that is a list of existing site conditions that can be marked onto your survey drawing.

• Use a compass point to work out your garden's aspect.
• Use a pH kit to check the soil's acidity and alkalinity. This will help you to find out which plants will grow best there. Sand and clay content will indicate how well-drained the soil is and how much excavated soil will bulk up.
• Make a note of garden features you need to remove, such as an old shed.
• Work out where there are wet corners (to drain or plant with bog plants) and shady corners (to create areas for cool seating).
• Note any manholes or outside taps.
• Mark any existing trees (their height and canopy spread), any trees from adjacent gardens that cast a shadow in yours and existing planting both good and bad.
• Your survey should show house walls, fencing and existing paving.
• Take photographs showing both good and bad views of the garden to help with your planning.

surveying AND PLANNING

One of the most important aspects of garden design is taking time right at the start to plan carefully on paper before beginning any of the physical work. Taking a survey of your garden so that you can make a detailed, scaled plan will help you enormously when you come to tackle the practical aspect of actually carrying out the job.

Taking measurements

Make a simple sketch plan (not to scale) on a pad to show the house, the boundaries and any existing features, such as trees or a shed. Then fix a tape measure to the side of the house and pull it out along the outside – start from one corner, at nought, and record a series of running measurements to show window and door positions. Add the measurements to your sketch. This process can then be repeated for all sides of the house.

The corners of the garden can be fixed by triangulation, which involves taking measurements from two points on the house to each corner of the garden. To do this, you can either use a long tape pulled out from the house to each corner or walk between the two points using a measuring wheel. Triangulation can also be used to fix the position of trees or drain covers in the middle of the garden. Measure along each boundary using running measurements to record the position of gates or any significant planting.

Recording levels

Even if your garden appears to be flat, it may not be. A small slope can be measured by holding a straight edge and spirit level out from the top of the slope and measuring down from the underside of the straight edge to the bottom. This is not practical for a whole garden; here it would be best to use a laser level (see page 145). In a small garden, you will only need to record a couple of levels adjacent to the house and the levels at each corner of the back boundary. A difference between the readings will indicate a fall but if the readings are all equal, then the ground is level. Take a further reading on a point that is fixed, so it won't be disturbed, such as the damp proof course (dpc) in the house wall.

Survey drawing

Do a survey drawing to mark on the existing features of your plot.

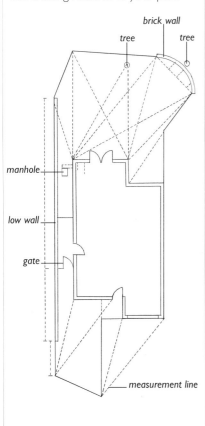

brick wall

tree   tree

manhole

low wall

gate

measurement line

Using a measuring wheel.

Use a laser level to measure the gradient.

Starting to plan

When your survey is complete you can draw up a plan to scale on a clean sheet of paper. Most small to medium gardens can be drawn up to a scale of 1:50 or 20mm:1m (¾in:40in), so you will not need a massive sheet of paper.

Start by drawing the outline of your house using a scale ruler to mark the running measurements that you have taken on site along each wall. Then fix all the corners of the plot onto paper using a pair of compasses. Mark onto the plan an arc line for each of the triangulation measurements – where the arc lines meet will be the correct position in each case.

Now start to plan the detail of your garden. Work on tracing paper laid over the top of your plan. This will enable you to make alterations on the overlay without spoiling the plan drawing underneath.

Ideas for the garden, including patios and lawns, can be drawn up as a series of overlays on the plan. While you are doing each of these sketch overlays you should start looking at the proposed areas in greater detail, making sure, for example, that the pathways that link the different parts of the garden are wide enough, even with plants tumbling over the edges to soften the overall effect. Look carefully at the existing site levels and begin to work out what size treads and risers you will need for any connecting steps. Try to look beyond the existing features and search for imaginative and practical solutions.

When you are satisfied that the right design has been reached, place a fresh piece of tracing paper on top of your series of overlays and transfer the complete outline plan onto it (see illustration, right).

Drawing a plan to scale

An outline plan of your garden can be drawn up to show proposed areas of different hard and soft landscaping features.

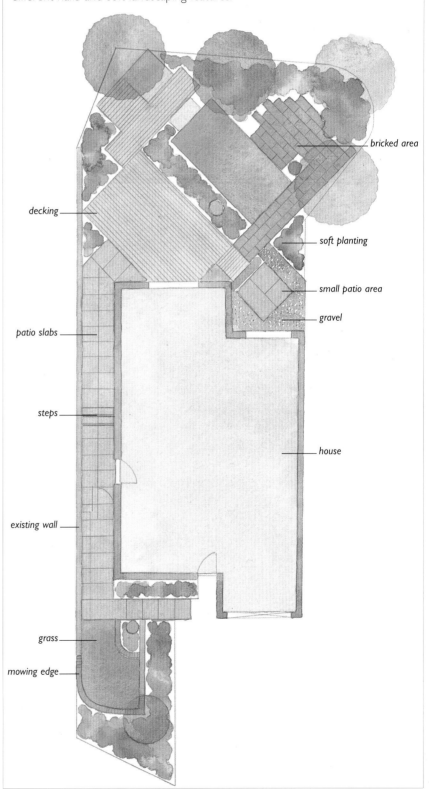

bricked area

decking

soft planting

small patio area

gravel

patio slabs

steps

house

existing wall

grass

mowing edge

surface DETAIL

It is important to think carefully about the surface colour and texture when planning your garden landscape because these decisions can have a significant impact on the finished result: for example, a blue slate path would look dramatic in a contemporary setting while a patio made out of granite setts would be more suited to a traditional, natural-style garden.

Points to consider

There is a wide choice of materials available and a variety of patterns possible for garden surfaces but before you go to buy your paving, consider the influences that will affect your choice: function, location, style and cost.

Function

Consider the function of your garden surface: paving for a utility area should be hard wearing but it does not need to be decorative. Second-hand paving slabs would be ideal for areas around the shed and compost bins. Stepping stones are fine if only used occasionally whereas hard wearing bricks would be more suitable for a path that is used frequently. Bricks or clay pavers could also be used to form steps with narrow treads for quick access while broad treads, perhaps in crushed gravel with a timber riser, could be used for a more leisurely ascent.

Location

The aspect where you plan to build a patio or lay a path is important. A natural stone terrace in full sun would be wonderful, but the same material in the shade of trees could become slippery and dangerous. The same would apply to decking, which also needs a sunny location to prevent

algae from making the surface treacherous – rough surfaced bricks or crushed gravel will give a better grip for paving and paths in shady areas. The area around a swimming pool will also require a surface that can cope with regular splashing without becoming slippery – brushed concrete, textured bricks or concrete paving slabs would all be suitable.

Style

The type of house, the local materials and the proposed style of the garden will all affect your choice of paving materials. Where possible, try to use indigenous materials for hard landscaping because sandstone paving, for example, may look somewhat incongruous in an area where slate is the native rock. Try to make sure that the materials that you choose are in keeping with the style of the garden: brick paths will look right in a cottage garden whereas concrete and stained decking probably would not.

Cost

Remember that the same effect can be achieved with more than one type of material of varying cost: for example, natural stone is expensive but there are some good imitations in concrete, which are cheaper.

Choice of materials

There is a wide choice of paving materials available today, not just in garden centres but also from stone suppliers, brick manufacturers, hardware stores and salvage yards. Consider too using the materials listed below in combination.

Natural stone

Sandstone is probably the most suitable stone for garden paving; it has a warm colour that mellows with age and it associates well with brick, timber, gravel and plants. Limestone is usually too soft to be used as paving, but slate on the other hand is a very dense, hard wearing material and can look terrific in a crisp geometric design.

Natural slate.

Pre-cast concrete slabs

There are many types to choose from in all colours, shapes and sizes. The subdued stone colours look better in the garden than more gaudy varieties. Textured slabs are excellent for a non-slip surface and look great laid in bands. Imitation stone slabs are also available.

Concrete slabs with bricks.

Bricks

Choose clay rather than concrete bricks as their soft colours are more suited to a garden. They work well for straight or curved paths, as a trim to other paving, or in patterns such as running bond, basket weave and herringbone.

Bricks in basket weave pattern.

Setts

Setts are widely available either as sandstone or granite blocks or alternatively there are some cheaper setts made from concrete that are very good. They are all hard wearing, and are ideal for making step treads and curved paths.

Granite setts.

Cobbles and pebbles

These are smooth round stones ranging from 20–100mm ($^{3}/_{4}$–4in), which can be laid loose for a beach effect or bedded in mortar for a pathway. They can make intricate mosaic patterns and are often bordered by bricks or tiles.

Cobble and slate mosaic.

Gravel

Loose aggregate, such as gravel, is an excellent material that is available as crushed stone from gravel pits. The size of gravel for surfacing ranges from 10–20mm ($^{3}/_{8}$–$^{3}/_{4}$in) and the depth of the surface need only be approximately 20mm ($^{3}/_{4}$in).

Loose aggregate.

Timber

Timber is a versatile material that looks good in informal settings. Log slices can be laid for stepping stones, or bark chippings used to dress a pathway, while timber decking forms a superb sitting area in a sunny aspect.

Stained timber decking.

planning AND ESTIMATING

Carrying out garden construction requires considerable planning; you cannot roll out on a Saturday morning without any preparation and expect to achieve anything worthwhile. Even if the project is only small, there may be as much organisation needed as for larger jobs: the same tools, safety checks and calls to builders' merchants will be needed.

Planning construction work

If there are several projects planned, then it is most important that they are built in the correct order. There is no point in constructing a beautiful brick path only to trek along it with wheel barrows and mixers to build a patio further down the garden at some later stage. Either build the patio first or, better still, lay a path of compacted road base to provide firm access and then lay the surface of bricks once the patio has been completed.

The beauty of preparing a landscape plan for the whole garden is that this allows you to plan the work in the right order. All the levelling and excavation work can be done in one go even if the finished surfaces for different areas are to be laid over a period of time. This is not only economical, as it avoids the haulage costs of bringing a machine back to your garden again, but it also avoids the risk of the machine damaging the newly laid paving.

Working to an overall plan also allows you to build individual areas to suit your budget in the knowledge that the area will be at the correct finished level. Without a plan, paved areas are often built in a piecemeal fashion in total isolation from each other, which results in some very odd, often dangerous, changes in level to connect them to each other. Your garden will look much more unified if you have spent time planning it out first.

Transporting materials along a path.

Estimating time

Once you have decided on the correct order of operations, you will need to plan your time to carry out the work. Unless you have some prior knowledge of construction work you will find the greatest danger is underestimating just how long a job will actually take. It is not a good idea to plan the construction of a patio on a Saturday and expect it to be finished for use for a party on Sunday. Depending on the skill involved in an operation, you may find that a day's work for a professional will be closer to five for an amateur. You should certainly plan to double your initial time estimates as there are unforeseen factors that can cause delay, notably bad weather or the possibility of machine breakdown.

Also remember that you cannot work right through until dark as you will need to allow an hour of daylight for cleaning tools and mixers. Bear in mind, if you can only work on the garden during weekends, that everything must be packed away for the week and machines returned to the hire shop if need be. So allow plenty of time when you do your estimate and then you may enjoy the feeling of finishing a day early.

Estimating materials

In addition to estimating time you will also need to estimate the quantities of

Use your plan to calculate how many slabs you need.

materials required for the job. This can be quite tricky and, if you have any doubts, ask for advice from a reputable hardware store. Unit

Calculating how many bricks you will need.

materials such as paving slabs can easily be counted off the plan.

To save counting all the bricks for a pathway, simply calculate how many are needed for one square metre (or square yard) and then multiply that number by the total area in square metres (or square yards) of the path. If the bricks are to be laid flat with mortar joints, you will need 35 per square metre (29 per square yard) while, if they are laid on their edge with mortar joints, you will need 50 per square metre (42 per square yard). It is a good idea to add an extra 5 percent to your estimates for all surfacing materials to allow for breakage.

Loose materials such as sand and gravel may be sold by volume in cubic metres (cubic yards) and are straightforward to estimate by simply multiplying the area by the depth. It can be more confusing when these same materials are sold by weight in tonnes (cwt) as one cubic metre (cubic yard) of sand will not weigh the same as one cubic metre (cubic yard)

of road base. Where materials are sold by weight, ask the supplier to advise you on how this equates to cubic metres (cubic yards).

Gravel is sold by volume.

Mortar may be sold as dry ready-mix in bags, requiring only the addition of water. This is ideal for small jobs and it is also easy to buy a few extra bags

Making mortar

Approximately 1 tonne or 1000kg (20cwt) of mortar is needed to fill 0.5 cubic m (²⁄₃ cubic yd) (see page 150). In the example below, the mortar mix is 1:6, one part cement to six parts sand (a total of seven parts) but this formula can be applied to different mortar mixes in order to calculate the amount of sand and cement required.

1 tonne (20cwt) of mortar covers 0.5 cubic m (²⁄₃ cubic yd).
1 part cement : 6 parts sand = 7 parts in total.
1 tonne (20cwt)÷7 = 143kg (3cwt) for 1 part.
143kg (3cwt) cement : 857kg (17cwt) of sand.
Therefore, allowing for wastage, you will need six 25kg (½cwt) bags of cement and 1 tonne (20cwt) of sand to make 1 tonne (20cwt) of mortar.

if you find that you need them. For larger areas of construction, it is more economical to buy sand in bulk together with individual bags of cement. It is, of course, important to know how much sand and cement you need to make up a quantity of mortar and again you could seek advice from your supplier. However, the 'making mortar' box (below left) may serve as a useful guide and will also help with your initial cost estimate.

Obviously the more construction work you carry out, the more knowledge you will gain. You will see that road base may compact down by approximately 10 to 15 percent of its volume while excavated soil may bulk up by 25 percent or more. Both these factors will need to be accounted for when ordering road base and a skip for the removal of soil. As you become more experienced, you will also become more accurate and confident at estimating the materials that you need for a job.

Ordering materials

Order all your materials well in advance of when you will need them as you cannot expect delivery the next day; you may be lucky but most merchants require at least two days' notice to deliver stock items. If possible try to organise for all your materials to be delivered in one load as this will save on the cost of haulage.

Machinery and any specialist tools can be hired by the day or the week and will also need to be ordered in advance to be sure of getting them in time. If you are unfamiliar with any of the equipment you want to use, hire shop staff will always provide a demonstration and run through all the necessary safety procedures.

tools and techniques

preparing THE PLOT

Once you have a completed plan you will need to transfer the measurements for the new paved areas from the plan onto the ground. To mark out the features on the whole site would be too confusing, so simply mark out the area of paving you are ready to build. You may find that you have to remove any unwanted plants before you can begin construction.

Marking out a rectangular area

1 First establish a base line from which all other measurements can be taken. You can use the triangulation method for this (see page 134). For a rectangular area away from the house, fix two points: one at each end of one of the sides of the area. Drive a peg in at each point and join together with a string line to form the base line.

2 Mark out the other sides at right angles to the base line. Make a large wooden right-angled triangle with sides in the ratio of 3:4:5 to form a perfect right angle. Set one of the short sides of the triangle against the base line and pull a string line out taut along the other short side. The line, tied round a peg, will be at a right angle to the base line.

3 Repeat this for the other side and join the two pegs with string to complete the shape. Finally, check the diagonals are equal.

4 Dribble sand or spray marker paint along the string line to show the outline of the area on the ground.

5 Then remove the string lines to allow for excavation but leave them attached to the pegs so they can easily be put up again when construction work starts. It would help if you set the pegs just outside the area of excavation.

Marking out a circular area

1 Use the triangulation method and on your plan draw a line from two points on the house wall (or from the boundaries if closer) to meet in the centre of your patio. To transfer this information onto the ground, use two long tape measures from the two fixed points, pull the tapes out taut to the measurements shown on the plan and bring them together to fix the position of the centre of the circle.

2 Drive a peg in at the centre point, tie a string line around it and then measure along that line to the correct radius of the circular paved area.

3 Tie a pointed stick or screwdriver to the line at this measurement and scratch out a circle on the ground with the string pulled taut. On lawn areas, you may have to scratch through the turf quite hard so that the line can be seen. Mark the scratch line with sand or paint for extra clarity, as shown for the rectangular area (step 4).

Marking out a curved path

Curved lines for pathways must be accurately marked out so do not be tempted just to lay a hose on the ground as a guide. You need to measure the curve out precisely.

1 Firstly, draw your proposed curved lines onto your plan. Then measure a series of off sets – lines that are measured at 90° from a base line to points at regular intervals along the curved line – and note their lengths on the plan.

2 Next, measure and transfer the off sets onto the ground. First transfer where your base line should be from the plan. Next, measure out from that line at the same intervals and distances as shown on your scaled plan, to fix the points for the curve.

3 You will need a long tape to run along the base line and a second tape to measure the off sets. A 3:4:5 triangle will ensure that the off sets are at 90° to the base line. You can then drive a timber peg into the

ground at the end of each off set to fix these points for reference purposes.

4 Run a line of sand from one peg to the next to indicate the proposed curved line. For a straight path, establish one edge as the base line and measure off sets out from each end that are equal to the width of the path to indicate the other path edge.

Ground clearance

You may need to do some initial clearance work before you are able to mark out the site with any accuracy. Remove all rubbish, bricks, concrete and unwanted plant material and cut down any long grass because it is

impossible to mark out accurately on this. All vegetation will need to be removed from areas to be excavated and, although short grass will rot down quickly, an application of weed killer (following the manufacturer's instructions carefully) will certainly help the process.

Areas of paving should not be laid over loose soil or soft ground, so any topsoil must be removed down to firm ground. If paving is laid on top of loose ground there is a high risk that the ground will settle and cause the paving to subside and crack.

Topsoil is, however, a valuable commodity so if it can be used elsewhere in the garden to make up levels in beds or elsewhere, then set it aside. If you cannot use the extra topsoil then do not bother placing it to one side but simply excavate straight down to the correct level and remove all the excavated material from the site.

Avoid the temptation to pave over the old patio and pathways as this is rarely successful. New paving that has been placed over existing surfaces may bring the paved area too close to the damp proof course, which could then let damp into the house. In addition, the levels of the old paving may be incorrect or may not allow for adequate drainage of the new surface. Perhaps more importantly, you will not be able to inspect the base under the old paving, which may be totally insufficient and will undoubtedly cause the new paving to settle and crack after a short period of time.

The best approach, when planning new construction work, is simply to clear out all old constructions and start afresh with the correct depth of base material.

setting OUT LEVELS

Before beginning any construction work, you need to establish the proposed finished levels of your paving in relation to the surrounding, existing ground level. Using fairly simple or more sophisticated equipment, there are various methods of measuring the levels and marking them out on your new site, all of which are described below.

Planning

The existing levels of your garden will have been recorded when the garden was surveyed (see page 134). This survey should indicate which way the garden slopes, if at all. Paved areas will need to be built with a slight fall (see page 146) to remove surface water and, if the paving slabs have a riven or uneven surface, the fall needs to be increased to avoid puddles forming (see pages 148-9). This fall needs to be planned at the outset as it will affect how much ground you need to excavate. If possible, plan the fall to be in the same direction as any existing fall on the ground because this will reduce the amount of soil to excavate and will also allow surface water to drain away more easily.

Ideally, patios should slope away from the house to ensure that any surface water is not trapped against the house wall. If this means that the patio would slope into higher ground, there are several options. A small area of paving, 1.8–3m (6–10ft) wide, could tip back to the house provided there are shrub beds against the wall into which any water could filter. Alternatively, introduce a fall running parallel to the house, which would take water into the beds to one side of the patio. If there are no beds, then lay a channel drain against the house wall, which will

direct water to a soakaway (see pages 146-7). Channels such as these may also be used if paving tips away from the house towards a retaining wall or bank. Paving and soil in beds adjacent to the house must be at least 150mm (6in) below the damp proof course (dpc) in the house wall to prevent damp creeping into the house. Paved areas that are at some distance from the house also need to be built on a fall and in this case the paving could be laid to tip towards the lawn or adjacent beds.

Measuring the surface fall

Setting out level pegs for paving requires a point of reference or a datum back to which all levels refer. Against the house, this could be the dpc, but in the middle of the lawn you will need to create a temporary reference point or datum. To do this, knock a peg into the ground just to one side of your proposed area of paving, making sure that it is clearly visible at 150mm (6in) above the existing ground level. Decide on the finished level of paving at one end of the patio (which may be the existing lawn level), then hold a spirit level across the datum peg, measure down to your proposed finished level and record the measurement. Remember that your paving will have

to have a fall across it so calculate how much lower one end of the patio will be than the other (see page 146). Add this drop to the first

Measuring the fall with a datum and spirit level.

measurement that you recorded and this will represent the difference in height from the top of the reference point to the finished paving level at the lower end of the patio.

Maintaining the surface level

You can now excavate the area to the correct depth below the finished paving level and lay the sub-base material (see pages 150-1) in position. When you are ready to start laying the paving, set up two string lines at right angles to each other, running along two sides of the proposed patio. You can re-use the lines you used initially to mark out the shape of the patio. Pull them taut and fix at the correct level of the paving by passing them across the top of pegs that have been driven in to mark the finished

String lines used to indicate the finished level.

paving level. You may just need to tap a nail into the peg to stop the line from slipping off.

These lines can now be used to indicate the finished level, the fall and the edge of the patio. It will also help to set in a temporary brick or peg at the end of the patio, away from the string line as this will give another finished level reference point to work to when laying the slabs.

A temporary peg is a useful reference point.

Working with larger patios

On a large patio, you may need several pegs placed throughout the area in a grid pattern, which will help enormously when laying slabs. Once you have pegs set up at each corner at the right level, then create a grid by running a string line across the tops of the pegs and knocking in additional pegs to the height of the line at intervals along its length. Pull lines from one side of the area to the other and repeat until the grid has been completed.

Creating a grid pattern.

Using a laser level

Setting in finished level pegs at some distance from each other using a spirit level, straight edge and tape measure is very impractical and laborious. Fortunately, there is a far quicker method – a laser level or other levelling equipment.

You can take a reading off the laser level when it is held on top of the first peg and then calculate what your next reading should be. The reading for the second peg will be the same as the previous one if the pegs are to be level, but must be calculated to include a fall as necessary. Place the staff on top of the second peg and continue

to knock the peg down until the laser records the correct level.

Reading a laser level.

Using the string method

There is an alternative to using a laser level, which does not require such sophisticated equipment. Knock in two pegs level with each other, about 1.8m (6ft) apart, and then pull a string line across the top of the first peg, over the second, to a position at the other side of your proposed paving where you will need to fix a third peg. By gently lowering the line until it brushes the top of the second peg you will create a level line that indicates the necessary height of your third peg.

Positioning the string line.

drainage

If water is not allowed to drain from paved surfaces, puddles will form and make the paving impractical because it will be slippery or icy. The water can also build up against walls to cause damp. If your paving falls towards a wall or bank, it is imperative to include in your plan a channel that will carry the water away to a gully and then to a soakaway.

Calculating the fall

It is important that a paved area has a sufficient fall to remove water but this should be subtle. There is no point in building a highly angled slope when something much more gentle would work perfectly well. The following figures can be used as a general guide:

Paving slabs (smooth and textured)
1:72 or 25mm (1in) in 1.8m (6ft)

Rough cut slabs, natural stone and bricks
1:60 or 25mm (1in) in 1.5m (5ft)

Granite setts and other uneven surfaces
1:40 or 25mm (1in) in 1.0m (40in)

Gravel surfaces
1:40 or 25mm (1in) in 1.0m (40in)

For example, a natural stone patio that is to be 4.5m (15ft) wide would need a fall of 1:60 and a drop of 75mm (3in) over its length. To create the required slope on an existing flat area, raise or excavate it by 75mm (3in). Raising the level may not be possible if it is then too close to the dpc in the house wall, so the far end of the patio would have to be dug into the ground in order for the patio to slope away from the house. This obviously creates a level change and the need for drainage.

Gravel areas

Gravel areas also have to be laid to a fall because, although they are free draining, water sits on the sub-base.

Paved areas

A fall in one direction only may be used on narrow areas of paving up to 6m (20ft) wide. Wider areas may need a fall in two directions that meet at a central channel connecting to a gully drain and on to a soakaway. Other areas may need to be dished; for example, a circular sitting area in a flat lawn. By lifting up the centre point you create a fall, but the circumference of the circle remains flush with the lawn.

Drainage channels and gullies

Open channels are available as purpose-made units or you can create a dish-shaped channel from bricks.

Some channels have a removable steel grid that helps keep debris out of the drain. The channels carry water to a gully pot that can be fitted neatly into the paving. A pipe is connected to the outlet of this gully, which leads to the soakaway. These pipes should be laid to a gradient of 1:40 for pipes of 100mm (4in) in diameter.

Soakaways

Soakaways are simply large holes dug into the ground and backfilled with large aggregate stones or gravel into which the surface water is piped. A geotextile membrane should be placed on top of the stones to

Soakaways

This cross-section shows the installation of a drainage pipe to lead surface water into a soakaway set under an area of lawn from which it is separated by a geotextile membrane.

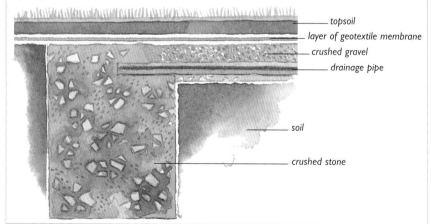

- topsoil
- layer of geotextile membrane
- crushed gravel
- drainage pipe
- soil
- crushed stone

separate them from the soil and turf that can then be replaced over the top of the area. The soakaway needs to be of a minimum size of 1 x 1 x 1m (40 x 40 x 40in), and it should be dug at about 3m (10ft) from the house. The base should be dug down at least 600mm (2ft) into permeable ground. This can be tricky in heavy clay areas with a high water table because the water will never drain away. In extreme cases you can employ a specialist contractor who will drill bore holes down to a permeable layer beneath the clay.

Piped agricultural line

As an alternative to a soakaway, you can create an agricultural line if you are laying an area of paving that has to tip towards a slope.

1 Excavate a trench along the length of the patio between the paving and the slope or wall. The trench only needs to be a spade's width and not too deep, although this depends on the overall fall. A geotextile membrane can be laid into the trench before setting in the pipe; this will extend the drain's life by preventing any soil from being washed into the pipe.

2 To ensure that the pipe drains correctly you will need to apply a fall of about 1:60 along its length. Over a 3m (10ft) length the pipe would, therefore, need to fall by 50mm (2in) from one end to the other. This means that the 7mm (¼in) crushed gravel that the pipe will be laid on will need to be built up by about an extra 50mm (2in) at one end to provide the fall. Spread your layer of crushed gravel along the base of the trench, adding more to one end, and position the pipe.

3 You should then backfill over the top of the pipe with more crushed gravel to about 50mm (2in) from ground level so that it is completely covered.

4 Once the trench has been completely backfilled with crushed gravel the geotextile membrane can be wrapped back over the top. As there is already membrane inside the trench, the whole of the crushed gravel and pipe system is then laid within this membrane, which will help to prevent it from silting up. The membrane itself can be folded over and neatly tucked under the edge of the paving.

5 If the drain runs along the foot of a bank, topsoil and turf can be spread over the membrane up to paving level. Or, if the drain is against a wall you can top the trench up with more crushed gravel to finished paving level.

steps AND RAMPS

The primary function of steps is to provide fast access from one level of the garden to another in much the same manner as stairs in a house. Outside in the garden though, steps can be an attractive feature: they can be broader and deeper than internal steps and they can meander and zigzag up slopes offering interesting routes from bottom to top.

Designing steps

You might use steps instead of a low retaining wall at a change of level allowing one area to flow into another without interruption. The same steps can provide an added attraction if they are used as seating or surrounded with plantings. Low plants can be grown at the side of steps to tumble down and soften the construction too.

Ramps provide even gentler access than steps from one level to another and are useful for wheelchairs, prams, strollers and lawnmowers. They are not always attractive and, with a maximum gradient of 1:10 (see page 146), can take up a lot of room in a

small garden. Ramped steps require less space as they combine ramps of 1:10 or 1:12 with low bump steps of about 10cm (4in) at regular intervals.

Planning for steps

Steps need to be carefully planned. The height of risers and the depth of treads are important considerations because otherwise the climb up the steps can be disconcerting and dangerous.

The maximum height for a riser should not be more than about 150mm (6in) while the minimum height should not be less than 115mm (4½in). A comfortable tread depth is 375mm (15in) though 450mm (18in) is

commonly used to fit the unit size of a paving slab. There is also a ratio of riser height to tread depth to consider, which means that the shallower the riser then the deeper the tread should be and equally the steeper the riser then the narrower the tread should be. A rule of thumb is 2 x riser + tread = 650mm (26in) although this can vary slightly.

Building steps

1 Before beginning construction, work out the height and depth of the steps required. Measure the height of the bank by holding a straight edge out horizontally from the top of the bank, checking it with a spirit level, and measuring down from the underside of the straight edge to the bottom of the bank. Work out the number of steps required by dividing the bank

Steps with brick risers

This shows steps that use brick risers built over the ends of the slab treads. A concrete foundation under the first riser gives strength to the structure.

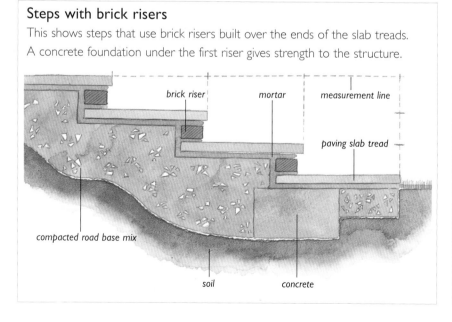

brick riser   mortar   measurement line

paving slab tread

compacted road base mix

soil   concrete

height by a sensible step height. Measure the length of the flight of steps along the straight edge, not down the slope, and divide this by the number of steps to work out the depth of each tread. If you need to change the dimensions of the steps, adjust them all by the same amount.

2 Clear the ground for the flight of steps and mark out their position. Excavate the bank, roughly cutting the steps into the ground.

3 Fix a peg at the bottom of the bank beyond the first tread and one at the top of the bank beyond the top riser. Tie a string line to these pegs, adjusting it down to indicate the final height of the treads. Check and adjust the shaping of the flight of steps against the string line, allowing for the riser and tread materials, and the mortar joints.

4 Dig a trench to make the foundation of the first step however wide you want your steps to be. Fill the trench with a firm concrete mix and level it off with the back of a shovel. Leave the concrete until it has completely hardened.

5 To make the first riser of the flight of steps, lay a row of dry pressed bricks end to end into a firm mortar mix (see page 152) on top of the concrete foundation. Joint the brick units with mortar as you go. Lay a second row of bricks on top of the first row if required, staggering the jointing pattern to make the step construction sturdy and secure.

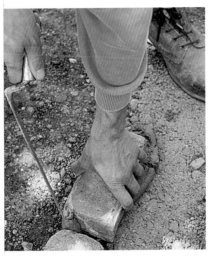

6 Lay the foundation for the first tread by backfilling the first riser with a layer of compacted road base and level it off. Point the joints between the bricks in front of the riser because these will be inaccessible once the tread has been placed into its position.

7 Cover the first tread with a thick layer of mortar. Position a slab on the tread so that it overhangs the riser by 50mm (2in). This will cast a shadow line, masking the mortar joint. Bed the slab down, tapping it so that the top just touches the string line. Go on to finish the first tread and point the joints.

8 Build the next riser on top of the previous tread and continue to build the steps using the same method. Ensure that they all just touch the string as shown. Check the depth of each tread and the height of each riser to ensure that you end up with the correct number of steps all built to the same dimensions.

base CONSTRUCTION

It is essential to lay paving on a firm base to get a professional finish. Otherwise soils that may be prone to shrinking will transfer such movement straight through to the surface of the paving and crack the slabs. So topsoil and all loose ground must be removed first and replaced by an even layer of compacted road base or concrete.

Excavation

Once the area to be paved has been clearly marked out and level pegs have been set up you can begin excavating for the base.

1 Unless you are intending to save the topsoil to be re-used, dig straight down to the correct depth allowing for the thickness of paving and mortar bed plus approximately 75–100mm (3–4in) for the depth of sub-base. Check the depth from time to time by measuring down with a steel tape measure from a spirit level held across the datum peg. If level pegs have been set up around the area to indicate the finished patio height, pull a string line from one peg to another and measure down from the string line to check the depth of excavation.

2 Transfer the planned fall across the surface of the patio (see pages 146-7) to the sub-base, making one side of the excavation deeper than the other. Begin by digging a trench along the back of the area, followed by one at the correct depth along the front and then connect the two trenches at the right depth by excavating the area between them.

3 Excavate an area that is slightly wider than the proposed patio to ensure that the sub-base extends underneath all the paving and to make the laying of the edge slabs easier. Dig out any soft spots further and fill with additional crushed stone.

4 Remove excavated material from the site and tip it into a skip. Use a wheel barrow with a pneumatic tyre to remove the material to the skip and, if you have to cross soft ground, set up a runway of scaffold planks to prevent the barrow sinking into the ground. Do not overfill it as this will make it harder to push and potentially dangerous on slippery boards. Make sure you hire a drop end skip, which is infinitely safer than trying to balance a wheel barrow on wet loading boards.

Materials

There are two layers of materials that form the base underneath paving. The first layer is the road base or sub-base, which is discussed here, and above this is the bedding material or mortar, onto which the paving is laid (this is shown in detail on pages 152-3).

Crushed stone

The material that is commonly used for a sub-base is crushed stone, which varies depending on the region where it was quarried. It is specified by its range of aggregate sizes – 38mm (1½in) down to a fine dust for example. This material is delivered loose or in 1 tonne (20cwt) bags.

It is best to avoid general builders' rubble for use under paving as it tends to consist of broken slabs, bricks and old lumps of mortar, none of which will compact down easily. The lack of fine material also prevents the road base from bonding into a cohesive layer and so settling may occur. This type of material is really only suitable to fill a deep excavation that can then be capped over with a strong mix of reinforced concrete.

Lean-mix concrete

An alternative to crushed stone is lean-mix concrete; a weak concrete mix in the ratio of one part cement to ten or twelve parts all-in-crushed gravel (mixed sizes of aggregate from a gravel pit), which can then be raked out and compacted in the same manner as crushed stone. Though this alternative is slightly more expensive it is the best material to use over soft ground.

Stronger concrete mixes are only needed to form a raft over made up ground, usually in a raised terrace. In this case, concrete in a mix of 1:6 should be poured through a mesh of reinforcing steel that is supported so that the mesh is sandwiched in the middle of a layer of concrete. The steel holds the concrete together in a raft to counter any settlement that would otherwise crack the paving.

Concrete being poured through a steel mesh.

Laying the sub-base

1 When you are satisfied that you have excavated to the right depth, barrow in the crushed stone and roughly shovel it into position. Measure down from the string lines as before, to check that the sub-base is at the correct level. Remember that the material will compact down by about 10 to 15 percent and should therefore be left proud to allow for this.

2 On large areas lay timber rails at intervals across the base of the excavation in order to help you place the crushed stone at the correct

depth. You should place the rails at the same depth as the finished layer of sub-base and use them as a guide up to which you can rake the stone. Then remove the rails and backfill their place with stone.

3 Use a plate compactor on the whole area to compact the material, using a hand rammer to deal with any awkward corners. After you have finished the compaction, check the depth again, spreading and compacting road base over any low spots. The area will then be ready for bedding down the paving.

A typical paving construction

This shows the different layers needed to construct a paved patio or path. The slabs are laid on a full bed of mortar over a sub-base of compacted road base.

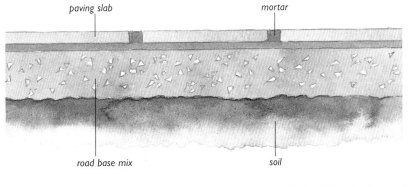

paving slab

mortar

road base mix

soil

bedding, pointing AND PLANTING

Paving slabs are laid on mortar, a mix of sand and cement. Mortar is also used for filling or pointing the joints between the slabs in some types of paving. Groundcover plants can be used to soften the edges of new paving while some can even be planted within the paved area to release their fragrance when touched.

Bedding material

Mortar is the bedding material that is spread over the sub-base (see pages 150-1) and onto which the paving units are laid. Mortar for paving is a mix of washed river sand, cement and water. Depending on the quantity of material that you require, you can either have the sand delivered loose, in 1 tonne (20cwt) sacks or in 25kg (55lb) bags for small jobs.

The mix of coarse sand and cement sets as hard as concrete and forms an excellent bedding course for paving. Sand on its own is not really good enough as a bedding material for paving as ground water or any water that filters down between the slabs will start to erode the sand and cause the slabs to settle. The only time that sand should be used as bedding is for interlocking brick paving units. Then, using a board, a layer of sand can be dragged out level (screeded) over the sub-base onto which bricks are placed and then vibrated down into the sand with a plate compactor. With this method of paving, the interlocking bricks act as a flexible surface. This paving is ideal for making driveways as it spreads the heavy load of a vehicle throughout the area. To be successful, however, it is essential to use a dry sand bed. The introduction of cement would create a rigid construction that doesn't have the same load-spreading qualities.

Mortar mixes

Mortar mixes are indicated in the ratio of cement to sand, with the most common mixes ranging from 1:3 to 1:12. A mix somewhere in the middle, about 1:6, is suitable for most types of paving. However, a much weaker mix of 1:10 is acceptable for stone paving because the flagstones are so heavy that they are almost self supporting. In this case, there is no real need to use a very strong mix – it would just be a waste of cement and money.

The amount of water in a mix is a matter of judgement – if the mortar is too wet, it may not actually support the paving units. Wet mortar is also messy to work with and can splash and stain the paving. The mortar needs to be just firm enough to support the paving units while they are tapped down to the correct level.

Fairly dry mortar mixes can be used for bedding small paving units such as clay pavers: screed out an area of mortar, place the clay pavers on top and tamp them down into position. In this instance, the dry mix can be a fairly strong 1:4 mortar in order to hold these smaller paving units firmly in place. The edges of patios or pathways can also be held firm in a technique known as haunching. Here, mortar or concrete may be spread out and smoothed along the outside edge of the patio to finish just below the surface of the paving in order to prevent any sideways movement.

Compacting clay pavers into sand.

A mix of cement and sand makes up mortar.

Mixing mortar by hand

For bedding mortar use a shovel to measure out the sand and cement. For pointing mortar it is essential that each mix is consistent in terms of strength of colour when dry and therefore it is better to use a dry bucket rather than a shovel as an accurate gauge of material quantities.

1 Shovel the correct amount of sand into a pile on a dry board and tip the cement onto it. Use a shovel to mix them until an even colour is achieved.

2 Make a crater in the middle of the pile and add water. Turn the dry mix into it, trying not to let any water escape.

3 You should continue to work the first lot of water in but, if it seems that the mix is still too dry, form a crater again and add a little more water. Keep turning in the material until the mix is moist, not wet, and can be easily worked with a shovel. Take care not to add too much water in one go as the mix may become too sloppy.

4 Next, slide a shovel underneath the mortar and turn it upside down. Continue to do this a few times before spreading it out on a board. Then move the shovel backwards and forwards through the mix using a chopping action. This ensures that the mortar is blended to an even consistency.

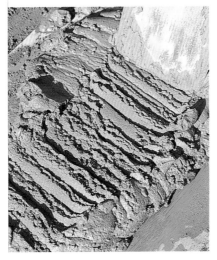

Using a mixer

A mixer will be preferable if you have a large amount of mortar to mix. An electric mixer is easier and quieter to use than a petrol machine. Set up the mixer close to your sand and cement

A mixer is useful for making a lot of mortar.

supplies but face it away from the area you are paving to avoid splashes. If you have to do the mixing on an existing driveway or paved surface, make sure that the wheel barrow is standing on a large board over a sheet of polythene to prevent mortar splashing and staining the surface. Ideally, mix up on an area of soil, lawn or old concrete.

You should limit the amount you do to what can be used in an hour or two; otherwise it will go off and be wasted. Once you have placed your mixture in the machine you will need to add water while it is running to achieve the correct consistency. The mortar should not be runny but should still fall off the blades.

Once your mix is ready, you can tip it into a wheel barrow ready for putting in position. At the end of the day, turn off the mixer and scrape out any excess mortar before adding water and a couple of broken bricks to agitate the remaining mortar loose.

Laying paving

There are two methods for laying paving stones with mortar: either apply five spots to the ground beneath each slab and tap them into position or lay a full bed of mortar and place slabs on top. The joints for both methods should be about 10mm (³⁄₈in) wide.

The five spot method

This method supports the slab on all corners as well as in the middle and makes it easy to tap the slab down into position. It does, however, create more of a problem when pointing up later as the pointing mix may disappear to fill in the void under the slab when pushed into the joints. There is also the possibility that water can sit under the slabs, resulting in the potential problem of slabs moving due to the effect of freeze-thaw action.

The mortar bed method

A full bed of mortar is the strongest method because the whole slab is supported and water is kept out. Spread a layer of mortar over the road base mix and use a trowel to create ridges and furrows in the mortar so that, when the slab is tapped down, the

The five spot method.

mortar has a space in which to move and you end up with a solid bed about 37mm (1¹⁄₂in) deep.

The mortar bed method.

Pointing techniques

This is the process of filling the joints between the paving slabs with mortar in order to keep the water from seeping down between the slabs and also to prevent weeds from growing up through the gaps.

Pointing up open joints

1 Mortar for pointing up paving needs to be much stronger than bedding mortar because it is subject to weathering and so if it is too weak, it may crumble due to frost action.

The most common mix is 1:4 (one part cement to two parts coarse sand, and two parts fine sand); fine sand is introduced so that you can rub the joint smooth. A slightly weaker mix of 1:5 or 1:6 may be favoured because this encourages attractive mosses to become established.

The pointing mix needs to be crumbly so make sure that it is not too wet. You should never do any of your pointing when it is pouring with rain or if the paving is wet as the mix may stain the paving.

2 Use a brick trowel to push the mix into the joints between the slabs, making sure they are completely filled.

3 Once all the joints are full, use a piece of pipe to rub the mortar smooth to form neat channels. These channels allow any surface water to run off easily rather than collecting. The channels will be less pronounced if a weak mortar mix is used in the joints, as mosses will soften their appearance.

4 After you have left the mortar to dry for a few hours any excess mortar that is on the surface can then be scraped off the surface of the slabs. Use a soft brush to sweep the paving

clean to ensure that no remaining mortar that would stain the surface of the patio will be trodden in.

Butt-jointed paving

There are some types of paving slabs and bricks that can be laid butt jointed, which means that they are laid tightly against each other without a mortar joint. Take care when using this method because it only takes a few grains of dry bedding mortar trapped

Laying butt-jointed paving.

between the paving to open up the joint, which will cause the jointing pattern to be ruined. After laying butt-jointed bricks, brush some fine dry sand over the surface of the paving to

Brushing sand in to seal the butt joints.

help form a tight seal between the bricks. You will not be able to use this method for stone paving and some concrete paving slabs with irregular edges because they cannot easily be laid tightly together.

Planting

There are many plants that associate well with paving in different areas of the garden and some of these plants can even withstand being trodden on occasionally. You can plant up areas around the edges or inside the paving. For example, helianthemum, aubrieta and cerastium will thrive in dry sunny terraces where they form low-growing

Plants can be placed among paving.

mats to creep over and soften the edges of paving. These plants all enjoy the dry, free-draining environment provided by gravel surfaces or the gritty compost that can be used to fill joints between paving. Plants such as these work well in stepping stone paths, patios and gravel walkways.

Where the joints between slabs are too narrow to introduce small plants, you can sow the seeds of herbs or alpines that will quickly establish to soften the paving. Varieties of the creeping thyme and the mat-forming chamomile, *Chamaemelum nobile* 'Treneague', can be walked on to release their wonderful fragrance. Other plants such as the blue grass *Festuca* 'Glauca', as well as many varieties of fern that are not mat forming, simply look great growing through a gravelled surface.

Plants also associate well with pathways in a woodland area, softening the edges of bark paths or growing up between slabs in stepping stone paths. Ajuga, lamium and gaultheria all do well in these positions. Ivy, periwinkle and soleirolia (Baby's tears) will also be successful but will need controlling as they are invasive.

Groundcover for sunny aspects
Armeria (thrift)
Aubrieta
Chamaemelum nobile 'Treneague'
Helianthemum
Saxifrage
Thymus (thyme)

Groundcover for use in the shade
Ajuga (bugle)
Hedera (ivy)
Soleirolia (Baby's tears)
Lamium (Dead nettle)
Lysimachia nummularia
Vinca (periwinkle)

good working PRACTICE

The logistics of building a small project in your own garden need to be thought through very carefully. You will want to make sure that everything is done properly and you should be especially vigilant with regard to safety issues. Follow the simple suggestions below to create a safe, well-run construction site while building your new garden surfaces.

Safety and protection

If you are not used to physical work then do not try to do too much in a hurry; warm up and stretch as you would for any other physical exercise. Remember to lift properly with your knees bent and your back kept straight and always ask for help when lifting heavy equipment or materials.

If you have long hair then tie it back, out of the way, especially when using machinery. Wear suitable clothes that do not restrict movement but do not flap either. A set of waterproofs is essential for rainy days as there is no point working while you are cold and wet. Always wear steel toe-capped boots for construction work and a pair of strong gloves when handling sharp-edged concrete slabs or cement.

You must wear goggles to protect your eyes when using a slab cutter or a hammer and bolster. A protective mask will keep out the dust and hearing protection would also be a very wise precaution.

If you use mains voltage electrical equipment on site then you must ensure that circuit breakers are installed to cut off the power should the cable become damaged. Hire shops will supply transformers, which are the safest option.

Allowing plenty of time to carry out tasks means that you can take proper care, whereas if you try to rush through a job it may cause you to leave potentially dangerous tools and materials scattered around that will cause other people harm.

Power tools, saws and other potentially hazardous equipment obviously need to be kept out of the reach of children and should always be locked away at the end of the day. Children like climbing over things so always make sure that your materials are stacked and stored properly.

It is also dangerous to be responsible for children when you are using noisy machinery, so make sure that they are being supervised well out of the way before you start any work and be sure to remove the ignition key when machines are not in use so that accidents cannot happen.

Excavations need to be covered over with strong boards and ideally the site should be cordoned off from the rest of the garden (see opposite).

The correct way to lift heavy materials.

Using a slab cutter.

Using a hammer and bolster.

Storing materials

If possible, try to unload materials next to where they are to be used to avoid handling them more than once. This is rarely possible and you may find you have to unload the materials onto the driveway first. Store loose materials such as sand and gravel on plywood boards away from each other – if they do get mixed, you will find it frustrating to try to lay slabs on mortar that contains the occasional piece of gravel.

Sand and gravel can be tipped off a truck or craned off in large heavy duty bags, which hold about 1 tonne (20cwt). Bagged sand and gravel is slightly more expensive but much more convenient as the bags keep the material clean and take up less space. Cement is delivered in 25kg (½cwt) bags and you should stack them on pallets or boards and cover them with polythene sheets, ideally in a shed so that they do not get damp. Arrange paving slabs on their edges, side by side, and stack bricks in piles. Keep sand and cement off driveways as they will stain the surface and move pallets of slabs as quickly as possible off a driveway as the weight can dent some surfaces.

Paving slabs should be stored on their edges.

Stack bricks neatly on top of each other.

Construction day

Keep an eye on the weather forecast when you are planning your days for construction as, although some jobs can be done in the rain, it is not much fun and you can end up making far more mess than is really necessary. Consider your neighbours, too; you may want to make an early start on a Sunday morning but they may not appreciate their one lie-in being interrupted by a noisy cement mixer. An electric mixer is actually quieter than a petrol mixer but it is still wise to plan all your noisier jobs for a more suitable time of day. Dust is a problem that cannot always be avoided so do check if there is washing on the line next door before starting up a slab cutter and consider using attachments that keep the disc dampened down to reduce dust.

Try to work logically and in sensible stages, giving yourself time for breaks in order to stand back, assess progress and plan the next task. Think each part of the job through before rushing in, especially when you are cutting slabs or other materials. And always double check measurements before making the final cut to save mistakes and expensive waste.

Completing the day's work

Leave plenty of time at the end of the day to clean the cement mixer and hand tools, particularly those that have been used for mortar and concrete as the materials will set hard and ruin the tools if you do not clean them off. Then make sure that you immobilise the machines and cover all the materials over safely.

Paved areas are best left covered with polythene sheets, held down by boards, especially if there is any chance of rain or a frost.

Ensure that the site is left completely safe by covering any trenches and excavated areas for paving with sturdy boards. Ideally, you should cordon off the whole area with brightly coloured marker tape or temporary plastic fencing. Lights may be unnecessary in your rear garden but they are an essential addition to lead any visitors safely past if your construction work is situated in the front of your house. Battery powered safety lamps, together with rolls of plastic fencing, marker tape and warning cones (which should always be placed round skips if you are using them), may all be obtained from most tool hire shops.

Plastic fencing cordons off construction areas.

tools AND EQUIPMENT

It is important to invest in good quality tools that will last you a lifetime. The tools required for garden construction have been placed in three categories here: kits for groundwork, paving and woodwork, while the section on 'hire tools' covers specialist machinery you may prefer not to buy. Each photograph illustrates the tool that is described directly above it.

Groundwork tools

Beetle Similar to a sledgehammer but with a round flat head, ideal for knocking in timber posts.

Crow bar A long and heavy iron bar for levering out old concrete or rocks.
Heavy fork It is much more useful to have a heavy fork than a light border fork when you are digging out ground.
Mattock This is similar in appearance to a pick axe, though the head has one flat blade, which is ideal for hooking out shallow trenches. It also has one blade that is similar to an axe head, which is useful for chopping through old roots.
Measuring tape, 30m (100ft) This tape is essential for surveying and setting out. It is particularly useful to have two such tapes for triangulation.
Measuring wheel This is a useful tool if you need to measure a large garden.

In such a case, it is much more practical than tapes.

Pick axe This is useful for breaking out hard ground or old concrete.

Shovel This is a multi-purpose tool for digging out soil as well as spreading road base, sand and mortar.
Sledgehammer This tool can be described as a long-handled, heavy

hammer and it is used for breaking up old paved surfaces.

Spade A heavy duty spade should be used for digging out.
Timber pegs These are short, pointed pegs that are needed for most jobs.
Wheel barrow You should aim to buy a heavy duty barrow with a pneumatic tyre suitable for carrying heavy loads over uneven ground.

Paving tools

Bolster This is a broad, flat-headed chisel, used for cutting bricks.

Broom A stiff broom is useful for cleaning off dirty paving, while a soft brush is essential for sweeping paving after pointing or brushing sand into paving bricks.

Bucket This is a heavy duty bucket, which can be used for water but also for measuring sand and cement in a pointing mix.

Club hammer This is a short-handled, heavy hammer, which is often known as a lump hammer. It is used with a bolster for cutting bricks and with a cold chisel for breaking old concrete. Its handle can also be used for tapping down paving bricks.

Cold chisel Used alongside a club hammer to break out old concrete.

Float This is a small, flat metal tool that is used for smoothing off concrete.

Goggles, gloves and hearing protection These should all be worn when cutting paving and when using concrete breakers.

Hacksaw This saw has narrow teeth and is used mainly to cut metal.

Line and pins This refers to short metal pins that can be pushed into soil or mortar between which a string line is pulled taut to indicate the edge and finished height of paving.

Measuring tape, 3m (10ft) This is a retractable tape that is essential for the detailed measuring of paving as well as woodwork.

Plastic sheets It is a good idea to purchase a few large sheets of plastic as they can be used to cover paving

once it has been pointed, in order to keep the rain off the surface.

Pointing trowel This is a small triangular-shaped trowel that looks like a brick trowel but is used for filling in the mortar joints in paving.

Rammer This tool is used to compact small areas of road bases.

Rubber mallet Used for tapping down flagstones, pavers and sleepers.

Set square A wooden triangle that can be used for setting out paving.

Spirit level A 900mm (3ft) long level is ideal, especially one with a bubble on the top edge, for laying paving.

Straight edge A planed length of timber essential for setting pegs to level and paving to the correct fall.

Watering can A heavy duty can is useful for watering in mortar.

Woodwork tools

Adjustable wrench This is used for tightening nuts and bolts for deck posts and beams.

Claw hammer Used for banging in nails and also for pulling out old nails.

Cordless drill This is a lightweight drill powered by a rechargeable battery, which is far more convenient than using an electric drill with a cable. It can be fitted with screwdriver attachments for the different types of screws, which makes light work of fixing and undoing screws.

Paintbrushes Always choose good quality brushes for applying stain to timber decks.

Panel saw This is a general purpose saw for most of your woodworking requirements. A smaller tenon saw can also be used for detailed joint work.

Plane This tool is used for smoothing down timber to produce a neat, planed finish.

Surform A similar action to using a plane is required with this tool, which takes the rough edges off sawn timber.

Try square This is a set square that is used for woodworking.

Wood chisel This is used for cutting out joints in timber posts when creating decking joists.

Wooden mallet Used with a wood chisel. You can hit the chisel with a mallet to create a greater force.

Using these tool lists
To save long, repetitive lists of tools appearing at the end of each project, only the necessary categories of equipment (groundwork and paving, for example) have been recorded. If one item from another section is also required to complete the project, it is listed individually.
Any necessary hire equipment is also shown at the end of the list. Therefore, you will need to refer back to this section as you are planning the projects that you wish to carry out in your own garden.

Hire tools

Chainsaw Logs and sleepers can be cut easily with a chainsaw. There are, however, strict regulations concerning the hiring of chainsaws. A company should only let a chainsaw out to a member of the public if they are convinced that it is the correct tool for the job and the customer demonstrates the ability to use it properly. The hire shop can actually refuse to hire out a saw if they have any doubts about the customer. They will give out protective equipment with the saw and this must be worn at all times when using the chainsaw. Make sure that you also follow all the instructions they give you as they are vital for your safety.

Circular saw If you have many beams and deck boards to cut then a circular saw is the best tool to use.

Concrete breaker An electric breaker is essential for breaking out areas of old concrete.

Concrete mixer It is far easier to mix concrete with a machine than by hand. Small mixers that fit onto a stand are the simplest to manage and transport. Both petrol and electric mixers are available – the electric is much quieter and therefore more neighbour-friendly.

Laser level This is an excellent piece of surveying equipment that can be operated by just one person. It can be hired very cheaply by the day.

Plate compactor This is the mechanical version of the hand rammer, and is mainly used for compacting large areas of rubble fill. However, it can also be used as a tool for bedding down paving bricks once they have been laid.

Skip loader This is like a little tip truck and can be loaded with soil and driven to the side of a skip. Then the load is raised up and tipped out.

Slab cutter This petrol powered machine is used to cut paving slabs. An attachment allows a hose to be fixed to it that dribbles water along the cut when in use to keep dust down.

Tracked excavator A whole range of excavating machinery can be hired, which will save you an awful lot of hand digging. Tracked vehicles are useful on uneven ground with rubber tracks being essential if you have to drive over any tarmac roads.

Vibrating rollers These provide great compaction but are unwieldy.

paths

planning for paths

As well as having the important practical function of linking areas of the garden, carefully designed pathways can make dramatic features. A straight path can provide a strong visual link between one end of the garden and another, drawing the eye along its length with definite purpose. On the other hand, curving, meandering paths can lead intriguingly into the distance, encouraging people to walk along them to discover what lies at the end.

Function and style Pathways usually have the practical function of providing access from one part of the garden to another. They are also essential for maintenance; for example, they could provide access along the back of a shrub border to trim a hedge. Often paths are multifunctional; one laid around the edge of a lawn provides access to adjacent planting and also negates the need for laborious edging. The same path may serve as a circular bicycle track for children. The style of path can be chosen to match the overall style and mood of the garden and this can be achieved by using the same material as the patio so that they echo one another. As paths lead away from the house, the materials can be spaced with gaps for groundcover plants to create a much softer appearance. As the atmosphere of the garden changes into a more relaxed style with drifts of naturalising bulbs, a mown grass path may be introduced or a path of bark chippings through more wooded areas.

Design choices Straight paths give direct access from one point to another although introducing a simple turn in the path around a clump of shrubs will add more interest without greatly increasing the distance. A zigzag path will make a long narrow garden seem wider, unlike a straight path, which will foreshorten the view to the end. A circular path will have a similar effect, allowing you to stroll around the garden rather than just take a quick walk to the end and back. The surface pattern of a path is another design factor to consider. Brick paths laid to a running bond along the length of the path accentuate the direction and stimulate quicker movement, while the same pattern laid across the path appears to broaden the width and encourages a more leisurely walk. This same effect can be created with rectangular paving slabs and even with a

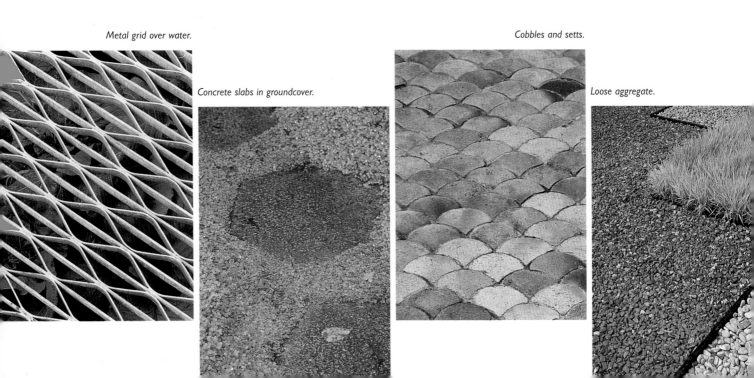

Metal grid over water.

Concrete slabs in groundcover.

Cobbles and setts.

Loose aggregate.

The style of pathway is key when designing your garden layout: the crisp clean lines of the smooth pale slabs across water (top left) would complement an urban or minimalist garden. The meandering timber pathway surrounded by natural planting (top right) would be more suited to an informal country garden. The straight brick path (above) draws the eye to the end but the repeat of the pattern and the elegant borders encourage the walker to linger awhile.

Bricks laid across the width of a path can make a pathway look wider and encourage people to take their time as they amble along it.

timber boardwalk. Surfaces such as natural stone setts or cobbles, which are not completely smooth underfoot, will tend to slow movement down, as will surfaces where groundcover planting has been allowed to grow in the joints or soften the edges. Stepping stones can be used for visual effect but must be laid close together if they are to be walked on. Mosaics of pebbles and ceramics laid in the surface of a path will create interest and so naturally slow you down. Other types of paving with a textured surface may be laid through shaded areas or on slight inclines where extra grip is needed. The width of a path will vary to suit its use. A broad path is often used where a slower pace is anticipated and 1.2m (4ft) is needed for two people to stroll comfortably side by side. Narrower paths are fine for quick access, while a single line of bricks may be laid to create a visual rather than practical link.

Types of pathway   Most garden materials can be used to form the surface of a path and even grass or plants can be grown to form a walkway for occasional use. Bark chippings work well in a woodland setting,

especially if laid over road base to prevent the path becoming too wet and muddy. Most loose aggregates can be laid as a path from the whole range of gravel to broken tiles, pebbles and even aluminium and copper granules, though they do need to be retained with an edging. Self-setting gravel is a useful material for less ornamental areas of the garden where a loose gravel may look out of place. This material is raked out and compacted with a wet roller to create a firm path with a natural appearance. Solid surfaces make the most durable paths, although some still need an edge restraint. Many types of paving brick and concrete sett are compacted into a sand bed and locked together to create a firm surface but it is the edging that prevents any joints opening up and the path failing. Other paving units such as natural stone flags or concrete paving slabs are bedded on mortar to form a rigid surface either as a solid path or laid through a flexible surface to create a strong directional line. Railway sleepers or log rounds can also be laid for the same effect. Small paving units such as brick or broken stone paving are ideal for curved paths.

The following projects illustrate the range of pathways that can be incorporated to suit the different areas of the garden – none require specialist help from contractors.

> *Stepping stones can be used for visual effect but must be laid close together if they are to be walked on.*

Timber is an extremely versatile material to consider when planning and building a pathway. Jagged lengths of timber, joined together in an uneven way (above left) provide an original and rustic walkway across a stream. On the other hand, stone slabs surrounded by a bed of gravel (above right) can provide a tantalising walkway to connect two areas of a garden.

Natural slate.

Setts in a running bond pattern.

Clay pavers in a basket weave pattern.

Log rounds with loose chippings.

stepping STONES

Stepping stones are ideal for making a path that is used only occasionally. They can be discrete, harmonising with the garden's natural lines or they can provide a strong visual sense of direction by leading the eye to a particular part of the garden.

1 Before cutting any turf, plan your desired pattern, laying the slabs out on the surface. Plan the spacing for the stride of the person who will use the path most often, with gaps that allow for a gentle stroll. If laying a path through groundcover, take care with spacing to minimise damage to the plants, as most will withstand only the occasional footfall. Of course, if stepping stones are being laid purely for their visual impact then the spacing is not so critical.

2 Once all the slabs are in position, mark them out using a spade to notch around the edges, then set the slabs to one side. Dig out the turf and soil to an area slightly larger than the slab itself to give room for a finger hold when you come to bed them in. Stepping stones through a firm lawn area require very little base construction, so you will only need to dig out about 50mm (2in) to allow for the thickness of the slab plus a shallow depth of bedding sand.

MATERIALS

Coarse sand

Road base

Mortar

Paving slabs: 450 × 450mm (18 × 18in)
300 × 300mm (12 × 12in)

Fine soil

Grass seed

TOOLS

Groundwork tools

Paving tools

1 Lay the slabs out in the desired pattern to get the spacing right before you start to cut the turf.

2 Use a spade to mark an area slightly bigger than the edges of the slabs to give room for a finger hold.

KNOW YOUR MATERIALS

Paving slabs can be laid in diamonds or squares or even in random sizes, and they do not need to be laid as single slabs either – broad bands of paving with grass or groundcover joints look equally effective in the garden. When paving slabs are made, pigments and aggregates can be added to the concrete mix in order to produce a range of muted colours, and different moulds create a variety of surface finishes too. You should therefore feel at liberty to experiment with the numerous combinations of colour and texture that are available to buy commercially. Try mixing various different coloured slabs together.

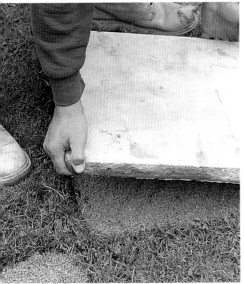

3 Gently lay the slab into position on a thin bed of coarse sand. A bed of mortar is not usually necessary when laying stepping stones.

3 | Next, spread a thin layer of coarse sand across the bottom of the first slab bed. Since the slabs for a stepping stone path are isolated from each other, it does not matter if they move a little once laid and so there is usually no need for a mortar bed. However, if the ground is loose, wet or made up, you could replace the sand with road base and a weak mix of sand and cement. Simply dig down to an additional depth of 75mm (3in) to accommodate the base.

Move one of the slabs into position, then tap it down with a rubber mallet or club hammer on a block of wood, until it lies flush with the lawn. It is essential that no slabs finish proud of the lawn surface, as this will form a trip and create problems when it comes to mowing. Slabs should also fit in with any slight falls on the existing lawn, though there is no need to employ a spirit level. Once all the slabs have been laid, you may need to make good around the edges with fine soil and grass seed.

wood chip and TIMBER ROUNDS PATH

Chippings of bark and wood offer a soft and fragrant surface underfoot, reminiscent of woodland walks, and are ideal for creating curved or winding pathways.

1 Mark out the position of the path according to your plan. The specifics of line and curve are not as critical with wood chip paths as they are with those built from slabs or bricks where joint sizes can be affected. Clear the ground of vegetation and remove loose soil down to a depth of about 100mm (4in). If the surrounding area is full of weeds, lay a weed mat, which will help to prevent them from growing up through the surface and also keep the road base from pushing down into the wet soil.

To make the edging, drive in timber pegs along the path edges. Then position the treated softwood path edgings and nail them back to the pegs at 1m (40in) intervals. Then scatter road base to a depth of 75–100mm (3–4in), rake it out and compact it down.

2 Next place the log rounds out on the pathway in their approximate positions and then move them to fit your

MATERIALS

Treated timber path edging
100 x 25mm (4 x 1in)

Pointed pegs 50 x 50 x 450mm
(2 x 2 x 18in)

Galvanised nails

Coarse sand

Road base

Timber log rounds

Path grade bark or wood chip

TOOLS

Groundwork tools

Woodwork tools

Rubber mallet

Club hammer

Timber straight edge:
75 x 50 x 1.8m (3 x 2 x 72in)

Plate compactor

Chainsaw

1 When you have laid the edging, scatter road base over the whole path surface to a depth of about 100mm (4in).

2 Lay the log rounds in approximate positions to fit the step length of the person who will use the path most often.

KNOW YOUR MATERIALS

Log rounds: These are slices of old tree trunks that can be cut from any type of timber, but hardwood rounds like oak, beech and ash are longer lasting than those cut from conifer trunks. Log rounds need not be too thick, between 75–100mm (3–4in), as any bigger than this would make them too heavy and the job would require additional excavation.

Wood chip: Comes in many chip grades, with some sold specifically as path grade. Bagged material can readily be bought from garden centres and large hardware stores, or delivered direct in 1 tonne (20cwt) bags. If you are covering a very large area, it is possible to obtain bulk truck loads direct from the supplier.

exact step length or the step length of the person who will use the path the most. Along a woodland walk, cater for a gentle stroll. If the log rounds are purely for ornamental effect, their positioning is less important. However, you will find it is more visually appealing if they are staggered rather than laid in a straight line.

3 Once you are satisfied with the line of log rounds, mark around each one with a spade or shovel, then put it to one side in order to dig out the road base from beneath. The aim should be for the log round to finish flush with the edging boards at the sides of the path. Dig out to the depth of the timber round, plus an allowance for sand. Any road base that is dug out should be spread over the path, while any excavated soil must be spread to one side to prevent any soft spots forming. Continue digging out the positions for all the log rounds.

4 Next scatter a thin layer of coarse sand under each round to help bed it down and to keep the base relatively dry.

There is no need for any road base under the rounds because they are sturdy enough without it and it does not matter if they move a little. Work each log round down into position by hand.

5 Lay a straight-edged piece of timber across each log round so that it stretches from one side of the path to the other. If the straight edge rests on top of the log round and on each edging board, then the round is level and you can move onto the next one. Otherwise, tap down the round with a rubber mallet until the straight edge sits flush across the path. Continue to lay and tap down all the log rounds in the same manner.

6 Now turn the straight edge along the length of the path, laying the timber across three or four of the rounds. Tap the rounds down with the mallet until they all sit flush with the underside of the timber. This will ensure they do not create an uneven hazard along the length of the path that might cause someone to trip and fall.

3 After deciding on the positioning of the rounds, put them to one side and dig out the road base and soil from beneath them.

4 Scatter a thin layer of coarse sand underneath each round and then work them down into position by hand.

5 Lay a straight-edged piece of timber across the path to check that the rounds are level with the edging.

Make good the foundation next to each log round by ramming the road base in with a club hammer.

7 Finally, using a shovel, spread bark or wood chippings over the surface around the log rounds to a depth of about 25mm (1in). You may find it easier to apply the final touches by hand to push the bark neatly around each timber round.

Alternative materials

Bark and wood chips form a soft, dry and non-slip path surface that is especially appropriate for children, who will find a soft landing on wood chips during the rough and tumble of play. However, if you are looking for a firmer surface dressing in a more formal part of the garden, then laying down crushed gravel will make a fine alternative to bark chippings and has the additional quality of providing a contrast in colour and texture to the log rounds.

The preparation of the road base is exactly the same as for a surface of wood chips, leaving a depth of about 25mm (1in) to be filled with marble. Crushed gravel, or crushed slate which is darker, both look good in a fairly natural setting. Shovel the crushed gravel into place and again work the stone down around each timber by hand to produce a neat finish. Use a soft brush to clear any loose stones from the tops of the rounds.

Alternative methods

If you are already using wood chips as a mulch (loose material used to insulate the soil) to the shrubby undergrowth of a woodland-style garden, you could simply extend the area of chippings away from the plants to provide a surface to walk upon, which in addition forms a link between the plants and path. This type of path is fine for occasional use, but it will not stand up to heavy wear and soon deteriorates if the ground is boggy.

For a less formal and adventurous walk in the garden, particularly appropriate for children, why not simply lay log rounds on their own as stepping stones in a woodland or through a bog garden.

6 Lay straight-edged timber along the path to make sure that all the rounds are even and to avoid the possibility of anyone tripping.

7 Spread a layer of bark or wood chippings over the path to a depth of approximately 25mm (1in).

Alternative materials: Laying down crushed gravel will provide a firm surface and offer a contrast in colour and texture.

sleeper and GRAVEL PATH

With bushy pockets of semi-wild plants appearing to reclaim the pathway, this type of sleeper path conjures up both the reassuring solidity and the romance of bygone railways.

MATERIALS

Sleepers

Road base

Galvanised metal for edging strips

Battens

Coarse sand

Crushed gravel

Groundcover plants

River pebbles

TOOLS

Groundwork tools

Hacksaw

Club hammer

Chainsaw

Rubber mallet

Rammer

Straight edge

1 Mark out the pathway and excavate to the full depth of a sleeper over the whole pathway, allowing for 125mm (5in) of road base and 25mm (1in) of crushed gravel. Wheel in the road base and spread it over the whole area. (Some of it will be removed to accommodate the sleepers but it is easier at this stage simply to cover the entire path base.) Compact down the layer of road base, leaving a gap of approximately 25mm (1in) below the finished path level to allow for the depth of gravel. Next, measure out the length of edging required for the path and get a blacksmith to cut the galvanised metal to length. Some form of edging is essential to prevent the erosion that will inevitably be caused by people walking close to the sides.

2 Position the metal edging strips along both sides of the path and bang them down to the finished height of the path using a club hammer. The strips can either be laid in

1 Once you have excavated the pathway area, you can begin edging your path. Here we are using metal to give a crisp, clean finish.

2 If you choose to, you can place the edging all the way along your path first, and then bang it down to the correct height.

KNOW YOUR MATERIALS

Sleepers: Available as either treated or untreated softwood or as hardwood for both new and secondhand sleepers. Softwood sleepers gain their durability by being heavily impregnated with tar, which also makes them rather dirty to handle. In shady conditions this may not be a problem but, if you are laying the path in a sunny situation, the tar may be drawn out of the timber in very hot weather. So hardwood is often the best choice.

Metal edging: Lengths of galvanised metal, approximately 2mm (1/16in) thick, can be cut to length by a blacksmith who will also be able to weld on the short metal spikes that allow the metal strips to be fixed into the ground.

the gaps between the sleepers or, as we have done here, in a continuous strip outside the ends of the sleepers, which avoids laborious cutting.

3 The next step is to measure out and mark the correct length of sleeper for the particular design of your path. As sleepers are normally 2.4m (8ft) long you might want to plan your design around 1.2m (4ft) lengths, which will help to avoid waste and still give a good width of timber to walk on. You should also consider whether you want to stagger the occasional timber in the pattern, in which case you will need to measure out different lengths of sleeper and cut the edging strips accordingly. The pattern of different length sleepers can be quite random, perhaps one long one followed by two short ones and then another long one. Staggering the sleepers introduces a sense of movement and creates a space at one end of the sleeper where you can plant groundcover, and it also stops the path from looking too much like a railway track!

4 Now cut the sleeper lengths according to your chosen measurements. You will first need to lay the sleeper on battens to keep it off the ground – it will take two people to lift a full size sleeper into position. If there are only one or two sleepers to cut you should be able manage with a bow saw. However, you might want to use a chainsaw to make light work of any cutting, especially if the path is long. Chainsaws are available for personal hire, together with all the protective clothing (see page 161), but if you do not feel confident, you can always employ a contractor to carry out this part of the job.

5 Carry the cut timbers to the path and lay them on the road base in their correct positions. When you are happy the layout looks right, mark around each one with a spade and set them to one side. Excavate a trench through the road base for each one, to allow for the depth of the sleepers and a thin bed of coarse sand. Spread the sand along the base of the excavation as this will help to bed the sleepers down and keep the base of the timber dry.

3 Next, you must decide on the lengths of your sleepers. Measure them out and mark them ready for cutting.

4 You are now ready to cut your sleepers. A chainsaw is the easiest tool for this job, but always wear protective clothing when using one.

5 Lay the sleepers in place to check their positions. Then move them to one side and dig a trench for each one to sit in.

6 Place the sleepers back in position and knock them down with a rubber mallet. Lay a straight edge from one side of the path to the other and along each sleeper, to check that the sleeper finishes flush with the path edging.

7 Once all the sleepers have been laid, turn the straight edge along the length of the path to ensure that the sleepers are all the same height. If one of them is standing proud, it may cause someone to trip up as they walk down the path. Adjust the heights as necessary.

 Use the excavated road base to fill in along the edges of each sleeper and compact it with a hand rammer. If you would like some sort of planting within the path then this is the time that you should do it. Scrape out planting pockets within the road base and fill with topsoil. Then plant your selection of groundcover plants.

8 Gravel can now be shovelled on and raked around the plants and between the sleepers. You will need to rake gravel right up to the top of the sleepers and metal edging at first, but it will naturally settle in time to reveal the top edge of the sleepers. Gravel may range from 6mm (1/4in) to 20mm (3/4in) and the larger stones tend to move less. As a finishing touch to this natural design, position a few river pebbles, available in bags from garden centres, in scattered groups around the clumps of plants. Choose natural colours for the gravel, such as limestone or slate chippings. Fine aggregate is used here.

Alternative materials

Some companies make small imitation sleepers either 1.8m (6ft) or 900mm (3ft) long, which are lighter and easier for one person to lift. They are machine rounded but flat on the top and bottom faces to make them easy to lay. Alternatively, you could use large pressure treated section timbers, perhaps 150 x 150mm (6 x 6in), which will give the look of sleepers but will be a lot cleaner.

 For this particular project we have chosen the crisp finish of a metal edge, but timber makes for an equally good edging material.

6 You can then place the sleepers back into position and bang them down to the correct height using a rubber mallet.

7 Once you have put all the sleepers in their final positions, use the straight edge to check that they are all at the same height.

8 Now you can put the gravel in the areas between your sleepers. We have chosen to use fine aggregate here.

boardwalk ACROSS WATER

On a warm summer's day a boardwalk across water allows you to sit and enjoy the magical quality of a still, reflecting pool, which mirrors the sky and trees while you dabble your toes in the cool water.

MATERIALS

Sleeper beams
150 × 75mm (6in × 3in)

Crushed gravel or coarse sand

Posts 50 × 50mm (2 × 2in)

Deck slats 125 × 37mm (5 × 1½in)

Galvanised nails 150mm (6in) and
63mm (2½in)

Wood stain

Chicken wire

Galvanised 'U' nails

TOOLS

Groundwork tools

Woodwork tools

Rubber mallet

Spirit level

Aluminium ladder

Scaffold plank

String line

Paintbrush

Polythene sheet

1 Laying half a sleeper beam bearer at each end is the simplest base construction for a single span boardwalk. First decide on the finished height of the boardwalk above the water, not so high that it needs to be supported above ground level on the banks at either side but, if you are bridging a natural watercourse, high enough to cope with any changes in the water level. The underside of the proposed boardwalk beams will give you the finished height of the supporting bearers. Cut a sleeper in half to give you the bearer for each end of the boardwalk then dig out a trench, allowing for the depth of the sleeper and a bed of crushed gravel or coarse sand. Lay the first bearer and thump it down with a mallet to the finished level. Check with a spirit level that it is level.

2 Excavate and lay the second bearer on the opposite bank. Then lay one of the beams across the water from one

1 Cut your sleeper to make two bearers for either end of the boardwalk. Dig out a trench for the first and lay it in position.

2 Repeat for the second bearer. Check the two are level by placing a beam across the water with a spirit level on it.

KNOW YOUR MATERIALS

Decking boards are available in
various different materials and
widths but treated softwood
slats measuring 125 × 37mm
(5 × 1½in) are ideal. The timber
is commonly available in 4.2m
(14ft) lengths, which may then
be cut by the supplier into four
lengths of about 1m (3ft) – this
would make an ideal width for
the boardwalk and will also save
you paying for wasted timber.
Before fixing the slats it would
be a good idea to give them a
coat of wood stain, to protect
against the elements and so
extend the life expectancy of
the wood. Stains are available
in a range of different colours;
blue wood stain was used in
this project to complement
the effect of water.

bearer to the other and use a spirit level to check that the two bearers are level. Knock the second bearer down with a mallet until both are level. If it is not easy to gain access to the opposite bank to complete this stage, then you could lay an aluminium ladder and scaffold plank across from one side of the water to the other, to act as a temporary bridge.

3 Fix the first beam in position by nailing through its side into the bearer using a long galvanised nail. Check that it crosses the bearer at 90° and fix the other end with a nail in the same manner. The beams need to be fairly substantial so use 150 x 75mm (6 x 3in) timbers, which will probably require two people to carry them. Position the second beam parallel to the first one by measuring and checking that the space between the two beams is the same at each end. The width across from the outside of one beam to the outside of the other should allow for deck slats to overhang at each side by about 75mm (3in).

4 The beams can then be firmly anchored by driving in long 50 x 50mm (2 x 2in) posts. Drive them in with a beetle or sledgehammer hard against the point inside the beams where the beams meet with the bearers, as far into the bank as they will go. Nail each post to both the beam and the bearer and then cut off the post to just below the top of the beam.

5 Cut each of the deck slats to the same length. Nail one slat of decking board into position at each end of the boardwalk, then pull a string line taut between them along one edge. Now start to lay the rest of the deck slats, nailing them into position with one edge just touching the string line. Use a nail or a pencil as a spacer to leave a small gap of about 3mm (1/8in) between each board. This gap is necessary to accommodate natural expansion of the timber and to allow for better drainage of surface water. At this stage, only knock in one nail at each end of the board and leave them proud in case you need to remove and re-align any of the boards.

3 Fix each beam securely into its final position by using a long galvanised nail to attach it to the bearer.

4 To firmly anchor each beam you can drive a post into each of the corners where the beam meets the bearers.

5 Begin to nail the boards into position. One edge of each board should align with the taut string line you have set up.

6 Work your way across the water, nailing in boards in front of you as you go. When you have completed approximately half of the boarding it is a good idea to lay out the remaining slats without nailing them down. This will show whether you need to increase or decrease the gap slightly between each board in order to fit all the boards neatly, without having to cut any of them down to a thin strip. If no adjustments are needed, fix nails at the end of each board so that they are all double nailed at both ends. Once all the boards are fixed, check along the opposite edge to the line to make sure that the ends there are all even too and, if any are not, trim them with a panel saw and sand them to make them smooth.

7 You will now need to check the entire boardwalk to see if you need to touch up any of the boards with stain, since cutting the boards may have resulted in some accidental removal of the stain. If re-staining is required, be sure to lay polythene over the water underneath to protect it from splashes, which would contaminate it.

8 As a final touch you may find it useful, especially if your boardwalk is positioned under trees, to tack chicken wire to the surface. To do this, stretch the wire taut over the slats and curl it around the edges before fixing it down with galvanised 'U' nails. This wire will not stand out much and will help to provide a good grip on the surface.

Alternative methods

Short areas of water can easily be spanned using large natural flagstones, perhaps sandstone or slate, whichever looks most appropriate. Railway sleepers also work well, since they are solid and long-lasting and require no complicated construction techniques, though two of them side by side are much safer than one. Stepping stones may be used as a fun alternative if the water is wide enough. These could be paving slabs bedded onto concrete blocks or natural boulders bedded at the base of the pool. For a wider span, a galvanised steel walkway could be used in a hi-tech design, or decking slats secured to solid timber beams may form an extension to an existing timber deck.

6 Continue laying the boards across the water. Be careful as you do this – take your time and nail the board in front of you as you go.

7 Having laid a polythene sheet on the water under the board, paint any areas of the boardwalk that need touching up.

8 To protect your boardwalk and to provide a good grip on the surface, you may want to fix chicken wire to the boards.

granite and
GRAVEL PATH

Patterned pathways make attractive and eye-catching garden features. Materials such as cobbles, bricks and setts are ideal for intricate designs or you could experiment by combining granite with different textures such as grass or crushed gravel.

1 | Mark out the position of the path according to your plan. Dig out to a depth of approximately 150mm (6in), which allows for a 100mm- (4in-) deep sett and 50mm (2in) of mortar or concrete.

   It is important to plan the dimensions of the pattern before you begin so that you end up with a regular repeat when you start to lay the stones. To achieve this pattern you need to allow 1m (40in) between the corners of each diamond. Lay out a section of the path dry to see how the pattern works and to establish the correct width of the path.

2 | When you are satisfied with the layout, you can start to lay one of the path edges. First, set up a string line to indicate the finished height and the line of the path. It is impossible to create two absolutely neat edges with a material such as granite setts, so position your line on the

MATERIALS

Granite setts: 90 × 90 × 90mm
(3½ × 3½ × 3½in)

Mortar

Road base

Crushed gravel

TOOLS

Groundwork tools

Paving tools

I Lay out a section of the diamond pattern dry so that you can work out the correct dimensions for the width of the path.

2 Use a club hammer to tap down the setts along the path edges. Use a stiff mortar mix and leave 10mm (³⁄₈in) between each sett.

KNOW YOUR MATERIALS

Granite setts: The natural appearance and hard-wearing surface of stone setts lend a sense of permanence to any garden. Of all the natural stone setts, granite is the most durable and most commonly used in urban settings, where it is often laid in a fan pattern or with cobbles for roadways. One benefit of using granite setts for a garden path is that, because they are so solid, they do not need to be bedded down on a layer of road base. Simply haunch the setts with mortar to prevent any movement.

Crushed gravel: With its warm colour, crushed gravel is just what is needed to break up the hardness of granite setts, and also provides a crunchy textured surface.

inside of the path edge because this is the side of the setts that will always be visible; the outer edge of the path will be covered with plants or turf. Make a stiff 1:6 mortar mix and trowel out the mortar to form a full bed alongside the string line. Position the setts in the mortar and tap them down with a club hammer until the tops rest level with the string line. Leave a joint of about 10mm (1/2in) between each sett, although the joints will vary because of the uneven edges of the stone.

Measure across to the other edge of the path and repeat the whole process. Once again, remember to position the string line on the inside edge of the setts. Do not try to marry up these setts with those in the opposite edge. This is not possible given the irregularity of the setts and would result in joints that are too wide.

3 Next, lay a row of setts as a header row at the end of the path to connect the two side edges.

Haunch up and along the outside edges of the header row and the edging setts with stiff mortar mix, finishing the mortar just below the top of the setts. This is done to support the edges from any sideways movement that might otherwise occur. If your pathway is to have a lot of heavy use, then haunch the edging setts with concrete rather than mortar in order to make them stronger.

4 When the edges are complete, once again lay a short section of the path pattern dry to double check the design. Move the setts around until the pattern is just right and all the sides of the diamond are equal and properly lined up. Now mark the setts along each edging with a chalk or pencil mark at 1m (40in) intervals to indicate where the points of the diamonds will touch the sides along the length of the path. You may need to adjust the space between each sett in the diamond to ensure that they match up.

5 Remove the dry laid setts and start to lay a bed of stiff 1:6 mortar mix. Tie a central string line along the length of the path to help centre the diamond pattern, although if

3 To keep path edges stable, spread a layer of mortar or concrete along the outside edges to just below the top of the setts.

4 Lay out the pattern again to check that it fits and mark the edge setts with a pencil where the diamond points touch the sides.

5 Use a club hammer to tap the setts into position in the mortar bed. Tie a string line along the path to help centre the pattern.

you find that this hinders the laying process then remove it because it is not essential. Begin to bed the setts back in position, laying mortar only as you need it and only under the setts, leaving the other areas empty. Tap the setts down with a club hammer. Continue to bed in the rest of the pattern. As you go, use a straight edge to ensure that all the setts line up neatly and finish flush across the top with the two edges of the pathway.

6 Before topping up the path to the finished level with crushed gravel, it is important to point the setts with a fairly crumbly 1:4 mortar mix. You could use a weaker mix such as 1:6, the same as that used for the bedding, because this will allow mosses to grow, which always look good in a garden setting. Push the mortar down well into the joints using a brick trowel before giving them a rubbed finish.

7 The following day, place road base in the areas between the diamond patterns. Do not attempt to do this any earlier in the process, otherwise you will risk dislodging the setts. Bring the road base to just below the top of the setts and compact it down with a hand rammer to form a solid base for the crushed gravel to be placed on.

8 Wait until the pointing has set completely to avoid damaging the mortar, before spreading the crushed gravel. Simply shovel the gravel from a wheel barrow and spread it between the setts to complete the path surface. You will need a maximum depth of approximately 25mm (1in) to create a firm surface to walk on.

Alternative materials
All manner of aggregates can be used for the surface in patterned paths such as this. Granite chippings will tone with the granite setts, producing a subtly contrasting finish, whereas woodchip will lend a more rustic character to the pathway. Or simply lay grass to really blend the path in with the garden, although this will only be appropriate for a path used less frequently, otherwise it is liable to become scuffed and turn muddy in wet weather.

6 Point the setts with a crumbly mortar mix. Use a brick trowel to press it down well between the joints.

7 Leave for a day before applying the crushed gravel between the setts, to just below the top of the stones. Compact it with a hand rammer.

8 Shovel the crushed gravel into position between the setts. Fill to a maximum depth of 25mm (1in) to make the surface firm.

straight brick path
WITH CORNER

The warm colours of clay bricks blend well with many other natural colours, while their angular shape is particularly suited for creating a path to complement an orderly, geometric-style garden.

1 | Work out the path position from the plan and excavate for the base (see pages 26–7), allowing 75mm (3in) for the road base and 85mm (3⅓in) for the depth of the bricks and sand bed.

Spread the road base mix over the base and compact it down. Then, set up a string line along one edge of the path to indicate the line and finished height of the path, which should be flush with the level of any adjacent lawn or beds. Lay a line of stretcher bricks, tightly jointed on a bed of mortar, and tap them down to the line. These edging bricks will give strength to the path by holding the dry laid bricks tightly together in place, preventing any sideways movement.

2 | Support the line of edging bricks by haunching them on the outside edge with a strong 1:6 mortar mix using coarse sand, or even a concrete mix of the same strength.

MATERIALS
Road base
Coarse sand
Fine beach sand
Cement
Paving quality bricks

TOOLS
Groundwork tools
Paving tools
Plate compactor
Screeding board

1 Lay a row of stretcher bricks along one of the path's edges to make the path strong and provide support for the dry laid bricks.

2 Haunch the outside of the brick edging with mortar or concrete to hold the bricks firmly in place.

KNOW YOUR MATERIALS

The small unit size of bricks is
ideal for laying a wide variety of
surface patterns, especially
curves, with the added benefit
that they require no excessive
cutting. Many paving bricks are
now manufactured as true
rectangles – 200 x 100mm (8 x
4in) – which enables patterns
such as basket weave to be
completed without the need
for jointing. A wide range of
paving bricks is available, so you
will always be able to find one
type that harmonises with the
house or the garden walls. Also
consider how the bricks will
look set against existing plant
beds or any planting you have
planned. Try to avoid concrete
paving bricks, which look
unnatural and tend to fade.

The mortar or concrete should finish just below the top edge of the bricks to allow soil or turf to finish flush with the paving.

3   It is possible to mark out the opposite edge of the path simply by measuring, but a safer method is to lay out the exact number of bricks across the width of the path, including the edging brick, in order to locate the true edge position. Remember to butt the bricks as there will be no joints. This should be done at both ends of the path, so that when a line is set up it runs parallel with the opposite path edge.

4   Lay the second edge of stretcher bricks in the same manner as the first and haunch up the outside edge. You can then lay the header course of bricks that will form the end of the path in mortar. Haunch up the outside edge of these header bricks too. These bricks can either be laid flat, as shown here, or on edge, which would necessitate the removal of some of the road base. The edging bricks

and the header course need to be left overnight to set firm before you proceed, otherwise they might be pushed out of position when you come to lay the paving bricks.

5   The next day, spread a thin layer of sand between the two path edges and screed it level with a screeding board. Cut this board from a piece of timber to fit over the path edges, so that it is deep enough to leave just the right amount of bedding. Ideally, the sand should be compacted to remove any soft spots and then dressed with another layer, which should be screeded so that the sand finishes approximately 6mm (¼in) up the inside edges of the path.

6   Position two or three rows of paving bricks into the sand along one edge in a running bond pattern. Remember that alternate bricks in the first row next to the header course will need to be cut in half to start off the bonding pattern. Tap the bricks down into place. Lay a block of timber (you could use the screeding board) from edge to

3 The safest way to measure the width of the path is to lay the exact number of bricks in position, including the edging brick.

4 Lay a header course of bricks at one end of the path and leave to dry overnight until they have set firm.

5 Spread a thin layer of sand between the path edges and use a screed board to level out the sand.

edge and tap it down so that the bricks finish flush across the width. On a long pathway, you could use a plate compactor to knock the bricks into position, but always stop about 1m (40in) from the laying edge to avoid loosening the bricks and the screeded bed. Continue laying bricks along the length of the path until you reach the far side of the first corner, taking care not to walk on the screeded sand.

7 In this project, the corners are made by butting each subsequent stretch of path along a straight joint with the previous stretch. Start the running bond for the next stretch of path with alternate half bricks as before. Continue to build the right-angled stretches of path in this way according to your plan.

8 When all the bricks have been laid, brush fine beach sand into the surface to seal the joints and help bind all the bricks together. Do not worry if some sand is left on the surface as this will freely wash down into any gaps whenever it next rains. If the joints are slightly open then some additional, grittier coarse sand can also be brushed in.

Alternative methods

Instead of creating corners with a straight joint across the path, the same running bond could turn the corner with a herringbone mitre, which does not require any cutting. Patterns like herringbone and basket weave are best suited to traditional style gardens, whereas the grid pattern of stackbond creates a more contemporary feel.

You could also lay bricks as a rigid construction on a mortar bed with all the joints mortar pointed. This will look very smart and will be in keeping with a traditional garden, but the pointing makes this method time consuming. It is far quicker to lay bricks butt jointed on a bed of compacted sand as has been shown here. This is ideal for long garden paths where excessive pointing might otherwise be required. However it is always best to use crisp-edged bricks to maintain a tight joint.

6 Lay the bricks in a running bond pattern, fixing the units firmly in place in the sand before tapping them in.

7 One way of making a 90° corner in a path is to create a straight joint and to cut half bricks to fit the turn in the pattern.

8 To seal the joints and bind the bricks together, brush fine beach sand into the surface of the path.

curved SETT PATH

Disappearing behind a riot of colourful plants, this curved path made from granite setts adds a sense of mystery and discovery to a simple walk around the garden.

1 | Mark out the path and drive in timber pegs to indicate both curved edges and the finished height of the path. Tie a string line onto the pegs for this purpose. In this project, the height of the path has been adjusted at intervals, by a simple step of one sett's height, to accommodate an existing gradient. Excavate down allowing a 100mm (4in) depth for the setts, 37mm (1½in) for mortar and 75mm (3in) for the road base. Spread the road base and compact it down to the correct level with a hand rammer or use a plate compactor for a long pathway.

2 | Make up a fairly dry mix of 1:6 mortar. Trowel it out on top of the road base just along the length of the outer edge of the path. Lay the edge setts on the mortar following the approximate curve of the string line, although you will have to adjust the position of the setts by eye to achieve a true curve. Carry on until you

MATERIALS

Timber pegs

Road base

String

Mortar

Granite setts

Timber

TOOLS

Groundwork tools

Paving tools

Watering can

I Mark your path with timber pegs and a line of string attached to them. This will serve as an edge as well as indicating the finished height.

2 Lay mortar around the outer edge and place the edge setts into it. You can use the string as a guide for the curve.

KNOW YOUR MATERIALS

Reclaimed granite setts look robust and have a timeless quality. The setts in this project are fairly evenly sized cubes measuring approximately 100 × 100 × 100mm (4 × 4 × 4in); longer rectangular setts are also available, which are useful for making less regular patterns. Setts will usually be slightly tapered and it is the smallest face of the sett that should be laid on the mortar with the other end forming the surface of the path. You can often see some old mortar still stuck to the base of the secondhand setts, which will help you choose the correct face. You could also use new setts, but they are expensive and will take time to weather and lose their raw appearance.

complete the edge and haunch up the outside of the setts with mortar to hold them firmly in position.

3 You can now determine the position of the inside edge of the path. The best way to do this is to lay a line of setts out dry, with spaces for mortar joints, across the beginning of the proposed path to establish the accurate width, then cut a length of timber to this same width to use as a gauge or spacer when laying the inside edging of the path.

4 Lay the end line of setts with mortar and then proceed with the inside edge. Use the timber spacer across the width of the path to ensure the width is consistent all the way along. Start by laying out an approximately 1m (40in) run of edging by eye and then tap the setts into their exact position after you have used the spacer to doublecheck their width. Do not try to line up the setts on the inside edge with corresponding ones on the outside; on the inner edge of a curved line this will prove to be impossible. Continue laying the edging setts to the

end of the path until the run is complete. Again, haunch up the outside of this line of setts to hold them firm.

5 You can now lay the main surface of the path on a bed of mortar. The easiest method is to lay lines, or 'runs', of setts along the length of the path, following the curve of the edges. Again, do not expect the setts and joints to line up across the path. If you try to lay setts across the width it will be difficult to avoid opening up large joints against the edge as you work around the outside of the curve, and you will also find that the setts get too tight against the edge on the inside of a curve, so work systematically lengthways.

6 Work your way down the path in 'runs' of around 1.8m (6ft) before starting the next line of setts. Continue in this manner until you have covered the entire length of the first section. Start off again laying lines for a further 1.8m (6ft) section and repeat until all the setts have been laid. As you approach the end of the path you may have to adjust some of the joints to ensure that you complete the

3 Lay the end setts out dry before bedding them in mortar; use this measure to establish the correct width of the path.

4 Use a piece of timber that is cut to equal the width between the two edges as a gauge for laying the inside edge of the path.

5 The rest of the path can now be laid. It is much easier to do this lengthways rather than across the width.

path with whole setts, without having to try cutting any setts and without leaving excessively large mortar joints.

The setts can be laid almost completely by hand, as they only need the occasional tap down with a club hammer to level them off. However, to make sure that all the setts are level, when a section of paving has been laid, place a piece of timber across from edge to edge and tap down with a club hammer. If you do not work in manageable sections but continue laying individual lines to the end of the path, you will find that the first setts in the line will have set firm before you have a chance to tap them down.

When laying reclaimed setts, as we have here, you should make sure that the best face is on the surface, not the one that was previously bedded in mortar. If all or some of the setts that you are using are wedge-shaped, the narrow part of the wedge should be the face that is laid into the mortar.

7 After laying all the setts, prepare a dry mix of mortar at 1:4 (or 1:6 for a slightly lighter appearance). Spread the dry mortar over the setts and work it into the joints with a brush. You must make sure that the mortar is well brushed in to avoid staining the surface of the setts.

8 When all the mortar has been properly worked in, lightly water the surface of the path using a watering can with a rose attachment. Do not use a hose or a watering can without a rose because the strong stream of water would wash the mix out of the joints and stain the setts. A light watering will produce a slightly recessed joint and give good definition to the edge of the setts.

Alternative materials

Reclaimed sandstone setts offer a warmer alternative to granite. They are supplied either as diamond sawn setts, which have crisp edges, or as tumbled setts, which have the edges rounded off for a more weathered appearance.

There are also some excellent imitation setts, manufactured in pre-cast concrete, which are laid on a sand bed and then vibrated into place with a plate compactor.

6 Continue down the path, placing 1.8m (6ft) runs of setts at a time. Make sure each run of setts is level before laying further runs.

7 Once the path is laid, you should prepare a dry mortar mix that will then be worked into each of the joints.

8 When all the mortar is in place, lightly water the surface to recess the joints and clean off any excess mortar.

edgings and trims

planning for edgings and trims

Although often similar in appearance and construction, edgings may be functional, whether retaining a flexible surface such as gravel or serving as a mowing edge to reduce maintenance, or purely decorative, such as a line of bricks laid flush along the edge of a patio. The lines between the two sometimes become blurred and in many cases a functional edging may also become a decorative trim.

Function and style The main purpose of edgings is to retain a flexible surface. They often act as mini retaining walls, holding back soil in flower beds or vegetable plots from adjacent paths. Mowing edges are installed to fulfil another important function – to avoid laborious trimming where a firm brick edge is set flush with a lawn. This same type of edge can also be laid where lawn is next to a wall, again for ease of mowing. If a paving slab is used for this purpose, on the other hand, the edge will become a pathway, enabling easy access to house windows for maintenance. Wide strips such as this may also be installed simply because the ground is often so dry in this position that nothing will grow. If the walls of the house are rendered or in pale brick then crushed gravel may be laid as a maintenance strip, rather than slabs, so that there is no splash back onto the walls. Gravel strips in this location can also act as catchment areas for water from gutterless roofs and then as a reservoir for irrigation systems.

Although not always highly visible, it is important to get the detail of edgings and trims just right as they must look good with the style of paving that they border, and form a common link with other materials in the garden. An obvious example is to use clay pavers rather than granite setts as an edge to a gravel path if clay pavers have been used elsewhere. In the same way, it would be wrong to choose a bland concrete edging instead of the traditional rope-top edging in a Victorian-style kitchen garden.

Design choices Edgings must be fit for their purpose; for example, timber path edgings are normally a minimum of 25mm (1in) thick, as anything thinner would bend and break. Timber of this thickness can be bent around curves, by making saw cuts on one face. Thicker timbers of

Slate surrounded by setts.

Metal edging against a stained deck.

Large pebbles laid against smaller aggregates.

A colourfully stained timber edge.

Edgings and trims can perform a functional or decorative purpose, or serve both. An informal arrangement of dark stones helps to retain a loose aggregate pathway (top left), while a pyramid of metal planters fulfils the same function between plants and a lawn (top right). A border of bricks along a pathway of paving slabs is, however, purely decorative as the box hedging performs the function of containing the planting (above).

Basket weave edging enhances the country-cottage feel of a profusion of colourful, cottage-style plants.

perhaps 50–75mm (2–3in) may be used on straight runs to form a much more obvious neat trim along the side of a path. Cost would also have an influence on design choices. For example, curved edges can be cheaply and quickly installed using treated timber boards; clay pavers or setts may look much better, retain the character of the garden but are slower to lay and much more costly in terms of materials.

Types of edging and trim
Pressure-treated path edging is readily available, can be laid to curves and, secured to driven timber pegs, is easy to install. It can be used to edge pathways of loose aggregate such as gravel or bark chippings, and may also be used as a temporary edging with mortar bedded bricks. As a permanent edging to sand-bedded bricks, timber boards that are about 75mm (3in) wide look good and are in the correct proportion to the width of the bricks. Logs laid along the edge of a pathway in a woodland setting are attractive and may help to retain soil banks but act more as a trim in defining the path than as a functional edging. Bricks are

> *Bricks are commonly laid as mowing edges and also form the ideal trim for paving.*

probably the ideal edging unit, providing a link with bricks used elsewhere in the garden and being easy to lay to curves. Bricks are commonly laid as mowing edges and also form the ideal trim for paving. They can also be run as lines through a patio for a purely decorative effect. Concrete path edgings are often best suited to pavements rather than garden paths. The simple flat-topped concrete path edging can be used effectively as a mowing edge but only along straight lines. There are some excellent imitation setts in pre-cast concrete, which are effective as pathways but can also bring continuity to a garden when used as edgings as well. Paving slabs can also be laid to form a mowing edge. You can position slabs around curved lawns without cutting them by opening up wide joints between them that can be laid to turf. A lawnmower can then easily pass over the slabs to mow the grass without any need for edging shears. Natural stone flags will serve the same purpose as paving slabs, while sandstone or granite setts may be bedded on concrete and laid to curves to form a hard-wearing edge. Large pebbles or small boulders look good when laid as a decorative trim to pathways of smaller aggregates. Metal strips, which can be cut for you by a blacksmith, are easy to install and provide a crisp edge to lawns.

Plants can be surrounded successfully by a whole host of edgings that create different moods. Old timber boards set on their sides enhance an informal planting that is complemented by colourful slate chippings (above left). For a more traditional look, bricks positioned in a herringbone pattern at the edge of a path (above right) act as an edging to the delightfully scented flowers in the bed beside it.

Pebbles form a decorative trim.

Metal edging finishes off this unusual pathway.

Decorative clay pavers form a perfect trim.

Clay pots on bricks make a raised bed edging.

timber EDGING

Timber edging is one of the simplest types of edging to lay. As well as combating soil and path erosion, timber can look very attractive: there is a wide range of wood stains available or you may prefer the natural wood effect. For a different look, you could try metal edging, which would complement a contemporary garden.

1 Timber edging can be used for either straight or curved paths. To bend the timber, lay a length out flat over a couple of pegs or battens, placed on the ground for support. Cut out notches with a panel saw, about 50mm (2in) apart, along one face of the board.

Mark out the position of the path according to your plan, knocking in pointed timber pegs at intervals of about 1m (40in) along the length of each edge line.

Set the timber edgings to the inside (path side) of the pegs, tapping them down with a club hammer, so that the edging sits just below lawn level. Fix the timber edging to the pegs with galvanised nails. For a curved path, position the timbers so that the notched edge is on the inside of the curve. For a neat finish, bend the middle rather than the end of the boards around the pegs.

2 Join together the lengths of path edging by cutting a separate short section of edging and butt the two ends

MATERIALS

Timber path edging: 3.6m × 100mm × 25mm (12ft × 4in × 1in)

Timber pegs: 450 × 50 × 50mm (18 × 2 × 2in)

Galvanised nails

Spiked metal edging strips

TOOLS

Groundwork tools

Woodwork tools

Club hammer

Block of wood

1 For a curved path, make a series of notches about halfway through the timber at intervals of approximately 50mm (2in).

2 When the boards are in position, saw the pegs down so that they are level with the edging and treat the cut ends.

KNOW YOUR MATERIALS

Timber path edging: This is usually treated softwood, available in 3.6m (12ft) lengths of 100 x 25mm (4in x 1in) sawn timber. Once cut, the timber can be stained or left natural.

Metal edgings: To create these metal strips, lengths of galvanised steel, approximately 2mm (1/16in) thick, can be cut to length by a blacksmith who will also be able to weld on the short metal spikes that allow the metal strips to be fixed to the ground. Though they are often painted an earth colour, these metal strips could equally be left in their original silver galvanised state.

on top of it. Then nail the three pieces together with galvanised nails to create the join. By doing this, you avoid having to nail two ends of edging to one peg and instead can arrange to fix pegs to the middle of the edging boards, which will result in a much neater finish.

Once the boards have been fixed into position in the ground, saw the pegs down to the top of the boards and treat the cut ends.

Metal edging

1 Cut a clean edge to the turf or shrub bed, before knocking the spiked metal edge into position with a club hammer and a block of wood.

2 Butt one length of edging up against the next one and knock it down as before. Continue in this way along the line until the edge is complete.

Metal edging: *Silver galvanised metal edging looks good here as an edge to the blue-grey slate path.*

toothed brick EDGING

Toothed brick edging can be used to create an ornamental, patterned trim for any path or patio, but it also fulfils the practical function of retaining loose materials.

1 First decide on the overall height above path level by which the edging needs to protrude in order to retain the adjacent soil. Ideally this will be at least 75mm (3in) to best show off the decorative style of the edging. A string line can now be set up along the length of the path to indicate the finished height.

Next excavate a trench along the side of the path, to a depth that allows for approximately two thirds of the brick to be below the finished path level, taking into account a 50mm (2in) bed of concrete. A mattock is a useful tool for excavating the trench, which does not need to be very wide.

2 Make a stiff 1:6 concrete or mortar mix using coarse sand. Trowel the mix into the trench and push the bricks into it, so that the top corner of each brick touches the string line. Position the first brick at a 60° angle and the rest will follow. Continue to lay the bricks, butting them tightly

MATERIALS

Well-fired paving bricks

Concrete or stiff mortar mix using coarse sand

TOOLS

Groundwork tools

Paving tools

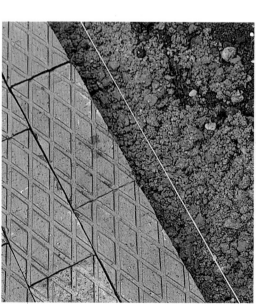

1 Work out the planned height of the brick edging above path level and set up a string line to indicate this height.

2 Set the bricks at a 60° angle in mortar. Use a club hammer to tap them down so that their top edge is just touching the string line.

Bricks may be used to edge paths in many different ways: laid flat, on edge, as stretchers (laid lengthways) and as headers (laid widthways). They are often mortared into place where they form an edge restraint to paths of sand-bedded bricks. In these instances, the edging does not stand out but finishes flush to form an integral part of the path. For this project, however, a toothed edge is created by laying the bricks vertically and at an angle. This style of edging is often used to retain the soil in vegetable gardens, but it should not be used against lawns as it is impossible to mow up to or over.

3 When the bricks are in place and have been haunched up, backfill over the concrete behind the bricks with soil.

together, without a joint. If necessary, tap them with a club hammer until they touch the string line.

3   Once you have completed a line of bricks, about 1.8m (6ft) in length, you can haunch up behind them with concrete to hold them firm. If the edging is laid before the path, haunching can be done on both sides of the brick, keeping it low on the inside to allow for the depth of the surfacing material. If you are laying a pathway of loose aggregate, where the edging is used to keep in the path material, the brick edge should be laid first. With a solid path, however, the edging can be constructed after the paving is laid, as it does not form part of the path construction.

   Continue laying bricks and haunching them up until the line is complete. Finish by backfilling soil over the concrete behind the bricks.

mowing EDGE

Where two different areas of the garden meet, why not set them off and make an ornamental feature with merging lines of curved brick edging?

1 Using sand or spray paint, mark out a general line for the first set of edging on the ground. Excavate a trench about a spade's width and to a depth that allows for 75mm (3in) of concrete and a further 60mm (2½in) for the depth of the clay pavers on a mortar bed.

Drive in timber pegs approximately 1m (40in) apart, around the outside of the concrete foundation, to indicate the finished height and to show the general line the edging should follow. It is, however, impossible to set a string line to a curve. Instead, the bricks must be carefully laid to a curve by eye.

There is no need for mortar if you are laying a short run of edging, as you can push the bricks straight into the concrete before it sets. On a longer run, however, you will need to lay the bricks into a bed of mortar (1:6 mix), otherwise the concrete will set hard before you have a chance to push all the bricks down. Wait until the concrete sets before laying the mortar bed.

MATERIALS

Pegs

Concrete

Mortar

Clay pavers

String

TOOLS

Groundwork tools

Paving tools

Slab cutter

1 Use the guide pegs and string to place your first line of pavers at the right height. The smooth curve will have to be done by eye.

2 Where two lines converge, you will need to cut the bricks to size. Raise them up to mark where they need to be cut.

The key idea behind a mowing edge is that it should be flat enough to be easily mown over, which avoids the need for laborious edge trimming. It is therefore essential that the edging is laid as evenly as possible and that none of the bricks or slabs stand up above the height of the lawn. Bricks are ideal materials for constructing a mowing edge because their small unit size makes them perfect for laying to the curved lines of a lawn. In this particular project clay pavers have been used to form a neat link with those that have been used elsewhere in the garden.

3 Once the bricks are pointed and haunched, remove any mortar and concrete from the middle, so it is ready for the grass to be sown.

2 To make the two lines of edging converge, lay the outside line of edging in the same way as the inside until the two meet. At this point the bricks will need to be cut to fit. Take the first brick to be cut and position it on the correct line but raised up and supported by a spare brick underneath, so that it overlaps the inside line of bricks. Mark with a pencil on the brick where the outer edge of the inside line of bricks will come to. Use a slab cutter to cut along this pencil line. Repeat as necessary.

3 When all the bricks have been laid, point them up either with the same mortar mix or a slightly stronger mix, and finish with a rubbed joint. The outside of each brick line should be haunched with concrete to hold it in place However, scrape out the mortar and concrete between the two lines of brick, in order to provide sufficient depth of topsoil for the grass to grow properly.

rock EDGE

Not all edging requires complicated construction techniques – a relaxed look can be achieved simply by laying down an informal edge of rocks and pebbles.

1 First, decide on the line of the edging. There is no need to set up a string line for this project because the edging will look better if an uneven effect is created, where the tops of the rocks are not all level.

Next, hook out a shallow trench for the rocks. No great depth of excavation is necessary, but the rocks will look better if they are partially buried rather than perched on the surface.

Now select and arrange the rocks. Rocks are too heavy to keep shifting from place to place, so it is well worth taking your time to select carefully those that will look just right the first time round. If you are working close to water or in a boggy area, it can be awkward trying to move rocks around by hand – a few shovels full of road base spread around the area will ease movement considerably.

If the ground is at all stony, it can be difficult to bed down the heavy boulders. Spread a shovel of coarse sand

MATERIALS

Rounded boulders

River pebbles

Coarse sand

Road base

TOOLS

Groundwork tools

Club hammer

Trowel

Hand rammer

1 Select your rocks and lay them onto a bed of coarse sand – make ridges and furrows in the sand to make it easier to work the rocks down.

2 Spread out mixed pebbles across the road base to create a reasonably flat surface and an even mix of pebbles.

KNOW YOUR MATERIALS

Any rocks will work as long as they fit in with the style of the garden. Rounded boulders or 'dinosaur eggs' look good, are easy to handle and tend not to be too large. They look attractive set next to an informal path of pebbles or 'beach' area beside a pool. They are available from hardware stores, stone merchants and garden centres, where they are sold by weight and can be delivered. Pebbles may be bought in small bags or delivered in large 1 tonne (20cwt) bags. Paths of mixed size pebbles ranging from 25–100mm (1–4in) look far more natural than a path of uniform size stones.

3 Once the pebbles and rocks are in position, shovel soil in behind them and ram this in with a club hammer to firm the rocks in place.

under each rock to ease the process. Push the sand around with a trowel to create ridges and furrows into which the boulder can be worked down.

2 After all the rocks have been placed and soil tramped in, ram down road base in front of the rocks and over the width of the proposed path, or 'beach' area, to form a firm base. Open up the bags of mixed pebbles and spread them evenly over the road base, pushing the pebbles around by hand. The aim should be to achieve a reasonably flat surface and an even mix of the different sized pebbles.

3 When you are happy with the pebble surface and the position of each rock, shovel in soil behind the rocks. This soil can then be rammed in with a club hammer to help hold the smaller rocks absolutely firm.

steps

planning for steps

Steps provide access from one part of the garden to another where a path or patio meets a change of level. The mood of the garden will be reflected in the style of the steps: stone flags and paving slab treads link well with patios that are made out of the same types of material in the ordered areas of the garden close to the house. Log risers and treads of bark chippings, on the other hand, are more suited to the relaxed, wooded areas further away.

Function and style A flight of steps may be purely functional, providing quick direct access, possibly in a utility area or perhaps up from the front door to the garage. A raised terrace will require steps down into the garden while a patio cut into a bank will need steps up through the retaining walls for access. Even a flat site will need steps, if only out from the house and down on to the patio. Interest could be added to a flat site by constructing a seating area that is raised above ground level, again requiring a step up for access.

Steps should certainly reflect the mood of the garden and relate to other materials that have been used. It makes sense to lead on and off the patio with steps that have treads of the same slabs that have been used for the rest of the paving. Bricks that have been used in the terrace retaining walls should also follow through into the step risers. When moving away from the harder areas of construction close to the house, the style of steps may reflect the more relaxed parts of the garden further away. In these areas, timber is the usual choice where it relates well to the more natural landscape and is often used to form the step risers with treads of gravel or bark chippings.

Design choices Steps designed for quick access tend to be quite narrow with a shallow depth of tread, while broader steps will encourage a gentler ascent where speed is not of the essence. Staggering a flight of steps up a bank creates far more interest than a straight flight, which is often too grand for most gardens anyway. Curved steps or those that have a change in angle are also inviting and, along with staggered steps, they are far easier to soften and partially obscure with planting, a feat that is impossible with a straight flight.

Curved timber decking steps.

Natural stone and pebbles.

Grey stone steps.

Stone slabs and brick risers.

It is important that the style of steps that you choose matches the mood of your garden. Curved steps with timber risers and gravel treads (top left) fit well in the cottage garden with lots of overhanging planting partially obscuring the steps. Similarly, the wild nature of the stone steps covered in ivy (above) are perfect in this natural-style garden. On the other hand, the clean, crisp lines of the broad curved steps (top right) complement the ordered style of the herbaceous borders nearby.

Weathered, broad stone steps covered in wild, informal green planting.

The character of the steps will also be affected by their edge treatment: they may have side walls for a smart appearance or, on the other hand, be planted at the sides for a softer, more relaxed look.

Well-designed steps will have a comfortable balance between tread depth and riser height and for safety reasons, the risers should be the same size for the entire flight. A broad, deep tread or landing can be planned halfway up a long flight of steps where a bench may be positioned at which to rest and take a breather. Shadow lines, where the tread overhangs the riser, will hide the mortar joint and give a clear definition to each step, while carefully positioned lights will illuminate the steps for safety and make them look inviting as darkness falls.

Step materials Extending the path or patio material on into the steps provides a strong continuity of design: to this end, treads are commonly laid in paving slabs, while the risers may be constructed from bricks used elsewhere in the garden. An alternative riser in traditional steps can be made from thin slates bedded horizontally with no

Steps should reflect the mood of the garden and relate to other materials that have been used.

visible mortar. This detail looks good with sandstone or slate flagstones for the treads.

Bricks are frequently used in the garden for walls, edgings and paths, so it follows that they should also be used to form steps. The bricks must be well-fired, hard bricks to withstand frost. They may be laid either flat or on edge and can be used to form both the riser and the tread. They are commonly laid to running bond across the width, thus making the steps seem wider and encouraging a gentle ascent, while bricks laid from front to back will tend to make the steps seem narrower and encourage quicker movement.

Sawn wooden slats can be used to make box-shaped steps, which associate well with raised decks, while larger sections of timber or even sleepers may be used for more informal steps in woodland areas with treads of crushed gravel or bark chippings. Log rounds work well in similar locations to form simple steps up through a wooded bank. A combination of materials can be very effective, using one type for the riser and another for the tread. Sleepers and other solid timber sections look superb as risers with treads of brick or granite setts. As an alternative to timber risers, large blocks of granite or sandstone can also be effective.

Stone slabs can be used to very different effect: they can have a formal appearance such as the short flight of broad stone steps (above left), punctuated by containers and surrounded by lush herbaceous borders, which encourage walkers to take their time as they move up or down. Stone slabs can also have an informal appearance, such as the curved steps in a seaside setting (above right), made out of slabs with uneven edges.

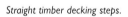

Straight timber decking steps.

Weathered stone.

Brick treads and risers.

Stone treads and terracotta tile risers.

sleeper STEPS

The long treads of this flight of sleeper steps encourage gentle strolling, while the combination of sturdy sleepers and crunchy slate chippings also makes for a pretty and inviting seat. Try fixing candle holders along the rise for instant ambience on a warm evening.

1 | Measure from the top to the bottom of the bank and calculate the number of steps required, taking into account the height of the risers and depth of each tread. Long treads were possible on this relatively shallow slope and were most appropriate for a stroll through woodland. Next, excavate for the first riser at the bottom of the slope and spread a thin layer of coarse sand on which to bed the sleeper. Two people will be needed to lift the sleeper as it will be extremely heavy and awkward to handle. Lay the bottom sleeper in position on its edge and thump it down so that about 75–100mm (3–4in) is buried, leaving a riser of 150–175mm (6–7in).

2 | Having laid the first riser and with the top level of the flight of steps already established, you can now roughly excavate the bank to shape. Cut the ground back from the first riser to behind the proposed second riser

MATERIALS

Sleepers

Coarse sand

Pegs

Galvanised nails

Road base

Soil

Slate chippings

Grass seed

TOOLS

Groundwork tools

Rubber mallet or sledgehammer

Spirit level

Rammer

1 Once you have excavated the space for the first riser and placed a layer of coarse sand on it, put the sleeper in position.

2 Continue cutting the steps out of the bank, placing a timber peg to indicate the top level of each step.

KNOW YOUR MATERIALS

Slate chippings: These chippings are especially effective as their blue colour contrasts well with the sleepers and they possess the rare quality of looking even better when wet.

Old railway sleepers: These are tough and uncompromising but are in fact easy to install, needing no concrete footings or mortar bedding. Sleepers are readily available either new or as secondhand materials. New ones are cleaner but more expensive. Sleepers can normally be purchased in dimensions of 2400 × 200 × 100mm (8ft × 8in × 6in). They are available as Grade I or Grade II. Grade I uses the best condition timber with very few twists or bows.

position, then carry on doing the same for the rest of the steps up the bank. When digging out, allow for a depth of approximately 50mm (2in) to be dug down on each tread, to make enough room for road base and loose aggregate. As you work up the bank, drive in a timber peg at one end of each level to indicate the finished height of each step. If you position them just outside where the sleeper will sit, these same pegs can be used to hold the sleepers in position.

3 After the rough excavation has been completed and all the level pegs are in position, you are now ready to set the second sleeper in place. Scrape out a shallow trench and spread a thin layer of coarse sand over it to provide a firm base for the sleeper. Use a rubber mallet or sledgehammer to thump the sleeper down to the height of the adjacent level peg.

4 Check the sleeper riser is level along its length with a spirit level and knock it down slightly further if necessary.

This process of bedding the sleepers on coarse sand, knocking them down to their peg and then levelling along their length should be continued up the entire length of the bank until all the risers have been laid.

5 Once all the risers have been laid, drive in two timber pegs on the front face of each riser (apart from the first one), just in from each end. You can re-use the existing level pegs for this purpose up one side of the sleepers. The pegs are needed to hold the risers firmly in place. Without them the sleepers would only be supported by the road base (except for the first one where the ground in front of it holds it in place). Drive the pegs in with a sledgehammer to about 100mm (4in) from the top of each riser and secure them to the face of the sleepers with galvanised nails.

6 Now bring in some road base as a base for the treads. The easiest method is probably to wheel barrow the material in from the top of the steps and tip out the road

3 After you have dug out all the steps, place the second sleeper. Use a mallet or sledge-hammer to drive it down to the peg's level.

4 Use a spirit level to check that the sleeper is level. Then repeat steps 3 and 4 with all the other sleeper risers.

5 Drive a timber peg into both the front corners of the risers in order to give them extra support.

base for the lowest tread first. Spread out the road base with a shovel and compact it with a rammer to give a firm 50mm (2in) base.

7 After the road base has been laid on each tread, cover the timber pegs with soil. The pegs are placed purposefully near the ends of each sleeper to ensure that they are unobtrusive and can easily be covered with soil. Loosen the soil at the sides of the bank, breaking down any steep vertical edges, and allow it to form a gentle slope down to the tread level. In the process, the soil will also tend to obscure the timber pegs. Add more soil as necessary to form a soft gradient down from the bank. Grass growing on the bank will probably spread to bind the new edges, but you may need to sow grass seed as well. Alternatively, some low groundcover plants would provide a more decorative edge and integrate the sleeper steps into the planting scheme of your garden as a whole. This can obviously be done at a later date, at your own convenience.

8 Finally, with all the loose soil tidied up, lay your chosen surface aggregate on each tread. In this project slate chippings were used. Again, the easiest way to carry this out would be to bring the wheel barrow full of stone in from the top of the steps and to work your way back up from the first step to the last. Spread out the aggregate with a shovel or a rake, brushing any loose stone off the sleepers. Crushed marble will provide a white, crunchy surface that stands out against the dark sleepers, while the colour of crushed blue metal will harmonise with the greens of the surrounding grass and foliage.

Alternative materials

A loose material such as crushed gravel works especially well in a larger aggregate of, say, 18mm (¾in) that will not be kicked about so easily. For a more hard-wearing tread, try laying granite setts. Machine rounded logs, which are smooth treated timbers with an even diameter that can simply be held in place with pegs, can be used to form the risers as an alternative to sleepers.

6 Next, use a wheel barrow to tip road base onto each step to create a base for each of the treads.

7 Cover up each of the timber corner pegs with soil to disguise them. Then tidy up any loose soil that is left.

8 You can now use the wheel barrow again to place your chosen surface aggregate onto each of the treads.

brick
STEPS

With so many different colours and styles available, and such a variety of patterns possible, brick is an incredibly versatile material. Brick steps provide a strong visual link with the house or with bricks used elsewhere in paving trims or garden walls.

1 Mark out the position of the steps, clearing the topsoil and any vegetation before excavating the shape of the steps. Calculate the number of steps required, the height of the risers and the depth of the treads. The riser height for paving bricks should be 184mm (7¼in) with a tread depth of 337mm (13½in). On one side of the steps put in a peg at the top and bottom of the bank to indicate the position of the first and last steps. Fix a string line between the tops of these pegs to show the leading edge of each step.

Most of the weight in a flight of steps will be transferred to the bottom step, so you will need to build the first riser on a concrete footing. To lay this, excavate a trench to about a spade's depth and backfill with a 1:6 concrete mix. Tamp the concrete to produce a smooth, level surface.

2 Make up a 1:6 mortar mix using bricklaying sand and trowel in a line along the concrete footing (i.e., the full

MATERIALS

Timber peg

String

Concrete

Mortar

Paving bricks

Short length of wood for tamping

TOOLS

Groundwork tools

Paving tools

Slab cutter

1 The first riser must be built on a concrete footing. To do this, excavate a trench, place the concrete in and tamp it down.

2 Lay a mortar mix along the concrete and then begin to lay your first line of bricks to create the first riser.

KNOW YOUR MATERIALS

Brick makes an ideal material to use for both paving and steps, provided it is suitably frost-proof. Some bricks that have a high rate of moisture absorption may be fine in walls where they are protected by a damp proof course and capping but will soon become saturated in paving and susceptible to freeze and thaw damage.

Bricks may be laid to different patterns and bonds such as running bond, which laid widthways will make the steps seem wider, but laid lengthways will make the steps seem narrower and encourage quicker movement. Stack bond is where bricks are laid to a grid pattern without the joints being staggered at all.

width of the step). Lay a line of bricks onto the bed of mortar to form the first riser, using a set square to ensure that it runs at 90° to the string line.

As you lay the bricks, butter up one end of each brick, then tap it into place. Buttering means trowelling a wedge of mortar onto the end of the brick that is to be laid against the previous brick, in order to create a mortar-filled joint. When the line of bricks is complete, use a spirit level to check they are even.

3 Once the first riser has been laid, set in a base of concrete behind the bricks to prepare for the tread. Mix up a 1:6, or possibly slightly weaker, concrete mix and then shovel it into place to the depth of the riser blocks. You can then smooth it out with a trowel to form a firm, level and solid base for the tread.

4 Next lay the bricks that will form the tread for the first step on a 1:6 mortar mix (or use a slightly stronger mix for a harder joint). The bricks in this project are laid on

edge and the tread is one and a half bricks deep, so you will need to cut a third of the bricks in half using a bolster or slab cutter.

Starting on the right, lay one full brick at the leading edge of the step, then lay a half brick behind it. On the left of these, lay one half brick at the leading edge of the step, then lay a full brick behind it. Continue working from right to left along the step, alternating the full and half bricks in this way. Take great care when laying the first brick that it lightly brushes the string line with its front top corner, as this brick will set the level for the whole tread.

5 Once the first tread has been laid, make sure that all the joints within it have been filled with mortar (this includes the riser joints). After you have done this, you can give them a rubbed finish with a short piece of pipe. Any surplus mortar that appears while achieving this rubbed finish can be removed when it is dry simply by brushing it off or by using a trowel to scrape off any more stubborn pieces.

3 Place a layer of concrete behind your first riser as a base for the tread and use a trowel to smooth it out.

4 Take care that the tread's first brick lightly brushes your string line. Then you can place all the rest of the bricks into position.

5 The joints of the tread must be filled with mortar. Once this is done, rub them with a piece of pipe to create a smooth finish.

6 Now your first step has been completed, you should shovel in concrete behind its tread to form the base of the next step. Roughly level out this concrete, and then use a trowel as before to create a smooth surface that finishes flush with the top of the brick tread.

7 You can now trowel mortar in a line across this concrete footing as done previously to create a bed for the second riser. Tap the bricks down into place, ensuring that there is a neat mortar joint showing between the bottom of the brick riser and the brick tread below. If there is not a good joint, not only will the riser be too low but it will be impossible to create a neat rubbed finish and therefore moisture could get under the bricks with the risk of freeze thaw damage. Use a spirit level to ensure that the riser bricks are all level and aligned.

8 Once you have laid all the bricks for the second riser, backfill with concrete behind the riser, levelling up to the top of the brick. Smooth the concrete off and again,

trowel mortar out for the tread bricks. Bed the first brick and gently tap it into place so that it just brushes the string line as before. Continue laying all the tread bricks, repeating the same pattern as used on the first step and pointing up the joints when you have laid them all down. Carry on with this process up the bank until the whole flight of steps has been completed. Finally, make sure that all the joints, including the risers, have been properly pointed and brush off any excess when the mortar is dry.

Alternative ideas

A combination of materials can look superb in steps. For example, bricks or granite or sandstone setts may be laid as the tread, and combined with a riser made from crisp sawn timber or dressed blocks of stone.

Containers placed on each step, either on one side or at alternate sides, can transform a functional flight of steps into a visual feature. For an even softer look try planting shrubs and other low plants alongside the steps to grow up and over the edge.

6 You can now place concrete behind the first step's tread, which should be levelled out and smoothed off.

7 The second riser's bricks can now be put into place. These should be tapped down, leaving a neat joint between them and the first tread.

8 As before, lay the first brick of the tread so that it brushes the string. Continue the whole process to lay the remaining steps.

timber DECK STEPS

Sawn deck boards have a smart yet natural appearance and are comfortable enough to double-up as warm, relaxed seats. Following a simple box structure, this flight of steps has been designed to run up a short section of bank adjacent to a deck patio.

1 Calculate the step dimensions so that standard width timber can be used for all risers and treads. Mark out the area and excavate down to the level of the proposed adjacent deck. Next, dig out holes for the front and back posts of the first step, each to about a spade's width. Set the front posts 225mm (9in) deep and 75mm (3in) above ground level. The back posts will need to be longer, overall about 400mm (16in), in order to form the front posts of the second step. Making sure the 50mm (2in) side of each post faces front, pour in a 1:6 concrete mix to two-thirds full and firm it around the base of the post. Mark out pencil guidelines on the front posts 75mm (3in) down and 25mm (1in) in from the outside edge. Cut along these lines and remove the timber sections from the outside of the post.

2 The sections of timber are cut from the front posts in order to form joints for the bearers, so the cuts need to

MATERIALS

Timber posts 75 x 50mm (3 x 2in)

Timber posts 75 x 75mm (3 x 3in) for the back seat

Timber bearers 75 x 25mm (3 x 1in)

Timber boards 100 x 25mm (4 x1in) standard width timber for decking and fascia

Concrete

Galvanised nails

Wood stain

TOOLS

Groundwork tools

Woodwork tools

Paintbrush

1 Set the front posts for the first step. Mark on each the dimensions of the bearer and then saw out the timber to leave a joint.

2 Hold the bearer between the front and back posts and, checking it remains level, mark the joint position on the back post.

KNOW YOUR MATERIALS

These streamlined timber deck steps require no foundations, which makes construction straight forward. Timber can be treated softwood, Western red cedar or possibly a hardwood. The decking boards may be varying widths depending on your design but do try to make steps that fit standard widths of boards, rather than trying to cut the boards down to fit. Timber merchants will be able to advise you on the most suitable timber to use but make sure that you do always buy pressure treated timber. They will also be able to supply grooved timber boards for extra grip. To save on materials, steps can be left open-sided, but to achieve a neat finish it is best to box in the edges.

be straight so the bearers fit flush. Timber bearers are placed along the side of each step to connect the posts of one step to the next and to support the deck treads. To get the bearers straight, place one in the joint of the first post and extend it back to the second post. Place a spirit level on the bearer and mark the second post along the top and bottom edge of the bearer, to show the position of the joint. Do this on both sides of the front step.

3 | Mark the joints for the bearers of the second step on the second posts. The bottom of the new joint should be 25mm (1in) from the top of the lower joint and it should extend upwards for 75mm (3in). Cut the new joint and trim the top of the post to the height of the joint.

For the lower joints, make two horizontal saw cuts along the pencil guidelines marked out in step two until you have cut halfway through the posts.

4 | Start to remove the timber from the lower joint by chiselling in from each side. Try not to take out too much

wood in one go and, when it has all been removed, use sandpaper to get rid of any splinters, so that you end up with a smooth joint to enable the bearers to fit flush.

5 | You can now tap into place both bearers for the bottom step. Nail the bearers into place using two galvanised nails at each joint. Continue this process for the whole flight of steps, notching joints in all the posts and fixing bearers in place. For additional stability, fix another beam between the two back posts of the top step, notching joints a couple of inches below the last bearers into the back face of each post. Once all the bearers have been nailed home, top up the post holes with concrete to finish just above ground level. Check that the posts are all upright with a spirit level before finally firming the concrete around them. Leave the concrete to harden overnight.

6 | You can now start adding deck boards to the step framework. Nail on the first deck board so that it sits over the front posts, having first cut it to size. Make sure the

3 *Having cut the top joint, make two horizontal cuts halfway through the second post along the guidelines marked out for the bottom joint.*

4 *After the horizontal cuts have been made, chisel in from each side to remove the wood from the lower joint section.*

5 *The bearers can now be slotted into the spaces you have made, and should be fixed securely with galvanised nails.*

leading edge of this board sits flush with the front edge of the posts. Cut all the deck boards to length and set them out on the first tread using a pencil as a spacer between them. Set them out until they sit evenly between the first board already fixed and the front of the second posts. Tap a nail through the end of each board into the bearer but do not drive it all the way home. This will ensure you are still able to lift and re-position the boards if the spacing goes awry. When you are satisfied that all the tread boards are in their correct positions, double nail both ends of each board. Continue to nail deck boards in this way until all the step treads are completed.

7 Now attach fascia boards to the front of each step to form the risers. Using timber the same dimensions as the deck boards, cut the fascia boards to length and nail them to the front of each step with two nails at each end of the boards. Position each fascia board so that it rests flush on the last board of each tread, with its top edge finishing flush with the tread of the next step.

8 Using fascia boards of the same dimensions, box in the step sides to conceal the ends of the deck board, giving a neat and professional finish to the steps. Try and plan it so that the board at the side of the first step extends past the side of the second step, and so on up the entire flight of steps, since this will look neater than having a joint at the side of each riser.

In this project, the top step has been extended to twice its width to form an open-fronted seat that is easily constructed. Set in a front and back post to the left-hand side of the seat. As this is an open-fronted seat, the posts will be seen and should look sturdy, so you should use 75 × 75 mm (3 × 3in) posts. Set them in concrete so that their finished height allows for a deck board to be nailed over the top. Cut joints into the left-hand edges of the post tops to hold a bearer. Nail the bearer into position and then attach extra long deck boards that extend across from the top step to form the seat. Complete by nailing 50 × 25mm (2 × 1in) fascia boards to the front and side of the seat to box in the deck boards.

6 Now start laying deck boards to form the treads. Place a pencil between each board to ensure that spacing is equal throughout.

7 Once the treads are all in place, measure and cut fascia boards and nail them to the front of each step to create the risers.

8 Box in the sides of the steps to conceal the ends of the boards. Try to avoid forming joints at the side of each riser.

natural STONE STEPS

You don't need to own a stately home to choose natural stone steps for your garden; they look just as impressive in the back garden of a smart town house and also fit in perfectly with the rural charm of a country garden.

MATERIALS

Concrete

Mortar

Walling stone blocks

Sandstone paving

TOOLS

Groundwork tools

Paving tools

1 | Calculate the number of steps, depth of tread and height of riser for the first flight up to the landing and from this point up to the top. The upper flight is laid at 90° to the lower flight. Mark out the position of the steps, clear the ground and roughly excavate the step shapes in the bank.
Working from the bottom, fix timber pegs along the side of the steps to indicate the finished height of each step. Fix the first peg at the correct height for the first step. Knock in the second peg to roughly the right height and then lay a spirit level across from the top of the first peg to the second. Measure up from the underside of the spirit level to the desired height of the second step and tap the second peg down to exactly the right level. Continue in this way, positioning marker pegs for each step up to the landing.

2 | For strength, lay the riser of the bottom step on a concrete footing. Excavate a trench to about a spade's depth and

1 Measure up from the bottom of a spirit level, laid from the top of the first peg back to the second, to gain the height of the second riser.

2 Having first laid concrete footings, place walling blocks on a mortar base to form the first riser and returns.

KNOW YOUR MATERIALS

The hard-wearing properties and frost-proof surface of sandstone paving make it the best material for the treads in a flight of stone steps. Sandstone is usually supplied in random rectangular flagstones that have been split out from large quarried blocks of stone. This type of flagstone has a rough cut face, so it may be slightly uneven on the surface. A sandstone with a smoother finish is available, called diamond sawn paving, which is more expensive but very smart. A textured surface can be given to this type of stone for extra grip. Sandstone may also be used for the walling blocks that form the risers and returns, normally 100mm (4in) wide in random lengths.

width before filling in with a 1:6 concrete mix. Spread a 1:6 mortar mix along the footing. The mortar can be made either with coarse or fine sand, but coarse sand may give a firmer bed for heavy stone blocks. Select walling blocks to show a good face at the front of the riser. Butter the ends of the blocks with mortar and tap them down into position. Lay more stone blocks to form the returns of the steps at 90° to the riser. Again, excavate a trench and fill it with concrete, then bed down the blocks on a mortar base, filling the joints with mortar as you go.

3 When the riser and returns for the first step are complete, backfill behind them with a 1:6 concrete mix and trowel out the concrete to finish level with the top of the blocks. Again, spread mortar of the same 1:6 mix used for the risers over the concrete base. Choose flagstones with good, square corners and lay them down on the mortar bed so that they overhang the stonework by no more than 50mm (2in). Tap these slabs down with a club hammer handle or rubber mallet, laying a spirit level

across to the timber peg every so often to check for the correct height. Lay the paving with a very slight fall towards the front so that it will shed any surface water.

4 Having completed the first step, backfill behind it with a shovel full of concrete to form a level base upon which to bed the second riser. Lay the riser blocks on a mortar bed, filling up the joints with mortar as well. You may have to lay some stone blocks underneath the side returns to get the desired height, depending on the gradient of the bank.

5 Backfill concrete behind the riser blocks, smoothing it out to form a firm base upon which to lay the next tread. Each flight can be formed from however many steps you would like or require, but for this project the second step forms the landing and is paved with larger flagstones accordingly. These larger flagstones will probably require two people to lift them into place.

Try to plan the paving of the treads so that the joints are staggered from one step to the next as you progress up

3 As you lay flagstones for the first step, place a spirit level across to the timber peg now and again to check for the correct height.

4 The next riser can be built now, although you may need to lay some stone blocks underneath the side to ensure the height is correct.

5 Each of the paving treads should overhang its riser by about 50mm (2in) to hide the mortar joints beneath.

the steps, and make sure that the tread overhangs the riser by approximately 50mm (2in). This is so that it will form a shadow line that will hide the mortar joint.

6 The flight of steps that leads up from the landing should be at 90° to the first flight. To get this angle correct, ensure that the second flight starts parallel with the far edge of the landing slabs by measuring the width of the landing in two places. The two measurements to the front of the next riser should be equal to ensure that this step is at right angles to the first flight. Check that the positioning of the next riser looks right by placing some stone blocks in position temporarily, then bed them down when satisfied.

7 In this project, the second flight of steps has been designed so that it is narrower than the width of the landing and therefore will be partially laid on the flagstones. Again, spread out a mortar bed and tap the stone riser blocks into position, ensuring that all joints are properly filled and that the blocks are correctly aligned.

8 Backfill with concrete behind the riser, smoothing off to a level finish before spreading out a bed of mortar for the next tread. The corner of this tread can be seen clearly, so be sure to choose a flagstone with a good corner. Continue to lay the remaining steps using the same methods as before and, when finished, point up the joints with either the same mortar mix or a stronger 1:4 mix and leave them with a rubbed finish. Clean off any surplus mortar when dry. The steps are now finished and you can plant up around them, place pots on the landing or, as here, position pots on each step.

Alternative materials

In this project we have used sandstone, but limestone is one possible alternative as a material for the risers. It is not, however, suitable for paving the treads as its surface may be damaged in frosty conditions. Slate, which ranges in colour from green through dark blue to black, can be cut in random pieces to form smart step treads with risers in slate blocks or thin pieces of horizontally bedded slate.

7 When building this next riser, which will be partially on the landing, you will still need to ensure the joints of the walling blocks are filled.

6 Once the landing has been built, you will need to measure across it to work out where to put your next step.

8 As this step is the first you see when turning the corner on the landing, make sure you choose the best possible flagstone.

patios

planning for patios

More than just a drab area of concrete outside the back door, patios have become the focus of family life in the garden. Stone terraces and streamlined timber decks are perfect for a lunchtime barbecue and candlelit dinner parties, while areas of textured paving form the ideal non-slip surface for children's play. A small secluded brick patio surrounded by perfumed shrubs may be the perfect place for a relaxing drink or a snooze on a comfortable bench.

Function and style A patio is a paved area of the garden that is normally sited near to the house and forms the centre of outdoor family life, both in terms of entertaining and relaxation. It helps to prevent mud from being carried indoors and offers a convenient location for eating outside. Sometimes the best position for a patio is a sunny location further down the garden, from where views can be enjoyed back over the garden towards the house. It is therefore essential that patios look right with the house and their location within the garden. A broad stone terrace close to the house allows space for dining outside, while a smaller paved area away from the house works well in materials such as brick or setts, whose small unit size is perfect for creating a more intimate and compact circular patio. Planting will help to soften the lines of paving and will also ensure that a patio feels comfortably enclosed and sheltered from breezes.

Design choices Patios must be in proportion to the scale of the house and garden. Avoid low perimeter walls along the edge of ground level patios as they are a nuisance for maintenance and serve no purpose other than to cut the patio off from the rest of the garden. Areas of paving set into a bank, however, will need retaining walls around the edge. A raised patio or terrace can be really effective for sitting out overlooking the garden when the ground slopes away from the rear of the house. Timber decks work particularly well in this situation and this type of construction also avoids expensive foundations and retaining walls. Simple designs usually look best. Instead of cutting slabs to a curved edge, for example, a cleaner effect can be achieved by staggering the edge slabs and planting against them to create a soft,

Decking interspersed with loose aggregate.

Geometric slab and sett design.

Coloured mosaic cobbles.

Coloured tiles and grey slabs.

The design style of your patio is a key consideration when planning your garden layout: the brick and slab squares (top left) provide an interesting contrast in texture and colour. The timber decking patio (top right) is perfectly set off with matching deck steps – these can provide a link from the patio to other parts of the garden, for example, the pebble path seen here. The geometric lines of the mosaic patio (above) are softened by the natural style of the flowering shrubs planted around the edge.

Irregularly shaped stone slabs, laid in a random pattern and surrounded by lush planting.

curved line. Flagstones and good imitations in pre-cast concrete work well when laid to a random pattern. Slabs laid to a running bond pattern or staggered joint introduce visual movement through the space, while paving laid to a grid pattern is more static, looking good in a courtyard and especially in a contemporary design.

Planting is a crucial part of patio design, linking the area with the garden and creating soft foundation planting to break the hard line against the house or perimeter wall. Fragrant shrubs and herbs work well.

Types of paving
A huge range of materials can be used to surface patios, including natural stone and many good imitations, which always work well with a brick trim and insets to form a visual link with a brick-built house. Natural stone is best laid in a sunny location to prevent the surface becoming too slippery. It usually has a rough surface, which can make it too uneven for small children to run around on without tripping. Natural stone can be supplied as sawn paving that has a more even surface and it can also be given a gritty textured surface for better

Combinations of different materials often work well for patios, particularly brick and stone paving.

grip. Pre-cast concrete slabs are also available with a textured surface, which is useful not only for areas of dappled shade but also in children's gardens where an even, non-slip patio is required. Small paving units such as bricks are fine for a courtyard or small sitting area but would look too fussy in a large patio. If you do decide to use bricks, then the clay type works much better than the concrete one. Natural stone setts are also available, sandstone being more even than granite, although they too are slippery in the shade. There are some excellent imitations, however, in pre-cast concrete. Imitation terracotta tiles link well with internal floors surfaced in the same material and, when surrounded with plants in pots, evoke a Mediterranean atmosphere. Decking in a sunny location looks superb but only when set against the right property; it may be out of place against a period home where natural stone would be more appropriate. Combinations of different materials often work well, particularly brick and stone paving. Loose pebbles set at the base of plants around a patio create a good transition from the hard paved surface to the surrounding soft landscape. Small mosaics look wonderful set into areas of paving, as do the sparkling points of light when small pieces of coloured glass are set into joints around darker paving.

You may choose to use one single type of material when constructing your patio: brick when used on its own, for example, is particularly well suited to creating crisp geometric patterns (above right). But you can combine two or more types of different materials: the timber decking patio (above left), for example, is complemented by a raised platform, which is made out of large, light grey concrete slabs, interspersed with small, dark grey bricks.

Multi-coloured tiles.

Slate in an informal pattern.

Grey stone slabs with grass and water.

Granite setts.

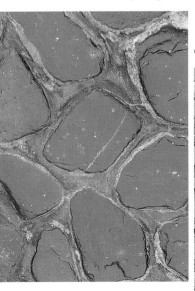

textured
SLAB PATIO

A patio laid with textured paving is ideal for a family garden if you have young children. It is also useful for other areas where a non-slip surface is required, such as around a swimming pool or in the shade of overhanging trees where moss may grow.

1 | Mark around and excavate the patio area allowing for a 75mm (3in) depth of road base and 75mm (3in) for the combined depth of the mortar bed and slabs. Textured paving can be laid directly onto a screeded bed of mortar covering the entire area to be paved, rather than placing the mortar in ridges and furrows under each slab.

After compacting a layer of road base, lay out screed rails across the road base at about 1.5m (5ft) intervals, depending on the overall size of the patio. The rails are lengths of timber of a thickness equal to the depth of the mortar bed, approximately 37mm (1½in). There is no need to fix the rails as their function is simply to support timber that is used for the screeding process.

2 | Make up a mix of fairly dry 1:6 mortar and tip it out onto the road base. Use a shovel to push the mortar around to a rough level before screeding. With a straight piece of

MATERIALS

Road base

Pegs

String

Timber screed rails

Timber straight edge

Mortar

Textured slabs

Fine beach sand

TOOLS

Groundwork tools

Paving tools

1 Having excavated and laid the road base across the area that will form your patio, position screed rails at 1.5m (5ft) intervals across it.

2 Put a layer of mortar on top of the road base and use a piece of timber, positioned on the rails, to screed it out flush with the screed rails.

KNOW YOUR MATERIALS

Textured paving normally comes in the form of pre-cast concrete slabs. The slabs are produced in a range of different textures, sizes and colours, so they are ideal for all types of setting, both traditional and modern. Use them to form random paving patterns or, if only a couple of sizes are used, then a more streamlined design can be created. Although slabs are produced in several colours, natural-coloured (which are almost white) and buff-coloured slabs give the most satisfactory results. As the slabs do not have a rough surface to imitate traditional natural stone, they look good when used in crisp contemporary designs.

timber laid across from one screed rail to the other, screed the mortar to the correct level.

Keep screeding the mortar until it is all flush with the tops of the rails. However, it is a good idea to screed out only as much mortar as you think you will be able to pave over within an hour, or it will be wasted because it will dry out and become unusable.

3 Once you have finished screeding, carefully remove the rails without disturbing the mortar and fill in the resulting gaps. You can do this by trowelling mortar into these gaps and then smoothing it off with the back of the trowel. Alternatively, rather than smooth with the trowel, you can gently run a straight edge of timber once more across the mortar to smooth off the filled-in gaps.

4 Set up string lines around the edges of the patio to show the finished height of paving. Do this by setting up pegs in the four corners and running the string lines around them.

You can now begin to lay the slabs. It is important to spend time getting the first slab correctly positioned since it will set the fall for all the others. Lay the slab in one of the corners, so it lightly touches the two string lines marking the edges, and very gently tap it into position.

5 Continue to lay the slabs in the same manner, building up your pattern as you go. Jointing patterns can be truly random, with different slab sizes laid with no attempt made at an obvious pattern. Some manufacturers print out examples of random patterns for different width patios, which is useful for ordering the right quantity of slabs for each size.

If you do not want to use a pattern at all then it is best to let the supplier know the size of the area you are planning to pave and they should be able to advise you on the correct quantity of each slab size, so that you are not left with too many big or small slabs that cannot be worked in. Whether or not you lay to a pattern, the most important thing to remember about

3 *Once you have removed the rails, fill the gaps that appear with mortar, smoothing them off with a trowel.*

4 *Set up string lines to indicate the finished height of the patio and then you can lay the first slab using the strings as a guide.*

5 *Lay all the slabs in a random style, incorporating the occasional small slab and placing others around it.*

random-style paving is that you should avoid long joints. To do this, try to lay occasional small squares around which the other slabs radiate.

6 Textured paving slabs have crisp, even edges, allowing them to butt up tightly against each other. The slabs can be laid with mortar joints but they are manufactured to be laid butt jointed, which gives a smarter appearance overall. When butt jointing slabs it is imperative to scrape away any particles of mortar from the slab edge so that the next slab fits tightly against it. If the slabs do not butt together well there is a danger that the joints will begin to creep, and this will make the laying of subsequent slabs much harder.

7 When all the slabs have been laid, smooth off the mortar around the edge of the patio with a trowel. The next day, after the slabs have set firm, you will be able to walk on them in order to spread fine beach sand across the patio, brushing it in with a soft brush to seal the joints. After a

few days the sand will combine with general dirt to form a tight seal, binding all the slabs together.

Alternative methods

Since textured slabs do not imitate natural stone they are ideally suited to gardens with a more contemporary feel. If you are aiming for a more uniform appearance than the random pattern described here, paving units in rectangles can be laid for pathways in 90° herringbone or running bond (see below). Both of these patterns will also lend a strong sense of movement to the patio. If you wish to create a geometric courtyard design, square slabs are more suitable.

Alternative materials

Many well-fired bricks have a sandy texture on their faces, making them useful for small patios and courtyards. Natural stone can also be bought with a textured finish for extra grip and sandstone, one of the best natural materials for paving, is also available with a grit finish.

6 *You must ensure that you scrape away any mortar that appears at the edges of the slabs, so they can be butt-jointed neatly.*

7 *When you have finished laying the slabs spread fine beach sand across them all, brushing it into the joints to seal them.*

Alternative method: *A more uniform patio can be created using rectangular paving laid in a running bond.*

circular PATIO

If you are yearning for a private space at the bottom of your garden that can make the most of a suntrap, a small circular patio is perfect for creating a sense of intimacy. And with kit patios now available that contain all you need to lay a complicated circular design without cutting any slabs, it could not be easier.

1 | Decide whereabouts in your garden you want to position your patio and then, using the triangulation method set out on page 142, fix the centre point of the circle in the lawn to mark the middle of the patio. Drive in a steel pin or timber peg at this point and tie a string line to it. Then attach a screwdriver or nail to the string the exact length of the circle's radius and pull the line taut.

You can now walk round the circumference of the circle scoring a mark on the turf to indicate the outside edge of the patio. Make the scraped line in the turf more visible by sprinkling sand along it or by marking it with spray paint.

2 | Start excavation by digging around the edge line, then work towards the centre from opposite points. This will ensure an even depth of excavation and avoid over-digging. If you start excavating at one side of the patio and work your way across it, there is a danger that your

MATERIALS

String

Steel pin or timber peg

Road base

Mortar

Circular paving kit

Timber straight edge

Clay bricks (if desired)

Crushed gravel

TOOLS

Groundwork tools

Paving tools

Plate compactor

1 Once you have measured out and scored the circumference of the circle on the turf, sprinkle sand on the outline to make it more visible.

2 Begin your excavation of the area by digging out around the perimeter. Ensure you allow for the layer of road base and mortar.

KNOW YOUR MATERIALS

Many paving suppliers now produce a variety of kit patios with imitation riven natural stone slabs that can be laid on their own or to form an interesting link with larger patios of the same material.

Many different patterns are available, but usually the circular or hexagonal patios provide the best result. Most types of pre-cast concrete slabs can now be obtained in units to make up a circular patio. The radial-shaped pieces in different dimensions can be laid to form one-, two- or three-ring circles, depending on the size of the patio. A good way to make the concrete appear more natural is to fill the joints with crushed gravel, as shown here.

excavations will get deeper and deeper. When digging out, allow for the thickness of the slab plus a 37mm (1 ½in) depth of mortar and a 75mm (3in) depth of road base.

3 Having finished the excavation, drive in four pegs just outside the circumference to indicate the finished height of the patio. Site the pegs at each end of two diameter lines that dissect the patio area into four equal quarters. Attach string lines over the tops of opposite pairs of pegs so that the lines cross over the centre point. These will provide reference to check for the correct depth of road base and to indicate the finished paving height. Make sure the string lines are set up accurately to show the alignment of the patio. This might mean that one of the lines runs parallel to the back of the house if that is how the patio has been planned. The other line should be set at 90° to the first one using a 3:4:5 triangle.

You can then shovel in the road base and compact it down using a plate compactor to give a sufficient clearance under the string lines for the paving and mortar.

4 Once a level base has been created you can prepare for the laying of the paving, which should always be started from the centre and never the outside. If you start laying slabs from the outside, there is the possibility that the inside slabs will not quite fit. The slabs will need to be laid onto mortar, so spread a few shovels of 1:6 mortar mix on top of the compacted road base. Then lay two of the centre quadrants side by side, with both their straight edges touching the string lines that you set up. You should tap them down until they sit flush with the string lines.

Then lay the first band of surrounding segment slabs, putting down mortar for each slab as you work your way around. Use the string lines as a guide for positioning and the finished height.

5 If your kit has more bands, you can go on to lay the second band of segment slabs in exactly the same way, using the first band as a guide for positioning. Each patio slab should be tapped into place leaving an open joint for pointing. It is often a good idea to lay the circle out dry to

3 Set up pegs and string lines to indicate the centre of the patio and its finished height, then lay road base and compact it down.

4 Start by laying the first two centre quadrants, ensuring their straight edges touch the string lines. Then lay their surrounding slabs.

5 The second band of slabs can be laid down next if there is one, leaving a joint between each to be pointed up later.

one side of the area, just to check how it all fits together. This will also ensure that you always pick up the correct piece to lay as you can just take the next one along.

6 Once you have laid the first few bands, place a timber straight edge piece across the slabs as work progresses to ensure that all the pieces fit flush with each other. Continue to lay the segments to complete one half of the circle first as you will find this easier than trying to work around the whole circle in one go.

7 Lay the second half of the circle, then, if desired, lay down an edging of bricks. We have chosen to use clay bricks here, which take a long time to lay but do give a smart appearance. You will need to lay the clay bricks on a bed of mortar once again, and should follow the curve of the paving around, keeping the joint between the bricks adjacent to the paving as tight as possible, so that the outer joint is not too wide. Haunch up the outside of the bricks when they are all laid.

8 Once all the paving units are in place, brush crushed gravel into the joints of the whole patio. This produces a softer appearance than mortar-pointed joints.

Scatter the crushed gravel with a shovel and use a soft broom to brush the material into the joints, leaving the joints slightly recessed so that the gravel is not kicked around when it is walked on. Sweep up any excess. You can now either lay new turf around the edge of the patio or plant up the area, as desired.

Alternative materials

Imitation brick or tile edges of about 600mm (24in) long are also produced for creating a trim to the paving slabs. They are certainly quick and easy to lay but some varieties can look like obvious imitations, though there are plenty of better quality ones available.

Mortar can be used to point up all the joints in the slabs, rather than the gravel. The best mix for this is 1:4 mortar. However, if you are happy for moss to grow through and soften the joints, a weaker mix could be used for this.

6 Place a straight edge of timber over the slabs you have laid to make sure that they are all flush with one another.

7 Once all the slabs have been laid down, you could lay an edging of bricks around them. Bed the bricks into a layer of mortar.

8 After the patio is completely laid, scatter crushed gravel into all the joints using a soft broom to brush it into place.

stone and BRICK PATIO

Sandstone is probably the best natural stone to use for patio paving. Its golden colour mellows with age, weathering beautifully and providing a real sense of permanence.

1 Mark out the patio and then set a datum peg to one side of this area. The patio should be level from side to side, and incorporate a fall of 1:60 from back to front. Decide on the finished level of the patio along its back edge and, using a spirit level and tape measure, be sure to check the measurement down to this finished level from the top of the datum.

Next determine the finished level of the front edge, applying the fall and check this measurement down from the top of the datum. The overall depth of excavation will be 175mm (7in), the sum of the paving thickness of 63mm (2½in), mortar depth of 37mm (1½in) and the foundation of 75mm (3in), allowing slightly more at the front of the patio for the fall.

2 With a strong spade, dig out a trench along the back, followed by one along the front of the patio area. Once

MATERIALS

Road base

Coarse sand

Fine sand

Cement

Random rectangular sandstone paving (1 tonne /20 cwt of 63mm/2½in slabs for 6 sq m/7 sq yd)

Timber straight edge

Selection of paving bricks

TOOLS

Groundwork tools

Paving tools

Stone cutter

Plate compactor

Concrete mixer

1 Set up a datum peg to one side of the area, against which all levels will be determined using a spirit level and tape measure.

2 After excavating the patio, apply a layer of road base and compact it down to a depth of 75mm (3in) with a plate compactor.

KNOW YOUR MATERIALS

Natural sandstone lends warmth to any outdoor area and it associates well with other materials and plants. Here, well-fired paving bricks add interest between the slabs and provide a subtle contrast of colour and texture, but hard, egg-shaped beach cobbles would work equally well. The rough, textured surface of the sandstone is produced by splitting the rock along its natural bed face, which is best for paving. Not only does this give sandstone a naturally ornamental finish but it also makes the patio surface less likely to become slippery in wet weather. The slabs are supplied by weight in random rectangular sizes with their rough edges trimmed or fettled.

these two trenches are at the right depth, the area between can be dug out to complete the excavation. Check the depth as work progresses by measuring down from a spirit level held across the top of the datum peg. The correct depth is the distance from the top of the datum to the finished level of the patio plus 175mm (7in). Excavate an area slightly wider than the patio so there is a sufficient base width of road base and also in order to make it easier for you to lay the edge slabs.

Spread road base over the area to a depth of 90mm (3½in) and compact it down to 75mm (3in) with a plate compactor. Measure down from the datum peg to check that the foundation is at the correct level of 100mm (4in) down from finished paving level. Add more road base to any low spots as this is cheaper than filling with mortar.

3 | Set up two string lines at right angles to each other to mark the back edge and one side of the patio, and also indicate the finished level of the paving along these edges. Take your time setting these lines out accurately

as they set the finished height and fall on the first few slabs from which the others follow.

4 | Make up a 1:6 mortar mix on which to bed the flagstones (although a weaker mix may be adequate). Start in the corner where the string lines meet and spread a few shovels of mortar over the road base. The mix should be a little firmer than that used for other paving in order to support these heavy flagstones. Use a trowel to create a series of ridges and furrows in the mortar screed so that the slab can be tapped down into place. Make sure that you have laid enough mortar so that when the slabs are initially placed on top, they sit about 6mm (¼in) higher than the finished level.

5 | Select a good sized stone slab with two edges forming a right angle for a cornerstone. Lay it gently, wriggling it down into the mortar bed. Push the slab down so that it sits just above the string lines. Next, gently tap it into place with a rubber mallet until both edges are flush

3 *Set up two string lines to indicate the finished paving level and line of the back edge and one side of the patio.*

4 *Use a trowel to make ridges and furrows in the mortar bed so that the slab can be tapped down to the right level.*

5 *Start with a cornerstone and position it gently into the mortar bed, pushing it down until it sits just above the string line.*

with the lines along the top. Get help to lift the heavy slab if necessary. Lay slabs either side of this cornerstone using the string lines and the first slab as a guide. Continue to pave the patio area, building up a random pattern and avoiding long straight joints. Create an even blend of sizes within the pattern, avoiding any large groups of small pieces. To form gaps into which the bricks and cobbles can be inserted, simply leave out some of the smaller pieces, but do make sure you clean out the mortar in these gaps promptly before it sets hard.

6 Lay a brick or slab at the finished level of the bottom edge of the patio to act as a temporary guide. Then place a timber straight edge measuring 3m x 75mm x 50mm (10ft x 3in x 2in) across from the top to the bottom edges of the patio to ensure that the tops of all the slabs finish flush with the underside of the timber. Tap down any uneven slabs with a mallet as necessary. Leave joints of about 10mm (⅜in) between each slab and scrape out any mortar in the joint before it hardens. Finish laying all the slabs, cutting any as necessary or leaving a toothed edge against planting areas. Cover and leave to dry overnight.

7 The next day, you can start to lay bricks in the gaps between the stones. First, scrape out some of the road base and then lay a bed of the same mortar mix. Place the bricks either laid flat or on edge. Tap down bricks to finish flush with the surrounding paving using a block of wood and a club hammer. If you are laying cobbles instead, set them in mortar to about two-thirds of their depth to ensure they remain firm and tap them down to finish flush with the paving.

8 Choose a dry day for pointing the joints to avoid smearing mortar over the slabs. Mix a crumbly 1:4 mortar (one part cement, two parts coarse sand, two parts fine sand). Pack it into the joints with a trowel so it is flush with the paving. Then use a short section of pipe to produce a rubbed finish. Scrape off excess mortar the following day and brush the paving, prior to hosing down.

6 Use a rubber mallet to tap the slabs down into place. Lay a timber straight edge across the patio to get the level of each stone right.

7 Use a block of wood and a club hammer to tap the bricks down so that they finish flush with the paving stones.

8 Use a crumbly mortar to point the joints between the bricks. Make sure that it finishes flush with the tops of the bricks.

cobbled PATIO

Laying cobbles to form intricate patterns is one of the oldest and most beautiful types of paving. Such patterns are stunning on a huge scale but work equally well for a small and intimate patio to create an atmospheric seating area.

1 Mark out your proposed seating area, excavating down to allow for 100mm (4in) of road base, a 37mm (1½in) depth of mortar and the depth of pebbles, which is likely to be about 50–75mm (2–3in). Spread and compact down the road base, building in a fall of about 1:40 towards the flower bed or lawn to shed surface water. Fix a temporary edging using 75 × 25mm (3 × 1in) timber boards attached to timber pegs, so that the top of the edging lies at what will be the finished height of the paving. These will support the cobbles as they set.

Screed a thin covering of mortar over the road base as it is necessary to have an even surface to work on. Then set in a second edging board, using a spirit level to make sure it is level with the first, to frame the border pattern.

2 Make up a fairly stiff 1:6 mortar mix and trowel it in between the edgings. Place the cobbles on end and push

MATERIALS

Road base

Mortar

Edging boards 75 × 25mm (3 × 1in)

Pegs

Black and white cobblestones

TOOLS

Groundwork tools

Paving tools

Board for tapping down on

Soft brush

Watering can with rose attachment

1 Put the two edging timbers in position, using a spirit level to ensure they are both at the same height.

2 Once a layer of mortar has been put between the timbers, put the cobbles on their ends and push them into it.

KNOW YOUR MATERIALS

Cobbles are small, rounded stones that may be beach pebbles or stones from areas of ancient glacial activity, rounded by the ice. Reject stones from gravel pits are also available as egg-shaped pebbles.

These range in size from 25–75mm (1–3in). Cobbles are available in many different colours, such as the blue, grey and white varieties that are used in this project. However, you can also get greens and browns for a more earthy feel. The

small size of cobbles makes them perfect for experimenting with more artistic garden surface design; combined with ceramics and pieces of glass they can be used to create wonderful mosaic-style patterns.

them down into this mortar. You must take care to keep the stones as close together as possible and lay them in orderly rows so that the overall pattern can be created.

3 After a short area has been filled with cobbles, tap them down with a club hammer over a piece of timber so that the tops of the stones finish flush with the tops of the edgings. Continue working in this way around the entire border, pushing stones into the mortar and then tapping them to the correct height as you go.

4 Change the direction in which you place the cobbles when you reach the corner of the patio, so that the lines of cobbles continue to run parallel. You will need to place more timber edging down to guide you as you did before. You can now actually remove the edging from the first section so that you can haunch mortar up against the cobbles to hold them firm. It is often best, however, to leave the outer edge until the end of the job, so that it can hold everything in place to set.

5 This project follows a similar patio design to the finished picture shown on the previous page, except that the diamond shapes are set against the edge of the patio to create smaller triangles. To lay the diamond pattern you will need to construct timber frames approximately 450mm (18in) square, from 75 x 25mm (3 x 1in) timber, and set them into position by measuring in from the corners of the border pattern to make sure that the diamond shape is straight. (In order to ensure that the patio is full of complete, rather than part, diamonds, you need to measure carefully before constructing the timber frames as they may need to be slightly larger or smaller than the measurements given to fit your patio size.) The pattern of cobbles in the diamond needs to touch the inside of the border and in order for this to work the frame must be set just into the border pattern. To achieve this, remove a laid cobble from the border pattern at both points where the corners of the diamond pattern will meet.

Lay a bed of mortar in the space to bring it level with the outside edge of the patio. Put the corners

3 Tap the pebbles with a club hammer positioned on a piece of timber until they are at the same height as the edging.

4 Having laid your second strip of cobbles using the same method as before, go back to haunch mortar up against the first.

5 Create a timber frame that you can then use as a guide to show you where your diamond pattern should be laid.

of it into the spaces you created in the border in order to prevent any gaps being left between the diamond and the border pattern. The cobbles should be replaced when you have finished.

6 Make sure that you use a straight edge or spirit level to check that the frame sits at the correct height before laying any of the cobbles. Once it is, you can then put the stones, starting with dark cobbles, into the frame by pushing them into mortar and gently tapping them down using the same method as you did for the border.

7 When the first diamond of dark cobbles has been laid, set into place the triangles of white cobbles either side of them. To do this, first remove the timber frame and pack mortar tightly around the dark cobbles to hold them firm. Position a timber board to run along the side of the diamond shape, meeting the inside of the border. This board will act as a temporary edge restraint while laying the cobbles and will show you where to place them.

Trowel mortar behind the board and push the white cobbles into place to form the triangular shapes. Carry on laying this pattern of diamond and triangles across the area until the whole terrace is complete.

8 When all the cobbles have been laid, make up a strong 1:4 dry mix of mortar and spread it over the surface of the stones with a shovel. Use a soft brush to work the mortar between stones, ensuring that none is left on the surface of the cobbles. Then, use a watering can with a rose to water in the dry mix, which will set to hold the cobble stones firmly in position. You will then be able to remove any remaining edging boards before preparing the surrounding area for planting or lawn.

Alternative uses

The same method that is shown here for fixing cobbles into a mortar bed to create a patio area can also be used for a decorative pathway or just a neat little detail to prevent corners from being cut across a lawn.

6 Use a spirit level, once the frame has been set in place, to ensure that it is at the right height before you start laying cobbles in it.

7 Set up a timber board as an edging for the triangle of white pebbles that will surround the dark diamond you have just laid.

8 Once your patio is completely laid, you should then spread a mortar mix over it, to hold the cobbles firmly in position.

decking PATIO

Decking creates an instant tropical feel and will stimulate you to enjoy warm days in a new way. This patio is fixed to the house providing easy access to a platform from which to view the surrounding garden.

MATERIALS

Treated softwood or Western Red Cedar

Timber beams 150 x 50mm (6 x 2in)

Timber posts 100 x 75mm (4 x 3in) or 100 x 100mm (4 x 4in)

Timber joists and fascia boards 100 x 50mm (4 x 2in)

Timber deck boards available in widths of 100 or 150mm (4 or 6in) and in thicknesses of 25 or 40mm (1 or 1½in)

Wall plugs and rust-proof screws or 100mm- (4in-) masonary anchors

Galvanised nails

Deck or stainless steel screws

Crushed gravel

Concrete

Wood stain

TOOLS

Groundwork tools

Woodwork tools

Spirit level

Circular saw

Paintbrush

1 The best way to fix a deck against a house is to screw a timber batten onto the wall – this will give a solid and level base upon which to fix the deck joists. The batten should measure 150 x 50mm (6 x 2in), which will be the same dimensions as the beams. The position for the batten can be calculated by measuring down from what will be the finished level of the deck, taking into account the thickness of the deck boards and the joists. Hold the batten level against the wall and drill through to mark the hole positions on the wall. If possible, try to plan it so that the holes will be in a mortar joint as this will make drilling easier. Set in wall plugs and attach the batten to the wall using long screws or, alternatively, use masonary anchors.

2 Before starting work on the rest of the decking frame, it is a good idea to clear and roughly level the area to be covered with decking, before spreading it over with

2 You will now need to measure out where your supporting posts should be. It is often best to set them at 1.5m (5ft) intervals.

1 To fix the decking to your house, attach a timber beam to the wall next to which the deck will be situated.

KNOW YOUR MATERIALS

Decking slats may be smooth or grooved to provide extra grip and the timber can be chosen from many different woods. Pressure treated softwood, usually pine, is relatively cheap and can be stained easily.

However, do check the wood before buying because very cheap softwood can be full of knots and have poor structural strength. Hardwoods have the advantage of incredible strength but they are also very expensive and difficult to

work with. Even though it is a softwood, Western red cedar is often the best decking timber because of its tight grain, built-in resin (which actually acts as a preservative) and its colouring that weathers to a beautiful silver.

crushed gravel. This will provide a clean surface to work on and the gravel will also help to prevent weeds from growing through underneath the deck, where they will be particularly difficult to access.

Having prepared the crushed gravel, measure out from the house to fix the positions for the supporting posts. Depending on the length of the deck, you may need two, three or even more posts positioned at approximately 1.5m (5ft) intervals along the front of the deck, parallel with the house. The posts should be 100 x 75mm (4 x 3in) or 100 x 100mm (4 x 4in) in dimension.

3 Dig holes for the posts at the correct distance from the house down to about 450mm (17¾in). Mix the concrete and, holding the post vertical, pour concrete around each post up to just above ground level. Check with a spirit level that the post is both vertically and horizontally straight. Each post should be cut off so that its top finishes level with the top of the batten on the house wall. Leave the concrete to set overnight.

4 Screw a 150 x 50mm (6 x 2in) beam (the same size as the batten on the wall) to the outside of each of the concreted posts, using two stainless steel screws for each post. Ensure that the top of the beam finishes level with the posts, which will also mean that it finishes level with the batten on the wall, provided the posts have been set at the correct height. This beam and the batten attached to the wall will support the deck joists.

5 Lay out the 100 x 50mm (4 x 2in) joists from the batten on the wall to the outer beam, at even spacings of approximately 450mm (17¾in). Nail the joists at both ends into the supporting beam and batten by angling two nails so that they cross each other (this is known as 'cross-nailing'), but only drive them home when you are fully satisfied that the joists are correctly positioned. You will need to make sure that a joist is positioned to support each outer edge of the decking area, and this may require slight adjustments to the positions of the joists in between to keep the spacing even.

3 Once you have dug the post holes and put the posts in, pour concrete around them. Use a spirit level to check that they are straight.

4 You can now screw the beams to the outside of the concreted posts. These will then be able to support the deck joists.

5 Begin to position the deck joists in even spacings and cross nail them to the supporting beams.

6 With all the joists fixed into position, nail a fascia board of the same dimensions across the ends of the joists, to provide a neat finish at each edge of the decking area. In this particular project the decking boards extend beyond the fascia, but you could fix a deeper fascia board allowing it to stand proud of the joist by the depth of the decking boards. This will then box in the ends of the decking boards and give a crisp appearance.

7 Set out the deck boards, making sure that the boards at each end of the deck area overhang the fascia by about 25mm (1in), which will provide a shadow line to give good definition at the edge. If the area to be decked is small, you can space out all the boards to see how they fit before screwing them down. If the area is too large for this, just fix the boards directly and adjust the spacing as you near completion. Plan the layout of the boards with staggered joints, as if you were laying bricks, as this looks better than long joint lines across the whole width of the deck. Make sure that the end joints finish centred on a joist.

8 Space the boards with about 6mm (¼in) gaps between them to allow for expansion, free drainage and air circulation. A nail knocked into a small piece of wood makes a good spacer. Use stainless steel screws or special decking screws to fix the boards in position. Start by fixing one screw at each end to hold the board in position and then double screw each end to firmly fix the board down. When all the decking has been completed, tidy up any cut ends by sawing and staining as necessary.

Planting ideas

On its own, the natural material of timber decking blends beautifully in a garden setting. You might, however, like to further integrate a decking patio into the overall scheme of your garden by planting strategically to soften the edges, or by allowing light foliage trees to grow through cut out spaces in the deck itself. If the scale of your patio is such that cutting plant spaces would cause too much disruption to the main area, there is always the option of positioning pot plants around the edge.

6 You can then use nails to fix fascia board to the ends of each of the joists. This will finish them off neatly.

7 The deck boards should be laid out next. You can adjust their positions until you are happy that you have got them right.

8 Use a piece of wood with a nail knocked into it as a spacer to ensure the decking boards are evenly spaced as you fix them.

maintenance
AND REPAIR

Once you have completed all of the necessary construction in your garden, it is important to ensure that the surfaces are maintained properly. If you do not repair any loose paving slabs, clean steps regularly and tidy away your tools, these features will become dangerous to all who use them. Follow the suggestions below to make sure your garden is a safe one.

Paving

If your paved surfaces have been laid properly then they should require very little maintenance, other than an occasional hosing down. All paving will inevitably accumulate dirt over a period of time and you may welcome this for the naturally weathered appearance it will lend to the surface.

Too much dirt, however, can cause surfaces to become slippery and this can be especially dangerous on natural stone paving that lies in shaded areas, where it will also attract algae. In this case it is imperative to clean off the surface with a stiff broom and a weak solution of cleaning fluid before hosing it down. It is also a good idea to cut back any overhanging plants from such an area to expose the paving to more sunlight to dry it all out properly.

Some clay paving bricks are particularly prone to efflorescence on their surface, which is the appearance of harmless white salts. Washing the paving down will not alleviate the problem as it is the damp that draws the salts to the surface. Use a stiff brush (not a wire one) to remove the worst of the powdery deposits when the bricks are thoroughly dry.

Jet washes

A jet wash can work wonders bringing a surface almost back to its brand new condition, but it is not ideal for all paved areas. The jet is so powerful that it may cause damage to the wood fibres on a timber deck, while any loose laid aggregates set between paving slabs will be sent flying.

A jet wash will reveal if there are any poor quality mortar joints in your patio, so if you do need to re-point then jet washing can present you with a quick method of removing any old and crumbling mortar.

Jet washing.

Repairing weathered joints

Make sure that all of the joints are cleaned out to a good depth, about 25mm (1in), before filling them again with a strong mortar mix. This is because if your new mortar is a shallow layer it will be quickly blown out by frost. Use a club hammer and cold chisel when you chip out the old mortar between the slabs.

Chipping out the mortar from a joint.

Replacing broken slabs

Any broken paving slabs or bricks in your patio should be removed and replaced quickly to prevent anyone from tripping on them, resulting in possible injury. A slab or brick set into the middle of a terrace is far harder to replace than one on the edge of it and you will probably need to break it out using a club hammer and bolster.

Once the slab has been removed, then chip out the old mortar bed, spread a depth of new mortar in its place and lower a new slab back into the correct position. Finish the process off by tapping the slab down firmly. This can be done by using a mallet or a club hammer that is hit against a block of wood placed on the slab. After the new slab has been put in, the surrounding joints can be re-pointed.

Re-pointing around a newly laid slab.

Sand-bedded paving bricks are very straightforward to replace, which is why this type of paving is often used in urban settings where access to utility services may occasionally be required. Bricks within areas of paving that have settled can be lifted out quite easily. You might need to break out the first brick to gain access to all the others, but after that the bricks can be removed quickly from the pattern as there is no mortar holding them together.

Removing the first paving brick.

Once a sufficient area of bricks has been removed, dry sand can be placed and screeded out before compacting, re-sanding and screeding to the correct level. The bricks are then re-laid and tapped into place to provide a seamless repair.

Re-laying sand-bedded bricks.

Steps

Paved steps must always be kept clean and in a good state of repair to prevent them from becoming treacherous to those who use them. Slate, gravel and bark treads may occasionally need topping up and raking out if they become worn with constant use.

If a paving slab tread is cracked or broken it must be replaced as soon as possible as it is very dangerous to leave it as it is. This is a straightforward operation if the slab is not bedded under the next riser, as you can just prise it out. However, if it is bedded under a riser you will need to cut it out to avoid dismantling the steps. Use a slab cutter to cut through the slab as close as possible to the step riser that is holding it in, then prise up the slab and chip out the mortar bed underneath with a club hammer and bolster. Try to clean out as much old

Using a slab cutter to remove a slab.

mortar as possible to give room for a good depth of new bedding mortar.

Cut a new slab to size and lay it in position, remembering to bed it with a slight fall to the front of the step in order to shed any surface water that collects (see pages 148-9).

Maintenance of tools

Looking after tools properly will not only extend their life but will also make the jobs for which you use them easier to carry out. Trying to lay bricks using a trowel encrusted with old mortar, for example, is irritating to say the least. All tools should be dried, oiled and stored in a dry shed or garage – tools that have been used with concrete and mortar should have all excess material removed before scrubbing and washing.

Keep all your tools safe and tidy, ideally fixed to the wall and not piled in a corner where it can be all too easy to trip over them. Woodworking tools such as saws, chisels and planes should be covered to avoid blunting. They should also be stored in a box out of the reach of young children.

As long as you are careful with your tools, the good quality ones that you invest in now will last you a lifetime.

BOUNDARIES

Toby Buckland

planning your garden boundaries

your GARDEN BOUNDARY

The concept of boundaries doesn't immediately appear to be a particularly inspiring one in the realm of garden design, but imagine how it feels to sit outside in your garden, enclosed by light-filtering trellis entwined with clematis and fragrant roses, and suddenly it takes on a whole new meaning. The right hedge, fence or wall can gift-wrap your garden, making a comfortable and beautiful place to be.

A combination of ground-cover and hedging entices you to explore.

The importance of boundaries

Boundaries are the key feature of a well-designed garden. They enclose its sides, separate one part from another, and define its focal points and views. Boundaries have a far-reaching influence, which touches all aspects of gardening, from where the sunshine or shadow falls, to the position of entrances. They even define a garden's atmosphere and how it feels. The right hedge, fence or wall gift-wraps a garden, whereas a poor one detracts from it, like ripped packaging.

When I recently moved house, getting a bigger plot of land was definitely the main incentive and stepping out into the new garden was like walking across a giant blank canvas, full of potential but largely empty. A walk out of the back door and across the patio led to the lawn which stretched to a perimeter of hedges and fences – all of which I owned and all of which were overgrown or falling down. Although distant, this motley mix of timber and foliage was the most magnetic part of the garden, drawing the eye and making the whole place appear untidy.

One year on and the picture is very different. At the back of the garden the old hedge remains, but in front a living wall made of willow meanders around. Last March, 20 bundles of red and pea-green whippy willow sticks were delivered. After a day of cutting and weaving and piling in topsoil, the ingredients had been turned into a living willow wall, blurring the boundary of the garden with the countryside beyond and demarking the space for a new small orchard.

In a space of just eight metres, the whole feel and function of the garden had been transformed.

That's just one change, there have been many others – a Leyland cypress hedge has been removed in exchange for a close board fence, tumble-down slopes retained with sleepers and bricks, and countless details added to smaller parts of the garden, which have made them more private, luxurious places to sit in. One of my favourites is the copper-clad wall – originally just rendered concrete blocks shaped into an arch, with the addition of a piece of copper, cut to size and magically aged, it is now an abstract picture painted in cobalt blue.

But more than simply adding detail, the new boundaries have broken up the garden, engendered the whole place with a sense of mystery and given each individual area a purpose.

Now when you step from the back door, paths between low hedges and walls entice you to explore the orchard, the cut flowers and the tropical garden – each with its own ambience and theme. While, more subtly, gates through internal divides tempt you into secret areas unnoticed until you chance upon them.

Using this book

This book is a practical guide to making your own garden boundaries, both around the perimeter of your garden and to divide it into smaller areas. It gives advice on building all kinds of walls, fences and screens, plus information on planting and customising living boundaries. As well as featuring step-by-step projects and chapters explaining the essential tools, techniques and suppliers, it is packed with original, inspirational photography to help you visualise how new boundaries could work in your own garden.

Consider how you can double up the function of your boundary, as seats or lighting.

The inclusion of an arch and a wrought-iron gate adds a magical touch to this beech hedge.

Boundaries explained

In design terms, boundaries have two major functions. These are physically stopping you in your tracks and/or blocking your view. Most perimeter boundaries form a physical barrier, but that doesn't necessarily mean that they obscure the view of a garden. Indeed, in front gardens the boundary is often low and exists simply to mark a change in property ownership and to discourage trespassers.

Visual boundaries (that block your view) needn't be solid and can be achieved by planting a bushy evergreen in front of a view. You can walk around the evergreen, but from behind its foliage you can't see out and, more importantly, no one can see in.

Design

Applying garden design to boundaries in your garden is largely about deciding the best place for screens and entrances through external divides, and whether views should be blocked or framed. The trick to good garden design isn't just getting things in the right place, though, it's about making them work really hard, so they double up in terms of function and have a lot of style. A retaining wall in the right place and with the right coping, for example, can double up as a seating area. Choosing appropriate materials to fit in with chosen themes and style is just as important.

For most people, many of these decisions are quite instinctive, because of our natural understanding of spaces that feel oppressive and others that feel too exposed. Every garden is different, so decide where you most like sitting in your garden and make your internal boundaries around these spaces. The same instinct comes into play when deciding where entrances should be sited and how high a hedge or fence should be.

This book has been created for inspiration, but it is primarily a manual, so use it while you work and don't be afraid to get sawdust and soil between the pages. Good luck!

choosing STYLES

The choice of garden boundaries is huge, and although researching in different books or on the web will give you an idea of which types are historically accurate or appropriate for your home, the decision is always a tug of war between personal taste and what the budget and the local planning department will allow.

Taste, or knowing what you like, is one thing, but recreating it in your own garden is another and if you're unsure, go on an 'enclosure expedition' checking out the boundaries in other people's gardens. It's no good just looking, you've got to take a mental note of what works and what doesn't and ask yourself why. Do the bricks clash with those used in the house? Are the hedges too imposing? Are the fences poorly built or so lacking in detail that they detract from the garden itself? Once you start, you'll notice the good, the bad and the ugly boundaries in every street, but most importantly, pick up tips and ideas about how to make the ones you like work in your own garden.

The starting point is to think of the purpose you want the boundary to serve. The issues to consider are discussed below.

Views

Assess whether there are any features, distant or near, such as large trees or power stations, that you either want to emphasise or obscure. If a boundary is close to you it needn't be very high to hide eyesores in the distance. So, as well as perimeter boundaries, consider using internal screens around seating areas and viewpoints.

Microclimate

Boundaries have a job to do filtering and enhancing the weather, so a stone wall in the right place will hold the heat of the sun well into the evening, while a soil-filled willow wall will always feel cool, benefiting plants that perform best in shady spots. When it comes to buffeting winds, a solid wall is not as effective as one that lets some air through. In fact, a fence with gaps, such as a picket fence, will slow the wind without creating turbulence as the air swirls over the top.

Security

Small gardens present the biggest problem when creating a secure boundary because you can't have a

high, dominant surround. But even a low, see-through enclosure will discourage cats and dogs from straying onto your property and present a visual deterrent to enter. A tall boundary will not deter a determined thief, but it will stop them eyeing up valuable items in your house and garden and slow their access.

Vertical gardening

Obviously walls and fences provide support for climbers and wall shrubs, but identifying your sunny aspects will give you the opportunity to grow tender or half-hardy, more unusual plants – not just climbers but shrubs and perennials that will thrive in the reflected warmth at the boundary's

A clean-cut serpentine hedge.

Pleached hornbeam form a vertical screen.

base. In addition, tall vertical plants can form a boundary in themselves. Some of the projects in this book offer ways to grow plants not just on boundaries but also inside them, due to the soil and built-in irrigation within that keeps plants watered. It's a way of raising up the garden, and ideal if you have a bad back or use a wheelchair as it elevates the flowers, bringing them up to sniffing height.

Intimacy

Boundaries can shield seating areas and patios from view of overlooking windows, and for the maximum effect the choice of boundary and its position are key. Where space is limited and sunlight is at a premium, as in many city gardens, a close mini-boundary along one side of a patio, rather than the whole area, is often all you need to make a seating area private. For this, the best boundaries are frosted glass screens or flower-covered trellis. Larger gardens can be made private by growing hedges and trees behind fences or around gates or mounding clematis or jasmine, to create an extra 0.6–1m (2–3ft) of foliage screening.

Nestle gates in foliage for an intimate feel.

Noise barriers

The thicker the boundary, the greater its ability to deflect noise. Soil-filled walls, dense hedges or thick wooden sleepers combined with dense planting and foliage, all help to make your space quieter.

Dense foliage creates an effective noise barrier.

Details

Boundaries offer incredible opportunities for detail, from copper cladding to trellis and pretty planting. By using luxurious or unusual materials, even the most tiny areas can be enhanced, leaving ground space free for decorative pots and garden furniture.

Entrances

Enclosures obviously require one or more entrances, and indeed it's these that make the focal points for vistas and views, and offer opportunities for pretty detailing in the garden. An entrance can say a great deal, and, depending on the message you want to get across, be imposing, inviting, prominent or concealed. The primary function of an entrance is of course to provide access, but a gate is a way of giving you that feeling of enclosure in what would normally just be a thoroughfare.

A staggered bamboo screen invites you to enter.

Seating

Boundaries create backdrops and can be a perfect place to position a seat. These may be designed into the boundary, perhaps in the corner of a fence, under a clipped arch in a hedge or on the top of a low retaining concrete block or sleeper wall.

Terracing

Boundaries are a way of retaining soil, transforming sloping gardens into levelled areas that are easier to maintain. They also offer ways of bringing in interest from steps, plinths topped with flowering urns and cascading water features.

Walls can incorporate shallow steps and plants.

choosing MATERIALS

Once you've decided on the function of your boundary, it's time to choose materials and a style that suits your location. Provided different parts of the garden are visually enclosed, so you don't see more than one at a time, you don't need to restrict yourself to just one type of material. Of course, it's best if you can link them in some way by repeating themes.

Treat your house as the most important boundary, dictating the flavour of the area around it, but also absorbing some of the character of the garden. Many designers forget that the house can be used to blend with the garden, as much as the garden should blend with the house. For example, a trellis screen could be made more relevant to the area around the patio by fixing some trellis to the house as well. Or if you are using a copper cladding on a wall (see pages 350-1), repeat the theme in copper-cladded window boxes and screens.

If you have a new house, often the boundary will be made up of just one type of fencing. It is a waste of money to remove it, so add detail to make it more interesting. For example, finials on top of fence posts, paint or trellis cladding can improve the look.

Internal boundaries can be treated in the same way, provided they have some link, as described.

Materials

There are dozens of materials for garden boundaries, each with their own personality. The criteria for choosing materials are: matching in with your existing materials and themes, preferred style, price and your ability to use them.

Timber

Timber is extremely versatile and is the easiest material to turn into boundaries because it can be cut to any shape. It's fairly inexpensive too. In a garden, timber creates a warm look and, as far as style is concerned, it is a bit of a chameleon – rustic or modern, left rough-hewn or given a lick of paint.

Weathered oak door.

Stone

Natural stone instantly ages a garden and lends a feeling of quality. Used with a little imagination, this effect of antiquity can be enhanced by combining with plants, or it can be given a fresh, modern look used with metalword (see pages 306-7). Local stone is usually the cheapest option and often blends well, but in enclosed areas, there is no reason why you can't use other more colourful stone or paint it with a colour of your choice.

Painted render.

Metal

Traditionally, metal is used to give a very formal front face to a garden. Ironwork railings and wrought-iron fences are best left to metalworkers, but it is possible to use some metals, like sheet copper and wire mesh, in DIY projects with little in the way of tools or specialist knowledge.

The effects that metal creates are fresh and contemporary, and so beautiful they wouldn't be out of place on the walls of an art gallery.

Louvred metal gate.

Living willow fence.

Sandblasted glass screen.

And because metal is relatively cheap to buy, the look comes without a huge price tag.

Stems

Willow and hazel are easy, quick and fun to work and allow you to be really experimental without worry. They also require the least preparation of the materials and while they don't last as long as more robust materials, you can expect 3–6 years out of them. Living willow has the advantage of rooting, and if kept watered, will last indefinitely. If it gets too big, chop it down in the winter.

Glass

Glass is mostly used for detailing in boundaries, for example, stained glass in trellis. If you're looking for a contemporary-style screen, sandblasted safety glass makes an ideal internal boundary that allows light to pass through and, combined with architectural plants, creates interesting silhouettes, in sun or night-time lighting. It equates to the price of a good brick wall, but is quicker to make.

Brick

Brick, with its warm and solid appearance, is the classic boundary material. Its variations are infinite: from the way it is laid to methods of pointing and brick bonds, not to mention the many colours and finishes of the bricks themselves. They do take a certain amount of skill to lay, though with practice, anyone can make a decent low wall. The cost is high, but you can save money when building your own with a few tricks of the trade (see pages 278-9).

Bricks are made from a number of different materials, with baked clay bricks being the most common. Their colour and texture varies depending on the type of clay used and the method of manufacture. Bricks are usually rectangular (though other shapes are available) and may be flat-faced, have holes through them or have an indentation known as a 'frog' on one face. Holes and frogs fulfil the same function: when filled

with mortar, they help to key the bricks together. Bricks vary considerably in price, so you should use 'common' bricks for areas of the structure that will not be seen, such as foundation work and inside retaining walls. These bricks have uneven colour and texture and are an economical choice for such elements. You can then use evenly coloured and textured but more expensive 'facing' bricks for the visible parts of the structure.

order OF WORK

Before starting construction, professional builders and landscapers write out the sequence of events needed to get the job done, known as the 'order of work'. It's a time-saver and pre-empts many possible problems, by ensuring you consider access, storing materials and making sure you've booked hire equipment for the day you need it.

Planning ahead

• Building regulations – contact your local council to find out if there are any regulations regarding the height, location, style or material of the boundary you are building.

• Stacking materials – if it will take some time to build the boundary, it is better to organise deliveries of materials for when you need them rather than leave them on the lawn.

• Hire equipment – whether it's a drill or a cement mixer, it's important to get tools when you have the time to do the work, so order in advance.

• Delivery dates and times – make sure you can take time off work, or if you can't, that you've given exact instructions about where the delivery is to be placed.

• Noise – check with neighbours when it's okay to have deliveries and use loud machinery and power tools.

• Access – what is the quickest and least troublesome route from where materials are delivered to where you want to use them? Are there any short-cuts? For example, by temporarily removing a fence panel, you can speed up the process.

• Timing – if you're building more than just boundaries, maybe putting in a path or a patio too, examine which element has the deepest footings. For example, a wall has deeper footings than a path, so it is always built before you put down paving. Trellis, on the other hand, doesn't, so it's best to put it in afterwards to keep access open and avoid damaging what you've just done.

Estimating materials

Once you've decided on your boundary – its style, materials and design – you need to estimate quantities and buy the materials. This is something that all good builders' suppliers will be able to help with, provided you know what materials you want. So, arm yourself with

Estimate how much of each material you will need.

knowledge – shop around, have a look at materials, take a photo of your garden or features to help you match materials or pictures from books or magazines that you are trying to copy. Visit salvage yards and metalwork shops, places you might not ordinarily go to, for inspiration.

Inevitably, you will have to modify designs from pictures and step-by-steps to fit your location, particularly if you are making projects such as trellis (see pages 342-5), Draw a sketch of your idea or, better still, a scale drawing, so you can accurately quantify. Scale drawings are done with a scale ruler. Remember that if you are building anything from timber, and it involves a lot of cutting to length, you should add an extra 10 per cent for waste.

The following are typical quantities for standard boundaries:

Walls

For 1 cubic m of blue metal you will need 1.4 tonnes of blue metal; for 1 cubic m of sand you will need 1.3 tonnes of sand.

For concrete footings you need proportions based on 1.25 tonnes blue metal to 0.5 tonnes of sharp sand to five 40kg bags of cement. For 1 square m of single skin wall you need 50 bricks, or 100 for full brick wall plus 10 for breakages. For 1 square m of concrete block wall (using standard blocks laid on their sides) you need 12.5 blocks.

1.25 tonnes of sand and 3.5 (40kg) bags of cement lay 1000 bricks. 1 tonne of sand and 3.5 bags of cement lay 300 blocks.

Close board fence

For every linear metre (3ft) of close board fence you need eight 150mm (6in) feather boards.

Feather boards.

Willow

One standard bundle of willow makes approximately 0.5m (1½ft) square of willow wall.

Willow wall.

Stone

You get 4 square metres (40 square feet) of wall per tonne (20cwt) of stone, depending on the exact stone.

Dressed stone.

How to buy

If previously you have concentrated on small-scale garden jobs, you'll be accustomed to buying materials in small bags and taking them home in the car. For larger jobs, you'll have a choice of how to get it delivered to your home, depending on the material in question, and this has an effect on cost.

Buying stone, gravel and aggregate

Stone, gravel, sand and aggregate are all cheapest to buy delivered loose, but that leaves you with the problem of storage and cleaning up; for instance, builders' sand will stain a driveway, so it must be contained on plastic sheeting. Slightly more expensive but far more convenient are large, white aggregate bags or pallets. This is definitely the best option if the job is going to take a while because it keeps out cats and weather, and looks neater.

Buying bricks.

Buying timber

Timber is sold in standard lengths and sizes, depending on the type of wood. This could be 3m (10ft) and 6m (20ft) for example, so if your job involves cutting it down to 2.5m (8ft) lengths, ascertain the standard sizes before buying to ensure you are not paying for waste. Timber is readily available from timber/builders' suppliers or, for older, more interesting wood, check out salvage yards.

Timber is delivered in individual planks, so if there is a lag time before installing it, keep it flat to prevent it from bowing. It is also important to protect it from the wet or it may twist out of shape.

Buying timber from a salvage yard.

tools and techniques

marking OUT

Marking out is the process of transferring the pencilled features on a drawn-up garden design into lines on the ground and creating reference points allowing speedy and accurate construction. It also allows you one last chance to alter your plans. Marking out is a job that is worth taking time over, as any errors can make building and quantifying problematic.

Making a 3:4:5 triangle

Creating a right angle on paper is easily done with a set square, but to transfer this onto the ground you need to do a little simple maths.

The technique was discovered by the Greek mathematician Pythagoras some 2500 years ago and involves making a triangle on the ground. If the base is 3m (9ft) long, the side 4m (12ft) and the diagonal 5m (15ft), the corner where the base and side connect will be a perfect right angle. The quickest way to mark this is with 12m (36ft) of measuring tape looped around a triangle of bamboo canes pushed into the ground. Hold the ends of the zero and 12m (36ft) mark on the tape next to one cane and

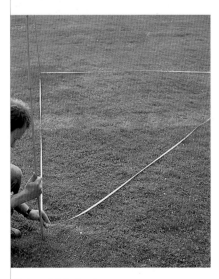

Make a 3:4:5 triangle.

move the other canes to the 4m (12ft) and 9m (27ft) marks to get your right angle. (The units you use don't actually matter as long as they are multiples of 3, 4 and 5; you could use 300, 400 and 500mm or 600, 800 and 1000mm, for example.)

External boundaries and not offending the neighbours

Boundary disputes are one of the main causes of conflict between neighbours, therefore it is essential to check deeds of ownership before commencing work on any perimeter boundary. It is also prudent to liaise with neighbours first about any changes you are making and to get permission to enter their garden while working on the divide. If you are replacing a fence, always build to the line of the old one and get your neighbours to confirm that your string marking lines are in the right place.

Marking and fixing fence posts

To mark out the line of a fence, fix the two end fence posts in position and run a taut line between them near their bases – you may need to tie back any overhanging branches or herbaceous plants that get in its way.

Starting at one end, mark the position of the intermediate fence posts. (Depending on the design of

Mark positions of posts on the ground.

the fence, the fence posts will either occur down its centre or be on the owner's side, so that the flat face of the fence runs along the boundary.) If any coincide with a drain or old concrete footing, digging a hole or hammering in a fence spike will be impossible, so either move all of the post positions along to avoid the obstacle or, if you are building a picket or close board fence, have a longer arris rail for that one section.

If you are building a panel fence, moving the position of the fence posts will more than likely mean that the end panels have to be cut down to fit the run (see pages 280 and 281).

If you're concreting the posts, dig the holes for all of the intermediate posts, making them 600mm (24in) deep and 150–200mm (6–8in) wide. Then, run another string line between the two end posts at their tops. If the end posts are upright, when each intermediate fence post is brought up against the top and bottom string line, it will be upright too. Finally, check that it is level side to side before bracing and concreting in place.

Use a taut line to position the posts.

Scribing an arc using a cane and string

Curved patios and paths, along with the boundaries that flank them, produce an informal look that blends easily with surrounding plants. Walls that double up as seating benefit from being curved as they allow people to face each other when seated; because they are curved, stability is increased. You can mark a serpentine or curved line on the ground by eye, but it is difficult to make it look natural. A more reliable method is to tie a length of string to a cane pushed in at the centre of your arc. Hold the string taut at the point you want the radius and use it as a guide as you spray ground marking paint or sprinkle sand along your line.

Scribe an arc.

Rather than being arbitrary about the position of the curves, aim to arc them around existing features of a garden, for example trees and seating areas, as this helps to unify and tie the features in a garden together.

Using fence spikes

Fence spikes take away all the hard work of digging holes. After marking out the position of the posts, use a sledgehammer to drive the fence spikes into the ground. Custom-made, plastic driving units are available which fit into their tops and take the impact of the hammer, preventing damage to the spike. These also have metal bars, which allow you to knock them back into line if they start to twist.

The trick to getting fence spikes upright is to check with a spirit level after every few blows with the hammer.

If they need straightening, hammer the driver against the direction they lean in to bring them upright. Once it is in the ground, hammer the post into the socket of the fence spike while ensuring that it is firm and upright. The best fence post systems have bolts which let you tighten the metal

Use a level to check the fence spikes are upright.

around the base of the post. These allow a little movement, making it easy to get the posts perfectly upright.

Tighten the fence posts in position.

As well as spikes, there are many different metal fence fixings including stirrups for bolting the base of a post to concrete, spikes that drive into the hole left after a rotten fence post has snapped and sockets for extending the height of your fence. They all work well but, if you use them, aim to disguise all metal spikes and fixings beneath evergreen planting or below soil.

concrete, MORTAR AND FOUNDATIONS

This section is about the two glues that hold the hard landscaping in a garden together – concrete and mortar. Understanding how to make and use them is an essential part of many garden DIY projects, including building walls, setting fence posts, laying paving and making water features.

The ingredients

Concrete and mortar have different applications. Mortar is used to fix materials such as bricks and paving stones to a level, while concrete is used for the foundations of walls, paths and fence posts.

Sharp sand

A washed sand with angular grains that fills the spaces between stones in concrete. The sides of the grains are angular, so they lock together, giving concrete its strength. A mortar made from sharp sand and cement makes a wear-resistant mix for laying and pointing paving stones, but is too stiff and hard to work for bricklaying.

Cement

The bonding agent that holds both concrete and mortar together. It is a caustic grey powder containing limestone, which crystallises and hardens when mixed with water.

Blue metal

Blue metal (crushed stone, shown here mixed with sand) is usually available in 10mm and 20mm diameter grades and can be used in concrete mixes or as aggregate behind walls to aid in drainage above agricultural drains.

Brickies' sand

Sand with rounded grains used to make mortar. Because they are round, the grains roll over each other, making it easier to tap bricks and concrete blocks down to level. It also contains a small amount of clay which makes it more pliable and sticky when wet.

Mortar and concrete mixes

Making concrete or mortar is like baking – you need a recipe and the ingredients in the right amounts. These are expressed as a ratio, for example 6:1 with sand always first.

When mixing, always measure quantities using a levelled-off bucket. Because you are constantly making new mixes, consistency throughout the job ensures that concrete is strong and that the joints in brickwork dry to the same colour. To make concrete for a foundation you need to make a 4:2:1 mix (4 parts blue metal, 2 parts sharp sand, 1 part cement). You can mix this by hand in a wheelbarrow or on a sheet of plywood, but it's easier and quicker with a cement mixer. To mix by hand, measure out 4 level buckets of blue metal and 2 buckets of sand onto a sheet of plywood. Sprinkle 1 bucket of cement over the top and turn with a shovel until the mix is an even grey colour. Create a crater in the mix and part fill with water, turning in the edges until the mix is wet and soft but not sloppy.

With a mechanical mixer, water is added first followed by the cement to form a slurry. This ensures that the blue metal and sand are completely coated as they are shovelled into the mixer. Add water as necessary and mix for at least two minutes to obtain a uniform consistency.

Masonry mortar consists of 6:1 brickies' sand and cement for above ground work and 3:1 for courses below soil level. It can be mixed by hand as above, but for large jobs hire a mechanical mixer to save time and

Mix mortar until the consistency is sticky.

your back. Add water until it becomes smooth but stiff enough to hold its shape when furrowed up with a trowel. Once the right consistency has been achieved, mix for a few minutes to create small air bubbles in the mortar. These help to make it workable and sticky. A test to see whether it is the correct consistency for bricklaying is to scoop a little onto a trowel, shake off any excess and turn upside down. If the mortar falls off, it needs either more water or more mixing.

Black mortar highlights the red bricks.

Additives are available including dyes which create coloured joints in brickwork and plasticisers which increase the air bubble content of mortar, making it more forgiving to lay and easier to mix to the correct consistency. Plasticisers can be bought premixed into the cement or as liquid for adding as you mix.

Plasticiser increases the air bubble content of mortar.

Foundations

For walls under 1m (3ft) high, the concrete footing should be at least 215mm (8½in) deep and never less than the thickness of the wall. The width of the foundation depends on how wide the wall is and whether it is a retaining wall. Freestanding walls need a footing 2–3 times their width while retaining walls need a footing at least three times their width, with the bulk of the footing behind the wall.

1 When digging the foundations use lines to mark out the width of the footing and dig down until you reach solid subsoil. The sides of the hole should be vertical, the ends square and the base at least 100mm (4in) deeper than the required depth of concrete (this allows the foundations to be buried out of sight).

2 Before pouring the concrete, hammer wooden pegs along the centre of the trench to the depth you want the concrete and check that they are all the same height using a spirit level. The pegs become a guide ensuring that the concrete is poured and smoothed to the correct level, making it strong and flat. It is therefore much easier to lay bricks/blocks once it has dried.

3 Pour the concrete to the tops of the pegs, slicing with a shovel to release any trapped air, then screed to the tops of the pegs with a length of timber. Because the concrete shrinks as it hardens, leave for at least two days before starting construction.

slopes and DRAINAGE

Changes of level, enclosed by hedges or judiciously planted evergreens, can blur the boundaries of a garden making it seem bigger while at the same time hiding all but its best views and features. Boundaries across a slope can create a sense of mystery too. Where levels are changed, consideration has to be given to drainage.

Measuring slopes

One of the biggest worries for DIYers is knowing the quantity of materials to order, or 'quantifying'. Provided you have measured up accurately, you will get all the help you need from your supplier. Measuring the length, height and width of the boundary is easy but it gets complicated if the ground is sloping and you want to build a wall into it. To calculate the 'fall', that is, how much the ground slopes, there are two methods.

Over a short distance place a 2m (6½ft) straight-edged plank at the top of the slope, and hold it out with a level on the top so it reaches over the bottom of the slope. When it's level with the base, measure from the base to the plank to give you the fall.

Use a plank and a spirit level to measure a fall.

For long, gentle slopes, hammer in a post at the top of the slope and fix the top of a hose 1m (3ft) high on the post. Run the hose along the ground to the bottom of the slope, then lift up this end of the hose and fill with water from a can. When the hose is full at both ends, the two ends are level with each other. Measure the length of hose you are holding up at the bottom of the slope and deduct 1m (3ft) to give you the fall.

Use a hose to measure a fall over long distances.

Fences and slopes

Picket, post and rail and close board fences can all be built to follow the contours of a slope perfectly. Panel fencing, because it comes in large 180cm (6ft) sections, will not; instead it forms steps between each new section of panel. Such steps are useful for making particularly large jumps in level, but are best avoided as they look ungainly and don't blend with the land they enclose. If you have a slope, the choice is between a close board and a picket fence that undulates with the ground or, if the slope is gentle, the fence can have a level top and an undulating base. Whichever you choose, for strength, always make the fence posts and the pickets/feather boards upright, sloping only the arris rails.

Walls and slopes

The large old walls surrounding stately homes were often built to follow the rises and falls in the land. Despite their longevity, such walls do not meet modern building standards as they have shallow foundations and are stuck together with soft lime mortar. This seemingly weak construction actually accounts for their strength, allowing the wall to move as the soil shifts beneath the footings. The building of sloping walls is best left to specialists.

Retaining walls

While a gently rising lawn may be easy to live with, a patio needs to be level and this means terracing into the slope and building retaining walls to hold back the soil.

Lining

If retaining walls aren't lined on the inside, the appearance of the bricks can be spoilt with a covering of white powder. This happens because water from the soil seeps into the bricks, carrying salts with it. When it reaches the face of the wall, the water evaporates and the salt is left behind. Water seeping through a wall will also make it vulnerable to algae which looks particularly bad on render and will make it prone to frost damage.

There are three ways to seal the back of a retaining wall from moisture. It can be given a coat of bitumastic paint, which is a modern quick drying version of pitch. On the down side, it is expensive, and to get an even coat the wall needs to be smooth.

Water-proof bitumastic paint.

Another effective method of lining is to cover the back of the wall with a waterproof cement sand render available from any builders' suppliers. It is time consuming but a good way of sealing the wall, and sloppy brick work. Finishing on the back of the wall provides a good key for the render.

The most economical way to seal the back of a wall is with plastic damp proof membrane (DPM). This tucks down against the wall and is held in place by the infill. Its only disadvantage is that it does not make a good seal around weep holes (see below).

Drainage

As well as holding back soil, a retaining wall slows down the movement of water and unless adequate provision for drainage is included, the ground above it will be wetter than it was before the wall was built.

Good drainage can be achieved in two ways. Firstly, weep holes are lengths of 15mm (¾in) plastic pipes cut to the width of the wall and laid every 900mm (3ft) between bricks in the second course above ground level.

Lay weep holes between bricks in the second course.

Better looking but more complicated is a land drain. This is a perforated 100mm (4in) wide pipe, set in blue metal or aggregate, on a slope of 1:70. The pipe connects to a land drain, known as a soakaway, which consists of buried rubble that acts as a sump from which water is absorbed into the soil.

Lay the drainage pipe and connect with land drain.

Soakaways should be located near the end of the wall but always at least 5m (16ft) away from buildings and a good distance from utilities such as drains, sewers and gas pipes. Whichever method you use, before backfilling the wall line the soil behind it with a geotextile layer. This is a fibrous material that keeps the soil particles from blocking the drainage pipes.

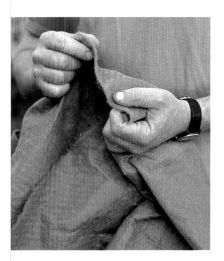
Geotextile membrane.

Backfill the bottom half of the wall with blue metal, then fold the geotextile layer over the top of the blue metal. Finally, fill to the top of the wall with soil.

bricks and BRICKLAYING

Bricklaying, like most crafts, involves many different skills that are simple on their own but when put together can seem daunting. However, by following the advice in this section and the projects on pages 296 to 311 you will be armed with all the knowledge you need to build freestanding and retaining garden walls up to 700mm (27½in) in height.

Brick types

Common bricks – economical bricks with uneven colour and texture for use where they won't be seen (for example, foundation work and inside retaining walls).

Engineering bricks – strong clay bricks with low water absorption for damp-proof courses and coping.

Facing bricks – bricks manufactured for display with few blemishes, even colour and surface texture.

Cutting bricks

Mark around the brick where you want to cut it and sit it on a layer of sand, edge side up. Using a bolster and a club hammer (also known as a lump hammer), strike the brick first on one edge then the other, going

back and forth between the two until it fractures in half.

Marking out

When building a brick wall, always chalk a line on the foundations to mark the face side and ends. To save having to cut bricks, make the length of the wall a multiple of the length of a brick – 230mm (9in) – plus the width of the joint – 10mm (½in). Work this out on paper or lay a dry course of stretcher bricks (see below) on the foundations leaving 10mm (½in) spaces between them to get your dimensions.

Laying the first course

Next set the end stretcher bricks in position on a trowel of mortar, tapping them down until the mortar beneath is 10mm (½in) thick and the tops are level with each other. Ascertain this by bridging between them with a taut line or a straight-edged length of timber and sitting a spirit level on top.

With the end bricks in place, run a line between them to mark their top front edge, holding it in position beneath two more bricks. This speeds up the rate of laying considerably allowing the bricks in the centre of the wall to be tapped level lengthways by eye. You then only have to use a spirit level to check across the wall.

Trowel mortar on the inside of the line and ripple its surface by zig-zagging the trowel's point along its length, creating a central channel. This spreads the mortar to the width of a brick and makes tapping the bricks level much easier.

Trowelling mortar.

Buttering the end of a brick.

Cutting bricks using a bolster and club hammer.

Turn the mortar to get air into it and trowel a small amount on to the end of the brick, smoothing the mortar to its edges. If the mortar keeps falling off, the mortar is too dry. Rectify this by splashing a little water onto the mortar and turn it in with a trowel.

Laying subsequent courses

Position the buttered brick (see opposite below left) up to the line and push it against the end brick to create a 10mm (½in) joint between them. Tap each brick down with the handle of a club hammer or trowel, until it is level front to back and its top edge is level with the line. Repeat this process until all of the face skin of bricks are in place (the last brick will need to be buttered on both ends). Lay the bricks at the back of the wall leaving a 10mm (½in) gap between the two skins (see below), checking for level across the wall as you go. Fill the gap with mortar and start the next course with two header bricks one at each end of the wall. Again, check that the joint is 10mm (½in), a storey rod is useful for this (see page 287), and run a line between them to mark their top edge. Now cut a 'queen closure' brick (see below)

Laying a queen closure brick.

and lay this next, to break the vertical joint, and continue laying until the next course is complete.

Build up the ends of the wall first to support the builders line and lay the bricks in the centre course by course.

Laying the second course.

As you work, collect the mortar that oozes out as the bricks are tapped down by running the point of the trowel along the face of the brick below, pulling excess mortar onto the trowel's blade. This and any that falls onto the foundations can be put back onto the mortar board for later use.

Leave any mortar that gets onto the face of the bricks until it stiffens (this takes an hour or so depending on the weather), then scrape it off with a trowel.

Pointing the joints

Next 'point' the joints, which involves smoothing over the dips and pits in the mortar to keep water out and make them frost-proof.

For walls in exposed positions make what is called a 'weather struck joint' by pressing a pointing trowel held at an angle down the vertical joints then across the vertical joints.

Weather-struck pointing.

Bricklayers jargon

Stretchers – bricks laid lengthways along the wall.

Headers – bricks laid sideways through the wall to bond the sides together.

Half bat – a brick cut in half across the middle.

Queen closure – a brick cut in half lengthways.

Joint – the mortar between the bricks.

Course – a row of bricks/blocks/stones in a wall.

Frog – indentation moulded into the bottom of some bricks, gripping them into the wall and making laying easier.

Single/half brick wall – a wall 110mm (4¼in) wide (the width of a brick).

Full/double brick wall – a wall 230mm (9in) wide (the length of a brick).

Soldier course – bricks laid on edge usually as a coping.

Coping – a protective top to a wall that stops rainwater from soaking into the bricks and making them soft and prone to frost damage.

Skin – the front or back course of stretcher bricks in a full brick wall.

'Buttering' – a term used to describe placing mortar on the ends of a brick for the vertical joints in a wall.

using TIMBER

Timber is versatile, relatively inexpensive and you don't need the carpentry skills of a furniture maker to create beautiful wooden boundaries. With a few basic tools, a little know-how and a tin of coloured wood stain, you can build a fence that captures the character of your garden while giving you and your plants shelter.

Timber joints

For many of the projects in this book it is necessary to make simple timber joints to fasten lengths of wood together in a neat, strong way. While making joints takes a little time, it is easy to do and the finished result is far more attractive than when more expensive metal brackets are used.

Half-lapped/notch joints

These joints allow two pieces of timber to cross and yet still be flush with one another. They are useful when building gate frames and for notching the arris rails of close board fences into their supporting posts.

To make a half lap joint

1 Lay the timbers across one another and mark both pieces where you want the joint. Then mark the depth of the joint. This should be half the depth of the timber if they are the same size or half the depth of the thinnest length.

2 To make chiselling out the wood easier, make repeated cuts through each timber to the depth of the joint with approximately 10mm (½in) between them. (The fastest way to do this is with a circular saw set to the depth of the joint, but it is easy to do with a wood saw.)

3 Remove the remaining wood from the joint with a broad chisel.

Mortice joints

Basically, these joints involve one piece of timber slotting into another, like a key in a lock. They are useful when making post and rail fences, close board fences where you want the posts to be visible from both sides and attaching picket fences to gate posts. To speed up the process, sharpen the ends of the arris rails into points to reduce the amount of wood you need to chisel from the post.

1 Mark on the fence post where you want the joint to be positioned. (Reduce its size if the arris rails are sharpened as above.)

2 Drill a series of holes through the post where you want the joint.

3 Chisel out the waste and slot in the arris rails, pinning them in place with a nail or screw.

Fixing timber with screws and nails

To prevent wood splitting, always drill pilot holes before tightening in screws. It is a good idea to borrow or hire an extra electric screwdriver so that you have one for the pilot bit and one for the screwdriver. Always use galvanised or coated nails and screws, as untreated types rust and leave stains.

Painting and preserving

Most shop-bought fence panels are ready-treated with preservative for a 15–25 year lifespan. If you buy timber to build your own fence, you can use untreated wood as long as you coat it with a wood stain or paint. This said, it always pays to buy pressure-treated timber for any part of the fence that will be in contact with the ground. Treated softwoods are rated according to the H (hazard) system, ranging from H1 (the least hazardous and durable) up to H6. As a general rule, H3 timber is suitable for rails and H4 for posts and gravel boards. Always wear a dust mask and gloves when sawing treated timber to protect yourself from the chemicals.

You can dramatically cut down the time it takes to paint a large fence (or trellis) by hiring a paint sprayer.

Fences and trees

If there is a tree growing along the line where you want to build a fence, don't nail the fence directly to it as when the tree sways in the wind, so will the fence; the health of the tree will also be damaged. Instead, put a post a metre or so back from the trunk and cantilever two arris rails to within several centimetres of it. For effect, a false post can go on the end propped in place by a diagonal timber

Situate posts well back from trees.

spiked into the ground behind the tree. Where there are branches, dips or holes can be cut in the fence to allow them to move in the wind.

Cutting down a fence panel

At the end of a fence run you may need to cut down a panel to turn a corner or to connect with a building.

1 Draw a line down the fence where you want the cut.

2 Screw a length of 45 × 19mm (2 × ¾in) batten to each side of the fence along the line.

Sawing the fence panel to size.

3 Cut the fence down with a saw.

Curved fences

To create a curve, use timber thin enough to be bent into an arc for the arris rails. To give the arris strength and to hold its shape it needs to be laminated. Bend it around a series of posts temporarily hammered into the ground around the arc, fixing it to the two end posts with a screw. Then paint the outer face with external wood glue and bend another length of wood over the top screwing it in place as you go. Allow the glue to set before detaching and fixing in position.

Fence jargon

Gravel boards – commonly used to underpin panel and close board fences. They form a barrier between the ground and the main fence, taking all the weather and rotting first.

Arris rails – sometimes called stringers, these are timbers that run between the posts and have pickets or feather-edged boards hammered to them.

Feather-edged boards – timber planks that are wedge-shaped in cross section to allow them to overlap each other.

incorporating PLANTS

Plants bring seasonality, character and individuality to even the most mundane of spaces and therefore deserve as much thought and care as any boundary detail. This section has been included to help you choose the right plants for your boundaries and to get them off to the best possible start.

Hedges

Planting a hedge is the quickest and most economical way to enclose a large area of your garden. Before planting, dig or rotavate along the line of your intended hedge, incorporating a barrow load of garden compost, well-rotted horse manure or commercially available soil improver every 4–5m (13–16ft). Then, plant your hedge, firm in the roots and water in.

The trick to getting hedges to establish quickly is to water through the growing season, particularly during dry spells in their first year after planting. To encourage the hedge to fill out, lightly trim the sides in early summer of the second year. Although

A smart, low front garden hedge.

it's tempting to plant the hedge and leave it to grow and reach the height you ultimately want it to be before cutting it back, it's better to trim its top half a metre or so below the desired height, to encourage it to branch out and fill out more quickly. Once the hedge is at the desired height it will be easier to trim as this method prevents the formation of difficult-to-cut thick branches.

With most hedges, you can get away with one major prune a year to remove unwanted growth. However, for the neatest look, especially with hedges such as box (*Buxus*), yew (*Taxus*) and topiary features, it's best to give a quick prune every couple of months. When trimming hedges over 1–1.2m (3–4ft), always make the sides slope inwards slightly to give the hedge an A-shaped profile. Otherwise, the top of the hedge will cast shadow over the base, making it gappy and showing the trunks of the plants.

Climbers and wall shrubs

To soften brand new fences and walls, climbers and wall shrubs are the obvious choice. The range is vast, so first decide what features you want your climber to have – flowers, berries, scent, evergreen or deciduous, autumn colour? Most of us want all

Climbers soften the square edges of a panel fence.

of these things but that's impossible from just one plant. However, by combining a couple you can have it all. Next, ascertain what will grow in front of the boundary. Even if you are unsure of your gardening knowledge, garden centres and nurseries can help you choose, if you find out the following:

• Aspect – which way it faces (whether it catches the morning or afternoon sun or none at all).
• Soil – sandy and free-draining, or clayey and sticky? Take a sample to the garden centre for advice.
• Exposure – is the site very hot and prone to dry out or very windy?
• Size and space – how much area do you need to fill, including base and top?

• How wet or dry is the soil? Does it sit puddled in winter and crack in the heat of summer, or is it permanently boggy or dry?

You should also consider what the neighbours grow well, because often similar plants will do well for you.

Bear in mind that climbers grow in different ways. Clematis will establish on top of the support, forming a cloud of foliage and flowers, so plant herbaceous perennials or smaller shrubs, like lavender (*Lavandula*), to fill the gap. Honeysuckles (*Lonicera*) and jasmine (*Jasminum*) become great sprawling mounds in front of the support and often look best when they cascade over from the other side, so are a good choice for internal divides. Wisteria, climbing roses (*Rosa*) and vines (*Vitis*) all lend themselves to training.

If you are building around a well-established plant, then you can always plan for it in your boundary design.

A scalloped wall to highlight the position of a tree.

Planting at the base of a boundary

Life at the base of a wall or fence is harsh, potentially in a rain shadow and what moisture there is can be sapped up by the boundary. So, give plants a good start by digging in lots of garden compost or commercially available soil improver to increase the soil's water-holding capacity. This will help drainage in wetter soils too. Plants bought in containers (as opposed to bare-root) won't grow into the surrounding soil for a few weeks, so need a reservoir of easily accessible water. Before planting, soak the root ball in a bucket of water until the air has bubbled out.

Then, dig your hole, at least 500mm (20in) from the base of the boundary to enable it to root into better soil away from footings and to give the roots space to grow. Sometimes it's hard to give plants enough water, so cut a plastic bottle in half, take off its lid and sink it into the soil, to act like a funnel, directing water to the roots.

This plastic bottle directs water down to the roots.

Supports or self-clinging

Some climbers like Virginia creepers (*Parthenocissus quinquefolia*), climbing hydrangea and ivies (*Hedera*) are self-clinging, and need only to be directed towards the boundary to pull themselves up. Others like roses, passion flowers (*Passiflora*) and honeysuckles require a support to wind around. Wires, fixed at 450mm (18in) intervals horizontally up the support, are a far better choice than trellis. Unless it's used carefully, trellis can spoil the look of a boundary and is unsuitable for many climbers. Wires, on the other hand, are discreet and versatile, running in any direction. They are also easier to remove, should it be necessary to maintain the boundary behind. Some climbers, such as clematis and honeysuckle, will weave in front and behind the wire, but where you are training climbers, try to avoid tucking stems behind the wire as it makes them difficult to move later.

Fixing vine eyes

Wires need to be held on a support with 100–150mm (4–6in) hooks which are screwed into the boundary, and are called 'vine eyes'. These hold the climber about 50mm (2in) away from the support, and allow air to circulate behind, helping to prevent fungal diseases, such as mildew. Always choose plastic-coated wire and tighten them in place using 'bolt tensioners' at the end of each horizontal wire. Or you can use vine eyes on their own to pin individual stems in place, tying the branches to each vine eye with soft twine.

good WORKING PRACTICE

When time is spent moving materials that are in the way or looking for tools, construction jobs become fraught, and the fun goes out of building them. This is why organising your tools and materials before starting any of the projects in this book is essential, enabling you to carry jobs out swiftly, safely and to a high standard.

Personal safety

Your own safety, and that of others, is the primary consideration when building any garden project. To protect yourself, wear strong gloves when handling materials with sharp or splintered edges such as stone, brick and timber, and always wear them when handling cement. Safety goggles are essential when cutting stone and bricks and should be combined with a mask when spray painting. One of the most common injuries occurs when tools or heavy materials fall on your feet, so always wear steel toecap boots. To protect your back, lift properly, facing the object as you pick it up with your knees bent and your back straight. Finally, don't overdo it. If you're not used to physical work, take your time and, if possible, persuade friends to help you. As with most gardening jobs, working with someone else always more than doubles the speed at which the job is done, especially when doing hard manual work, such as digging foundations or carrying materials.

Site safety

Because boundaries tend to be relatively large, you're going to have to bring a lot of materials into your garden. Make sure that access is easy by tying back shrubs and trees that would get in your way as materials are barrowed through and use planks of wood supported on bricks to ramp up low steps. Taking time to make the access to your garden as open as

Use planks to barrow up low steps.

possible will make carrying the materials easier and safer.

Treat moving materials as a separate job to the construction, stacking them in neat, stable piles near to where you need them. Doing this prevents unnecessary legwork during construction and means materials won't topple over.

If you or your neighbours have children and you are replacing a perimeter boundary, they must be considered at all times. To a child, a stack of bricks, power tools, chisels and hammers presents an irresistible opportunity for fun. So, ensure that tools are kept well out of their reach and if necessary cordon off your working area with a temporary plastic fence.

Always lift with your knees bent.

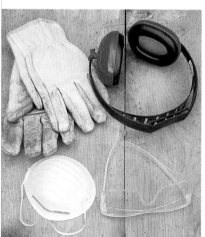

Safety equipment.

Safety at-a-glance

Always lift properly with your knees bent and your back straight.

Be sure to wear steel toecap boots.

When cutting stone and bricks always wear goggles.

Strong gloves must be worn when handling materials with sharp or splintered edges.

Keep all tools well out of reach of children and cordon off your working area with a temporary plastic fence.

Tools

The list of tools you need is included with each of the projects. If you don't own them, hire them – the extra cost is worth paying as it will make building much easier. If you hire tools, book them a few days before you need them along with any necessary attachments, such as saw blades and safety equipment. When they are delivered, read the instructions and practise how to use them.

Check that all the tools you need are in working order and at the end of each day clean and store them

Cleaning off a trowel at the end of the day.

away in a secure place where you can easily lay your hands on them the next day.

Organising your work

Give yourself plenty of room, so that you can work comfortably. Do this by allocating different parts of your garden to different jobs involved in the construction of your boundary. For example, create a space for a workbench that allows you to move freely around it especially if you are cutting timber. Allocate another for mixing mortar. This should be near where the sand is delivered, in an open spot that is easy to barrow to and away from, and where splashes of cement from the mixer won't cause any damage. For projects such as building trellis, screens and gates, you also need a space to lay them flat while you work. This can be a drive, patio or lawn, but should be as near as possible to their finished location.

As you work, stand back from the job regularly to check that string lines are level and in the correct place and to help you plan the next stage. The trick to building things well is to be methodical and give yourself plenty of time to enjoy what is a creative process and to make sure each stage is finished properly before moving on to the next.

The other thing to remember before cutting anything to length, whether it is timber, metal or stone, is the old adage – 'measure twice and cut once'.

Leaving the job

At the end of the day clean off tools – particularly those that have been used for concreting or bricklaying –

Place open bags of cement in bin liners.

before the cement dries hard. Open bags should be placed into a bin liner and brought into a shed or porch for the night. Protect concrete footings and walls built during the day as well as unopened bags of cement from rain with plastic sheets. It's also good practice to cover stacked bricks and blocks because mortar sticks to them more readily when they are dry. Cordon off any foundations with brightly coloured marker tape or cover over with timber boards and lock away tools and equipment.

Cordon off foundations with marker tape.

tools and EQUIPMENT

With the right tools, you're halfway towards getting the job done quickly and well. Some tools, such as spades, are a good investment as they are sure to be reused, while others can be hired for specific jobs. Here the tools have been split into categories: groundwork, masonry and bricklaying, and carpentry, and there is a section listing the tools most economical to hire.

Groundwork tools

Sledgehammer This long-handled and weighty hammer is a crude but very effective tool. Its uses range from simple demolition to driving fence spikes into the ground and tamping concrete around the base of posts.

Ground marking paint A water-based aerosol paint for marking out plans and fence lines on the ground. A good aid for visualising designs before starting work.

Bamboo canes Useful for setting out the features in a garden plan before construction starts.

Mattock This looks like a pick axe and can be used for digging, but it has a flat blade that is perfect for scooping soil from trenches. It also has a blade that is useful for chopping through old roots and breaking heavy clay soils.

Measuring tape This is useful for garden surveying and speeding up marking out a design on the ground.

Fencing bar/crow bar An iron bar used for making holes in the ground and breaking through buried stones.

Wheelbarrow An essential piece of kit used for all construction. Choose a model with a pneumatic tyre and a metal bucket. The place to buy is a building suppliers, as the barrows stocked by garden centres are often too weak for construction work.

Masonry and bricklaying tools

Bolster A steel chisel with a wide, blunt blade for cutting bricks, concrete blocks and stone.

Builders' line/string line A strong woven line for marking out levels when laying bricks or for the tops of fence posts. It can be tensioned to make straight lines.

Club hammer/lump hammer A heavy hammer for demolition and for driving a bolster when cutting bricks.

Level Enables walls and fences to be built perfectly upright. There are long ones for finding horizontal lines over a wide area, short ones for working in confined spaces, and 90° levels with two sets of bubbles used for positioning over the corner of a fence post to indicate if it leans to the left or to the right or forward to back.

Builders' pins These are pointed metal pegs that can be driven between bricks or into the ground for tying off a builders' line.

Pointing trowel This is a small triangular-shaped trowel used for smoothing the normal joints of brick work.

Bucket Essential for accurately measuring quantities of sand and cement by volume, tipping water and hand washing tools clean at the end of each day.

Mortar board A mortar board for brick laying or block laying is usually made from a square piece of plywood approximately 60 × 60cm (2 × 2ft). It acts as a place to pile mortar within reaching distance of where you are working and forms a convenient flat surface to load the trowel from.

Storey rod A gauge made from an off-cut of wood that is used to check that mortar joints in a wall are the correct depth. It is particularly useful when it comes to building walls with two skins because it helps to keep their joints at the same height as they are built.

Carpentry tools

Beetle A rustic mallet, traditionally carved from the branch of an elm tree. Tools such as this are no longer commonplace but are a joy to use as they can be weighted perfectly for their purpose and the person using them. However, an ordinary store-bought mallet would suffice.

Chisel Available in various sizes, chisels are used for cutting timber joints. For fencing joints, a 20mm (¾in) blade is fine. Keep the blade sharp and work with a wooden mallet – metal ones are hard to use accurately and will crack the chisel's handle.

Circular saw The ideal tool for cross-cutting timber to length and for cutting planks into strips. It comes with a metal guide bar (fence), which clips over the edge of the plank, keeping the blade straight. This saw is battery-powered, so you can use it away from a source of electricity, but it is less powerful. If you are cutting thick timber with access to electricity, hire an electric model.

Jigsaw A useful electric saw for cutting curved and straight lines. It comes with interchangeable blades for sawing timber, plastic and sheet metal. The trick to accurate cutting with a jigsaw is to look over its top at the blade while working. Doing this enables you to guide the saw more easily and adjust its position if it strays from a line.

Mallet A wooden hammering tool for knocking timber joints and fence posts into position without marking them and for driving wood chisels.

Panel saw An all-purpose saw for cutting timber to length.

Work bench Choose a model with a large top and clamps for holding materials while you work.

Residual Current Device (RCD) Sometimes known as a circuit breaker, an RCD is an essential piece of safety equipment for use with all electrical power tools. It can turn off the supply of electricity if it detects that the power cable has been cut or the tool developed a fault, thus reducing the risk of electrocution. The power tool is simply plugged into the RCD, which in turn is plugged into an electrical socket.

Router A power-tool with a spinning blade, used for bevelling the edges of timber boards. Different blades can be used to achieve a range of finishes.

Surform A useful tool used for planing timber. It has a blade reminiscent of a cheese grater – ideal for removing sharp edges from timber boards.
Try square This is a set square that is used for woodworking.

Hire equipment

Any tool can be hired, from screwdrivers up to tractor-mounted excavators, rented out on a daily rate. To save money, only hire tools as you need them and choose a hire firm that will deliver and collect the tools when you have finished with them. When hiring equipment with a petrol engine, such as a cement mixer or auger, check whether fuel is supplied and, if you don't own one already, hire a fuel can to keep it topped up.

All mechanical hire equipment comes with safety instructions and it is your responsibility to read them. However, safety equipment such as protective goggles, ear muffs and dust masks are often supplied separately.

Although hiring tools will make any job more expensive, they will save time and will reduce tedious or back-breaking work such as digging holes for fence posts or foundations.
Cement mixer Mixing concrete and cement by hand is a back-breaking job that a mechanical mixer will do for you. Always hire an electric mixer where there is a power supply as they are quieter than petrol models and easier to start.

Post hole spade An ingenious long-handled excavating tool for digging deep, steep-sided holes for fence posts. Inexpensive to hire and a real time saver.

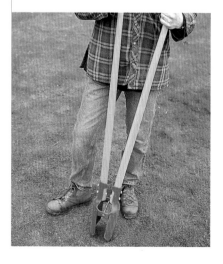

Paint sprayer An economical tool to hire that will save hours of brushwork (even days if you're painting trellis) and reduce the amount of paint you use. Always wear a mask.

Petrol auger The fastest way to dig a line of holes for fence posts is with one of these. As the blade turns it screws into the ground pushing out the soil. You have to be strong to use one alone, but most can be operated by two people.

Trenching spade A reinforced spade with a flat blade for digging straight-sided holes and foundations. Hire if your plans require lots of digging.

Turf remover Worth hiring if you are creating borders next to a boundary or making over a whole garden. This machine will save you the blisters and time it takes to cut away grass by hand.

Hardware

Decorative nails Thick iron nails with ornamental heads, which give a stud-work finish to gates. They can be bought in various lengths and rust proofed to prevent black stains from developing as the iron reacts to the timber. Because they have wide shanks, they need pilot holes to prevent the timber from splitting. To clamp lengths of timber together, use long nails and bend ends over.

Drainage pipe/agricultural line 100mm (4in) This collects water through holes in its side. It is laid underground in a bed of gravel or blue metal, and connects to a land drain. To carry water effectively, drainage pipes must be laid with a slope of 1cm (½in) for every 70cm (35in) in length.

Fencing spikes These are metal sockets for fixing fence posts. As well as spikes for hammering into soil, they can have plates or wings for bolting/setting in concrete and short wedge-shaped spikes, which are hammered down the sides of broken fence posts to repair them.

Hinges and latches There are many different types on the market and your choice will depend on whether you want them to be discreet or decorative. For outdoor use, though, always go for those protected with rustproof paint.

Fence spike driver A protective plastic block that is inserted into the socket of the fence spike while it is driven into the ground.

Staples C-shaped nails used for fixing wires and screen cladding to fences. Always choose galvanised staples as they won't rust.

Brick ties Loops or lengths of curved galvanised wire that are laid between courses and used to lock walls made of two independent skins of brick or blockwork together.

Using these tool lists

To save repetitive lists of tools appearing at the end of each project, only the necessary categories of equipment (masonry and bricklaying, for example) have been recorded. If any item from another section is also required to complete the project, it is listed individually. Any necessary hire equipment is also shown.

walls and edgings

planning for walls and edgings

When you visit the gardens of a stately home, inevitably many of the garden rooms are enclosed by venerable old walls. Long-lasting and solid, walls impart a feeling of permanence and reassurance. Edgings are another feature often seen in such locations and are very easy to construct in your own garden. They can be purely decorative or perform a function as well, such as retaining a flexible surface such as gravel.

Function and style This book concentrates on low walls as they are most manageable for DIY work and do not usually require planning permission. The maximum wall height allowed before regulations apply is usually between 600mm and 1m (2 and 3ft), but always check with your local council. Low walls are most suited to front gardens or low internal boundaries. Many also make good retaining walls, suitable for creating terraces on sloping sites.

The materials used for walls are many, from bricks, stone and timber to railway sleepers and gabions. Which you use depends on budget, ability and the style that suits your space. The larger the basic element of the wall, the quicker it is and the less skill it takes to build. Large units are also cheaper. On the other hand, small units are more versatile for creating curved and serpentine boundaries.

The main purpose of edgings is to retain a flexible surface. They often act as mini retaining walls, holding back soil in flower beds or vegetable plots from adjacent paths.

Although not highly visible, it is important to get the detail of edgings just right as they must look good with the style of paving that they border and form a common link with the other materials in the garden.

Design choices Walls are either formal or informal in appearance, depending on the material used. A smooth rendered wall coated with a glossy paint has a crisp, formal look, whereas a random stacked stone wall with plants cascading from it presents a much softer, natural face.

Stone laid in courses can look architectural enough to blend with buildings but still soft enough to harmonise with plantings. A soil-filled dry stone wall is more like a hedge than a wall, because of the way it becomes festooned with plants. Rendered and brick walls both blend effortlessly

Stone wall of various heights.

Old-style garden wall.

A wall to harmonize with the house.

Soil-filled dry stone wall.

One of the most common uses for walls and edgings is to hold back soil. They create interesting internal divides, separating a path from a gravel garden (top right) or retaining the soil adjacent to a stepped path (above). Low walls also make excellent seats and can be used as shelves for pots of plants (top left).

Country meets classical – the undulating face of this dry stacked stone wall contrasts beautifully with the straight-edged pier.

with houses, but depending on the finish and colour of the brick or render, can enhance a cottage garden, city garden or even a Mediterranean theme. There are plenty of home-spun details that give a wall a personal character, such as incorporating bottle ends during construction.

A low wall is the strongest of any physical enclosure, even if it is no more than 1m (3ft) high. This is especially the case around a patio because you are normally sitting down, and anything solid that's higher could make the space feel oppressive.

Edgings must be fit for their purpose. For example, a timber edging should be at least 25mm (1in) thick if it is to be bent into curves but not break. (Do this by making saw cuts on one face.) Cost will also have an influence on design choices, with bricks being more expensive and slower to lay than timber edgings.

Types of wall Brick – there are thousands of different types of brick and various patterns in which to lay them. Warm and established in character, brick works well near houses. There are also special bricks for coping and corners.

Rendered – render can give an ugly wall a new lease of life, or give an economically made concrete block wall a more attractive finish. It's also a chameleon – leave rough for a mud wall look, smooth for a crisp urban finish, or undulate the surface to replicate the appearance of the rendered stone walls of a Moroccan villa.

Sleeper – sleepers are popular for walls, steps and paths. They are straightforward to lay and their warm, chunky look is suitable for all styles of gardens.

Stone – sandstone is the most common type used for walling. It can be bought as random stone or 'dressed' boulders, that is, shaped into blocks. Dressed stone creates a wall with regimented courses and is easier to lay, while random stone has a more rustic appearance.

Gabions – gabions have long been used to shore up banks and the sides of watercourses. In a garden setting, they can be filled with interesting types and colours of stone, such as slate and dressed stone.

Types of edging Pressure-treated timber path edging is readily available and can be laid to curves. Thicker, 75mm (3in) timber boards look good laid next to straight brick pathways, since they are in the correct proportion to the width of the bricks. Bricks themselves are probably the ideal edging unit, and are easy to lay to curves. Alternatives include concrete pavers, large pebbles and metal strips.

This rendered concrete block wall (above left), painted in warm terracotta is the perfect backdrop to the cypress and citrus trees in this Mediterranean themed garden. The concrete block raised pond (above right) is softened with render and painted vibrant red. It has an almost plastic look and makes a lively contrast to the soft planting at its base and the curly-leaved sedge in the water.

Rammed earth wall.

Gabion wall.

Contoured stone.

Chunky stacked timber sleepers.

sleeper WALL

Railway sleepers have a myriad of uses in the garden, and make good-looking low walls that are quick to build. Their wood is warm and chunky, and when used for a retaining wall it doubles up as a seat and somewhere to display pots of flowers.

1 Mark out the position of the sleeper wall and excavate roughly 300mm (12in) of soil from the bank to give you room to work behind. Level and firm the ground before laying the bottom course of sleepers on edge. The sleepers then act as a guide helping you to locate the positions of the 50 x 50mm (2 x 2in) timber pegs that support them. Hammer one peg into the soil every metre (3ft) driving it in until it is about 75mm (3in) lower than the finished height of the wall. (When cutting pegs to length, ensure that the points on their ends are even otherwise they will tilt when driven into the ground.)

2 Where the sleepers meet at a corner, mark and cut them with a saw so that they fit perfectly together. To ensure that your cuts are straight, mark right around the sleeper to guide you as you saw through the timber. As you stack the sleepers back in position, make sure the

MATERIALS

New sleepers

500 × 50 × 50mm
(20 × 2 × 2in) treated
timber pegs

100mm (4in) screws

TOOLS

Masonry and bricklaying tools

Drill

1 Having laid the first course of sleepers on edge and back-filled with soil, hammer pegs behind them as a support.

2 Next mark and cut the sleepers that meet at a corner. Doing this gives a much neater finish than a butt-join.

KNOW YOUR MATERIALS

Because reclaimed railway sleepers are impregnated with tar, they are unsuitable for use as seats or any place where you will brush against them and pick up the tar on your clothes. For this reason it is much better to buy new sleepers that are made from treated pine, because they are clean and can either be painted to match the colour scheme in your garden or left to turn sun-bleached white, as seen in this project. If you do choose to use reclaimed sleepers, always buy grade 1 sleepers (they are graded 1–3 according to their condition). Avoid any with gummy patches of tar, and cover their tops with strips of decking.

3 Once the sleepers are in position, drive a screw through the back of each peg into the sleepers. Finally, back-fill with soil and plant.

joints between the second course of sleepers don't overlap with the first, so that the two courses lock together.

3 With the sleepers back in their final position, check that they are upright with a spirit level and fix them in place with 100mm (4in) screws driven through the back of each peg into the sleepers. Back-fill with soil and plant behind the wall. Then lay decking or gravel at its base.

Drainage

Joints in sleeper walls aren't sealed and allow excess water in the soil behind them to escape. Therefore they don't need extra drainage holes or pipes to take the water away.

Tall retaining walls

For walls above knee height, increase width and strength by laying the sleepers on their sides and use the same size timber as posts concreted into the ground. Use galvanised bolts to hold them together. Also remember to check with your local council regarding regulations.

soil-filled STONE WALL

A stone wall is the ultimate boundary as every single rock is unique and no two people would lay them in the same way. As well as the qualities of warmth and inherent charm offered by the stone, practically speaking you cannot get a more solid boundary than this.

1   This wall differs from the rustic stone walls used for stock enclosure in country areas as soil is packed into its centre. This means plants can root into it, creating a colourful garden feature as well as a boundary.

Mark out the base of the wall on the ground using sand or ground marking paint. Make the width 600mm (24in) and for strength give it a curved or serpentine shape. Then use a spade to dig out the top 150mm (6in) of soil to give you a firm even base to build from. Pile the soil close by for use later on.

2   Before building, organise your working area by laying out as many stones as space allows so that you can quickly pick and choose between them. The rule is that once a stone is picked up, it should never be put down unless it's in the wall. Although this is sound advice, you won't get it right every time, even after practice. However, it

MATERIALS

Dressed stone blocks

Topsoil

Plants

Soaker/micro irrigation hose

TOOLS

Masonry and bricklaying tools

Spade

Length of wood

Brick hammer

1 Having decided upon the shape and size of your wall, mark out the base on the ground and dig out 150mm (6in) of soil.

2 Lay the first course of stones along both edges of the footing, fitting them snugly together.

KNOW YOUR MATERIALS

There is an old saying 'stone for walls doesn't travel far' that is as true today as it ever was because the cost of haulage is high. So, when it comes to choosing stone, always source it locally to save money and to ensure that it blends with your surroundings. This is less of an issue if you live in a city where its use in residential buildings is limited, but, if you do have stone in your garden already, try to match the wall with it, otherwise there is a danger that your garden will become a hotchpotch of different materials that lack harmony. Always ask your supplier to help quantify how much stone you'll need, as the amount will vary according to the size and type of stone used.

does make a lot of sense to do as much sorting and choosing by eye as possible. Start the wall by placing stones of similar height along both edges of the wall, leaving space between them.

Note: the space between the stones equates to the width of the footing mentioned in step 1.

3   Fill the space between the stones with the soil from the footing, packing it down firmly with a length of wood. I like grass to grow from the sides of soil-filled stone walls, as it softens the edges of the stone, but if you prefer a crisper appearance, weed out any grass roots or use weed-free topsoil instead.

4   Lay the second row of stones, staggering the joints with the first and sloping the face of each stone gently towards the centre of the wall – aim for a slope of about 10° from vertical. If each course is laid in this way, the wall will be A-shaped in profile, which increases its strength as the two faces prop each other up. When

laying this course, deliberately leave planting gaps every few stones. (Putting the plants in at this level gives them room to trail.) To further strengthen the wall, bridge long stones every metre or so between the two faces to tie them together. Then pack with soil as before.

5   As you build, try to make the ends of the stones fit snugly together (except where you want planting holes). Any sharp points or lumps can be chipped away with a brick hammer or a bolster.

6   If any of the stones rock or where the gaps are large, use slivers of stone to wedge them in place or bridge large spaces. If you don't have enough small pieces, go to step 8 and cut a few coping stones to create some.

Another method of locking the stones together is to use mortar between the gaps on the inside of the wall where it won't be seen. It is particularly useful for fixing stones with difficult rounded edges and for giving stonework adjacent to entrances rigidity. Use a 4:1 sharp

3 Ram soil between the stones using a length of wood. This packs them in position and creates a firm base.

4 When laying the second course, place long stones between the two faces to further strengthen the wall.

5 To fit the stones snugly together, chip off sharp points or lumps from the ends, using a brick hammer or bolster.

sand and cement mix and work into the gaps between the stones with a pointing trowel (see page 287).

7 Before planting, stand the pots in a bucket of water to ensure that the root ball is wet. Remove the plants from their containers and wedge them between the stones, firming soil from the heart of the wall around them. In this wall house leeks, sedums, sea pinks and saxifrages were planted in sweeps and drifts as though they had colonised the gaps between the stones over time to give the wall an established appearance. For a lush effect, you could use low-growing grasses such as grey-leaved fescues and yellow sedges, or a traditional alpine mix including blue aubretia and yellow alyssum. Alternatively, plant grass seed between the stones for a natural country bank look.

8 Continue to build up the wall, leaving gaps for planting as you go along, tying the two faces together with long stones as before and packing with soil. For the final course, don't use any long stones and simply pack with soil. This allows enough space for a soaker hose to be placed in the top (see pages 362-3 for details). To make a coping, cut the stone into 30–50mm (1–2in) slices by laying it on the ground and striking with a club hammer and bolster along the strata. It is easy to do if you cut the stones in half and half again until they are the width you want. If you try and take off the slices from one side of the stone only, the tensions inside it will cause it to fracture.

Alternative ideas

For stability, a soil-filled stone wall shouldn't be over 1.2m (4ft) high but if you want to build one as a perimeter boundary for privacy you can adjust the design so that a hedge can be grown in the top. Do this by making the wall squatter and wider, about 0.6 × 1m (2 × 3ft). Good plants for this are trees such as hawthorn (*Crataegus*) and elder (*Sambucus*) with scented honeysuckle (*Lonicera*) scrambling through it.

6 Use slivers of stone to fill any gaps and to wedge any stones that rock or move firmly into the wall.

7 When laying the second course, leave planting gaps between the stones. Firm plant roots into the soil in the centre of the wall.

8 Having laid the final course, split the stone to make a coping, using a club hammer and bolster.

block and RENDER

The vivid paint colours in modern garden designs such as Mediterranean blue and earthy ochre have given the rendered wall a new lease of life. Once again held in regard for their smart, flawless finish, they are surprisingly easy to build.

1   Use ground marking paint to mark out the position of the wall on the soil and lay the foundations (see pages 272-5 for details on specification). Screed the surface of the concrete flat with a length of timber and allow at least two days drying time before building to allow the concrete to harden fully.

2   Organise your building area by stacking blocks within easy reach of the face of the wall and set a timber mortar board on a few blocks next to where you're starting. If you are building a curved wall (like the one pictured right), cut some of the blocks in half by sitting them on soft ground and striking them with a club hammer and bolster right around where you want to make the cut. Making the blocks smaller in this way allows you to create a smoother arc on the curve.

MATERIALS

High density concrete blocks

Blue metal

Cement

Sand

12mm (½in) plastic pipe for weep holes

Bitumastic sealant

Plastic damp-proof membrane

TOOLS

Groundwork tools

Masonry and bricklaying tools

Metal and plastic float

Timber mortar board

1 Once you have marked the position of the wall on the ground, lay the foundations. Use timber to screed the surface of the concrete flat.

2 Use a club hammer and bolster to cut some blocks in half. Having smaller blocks allows you to create a smoother arc on the curve.

KNOW YOUR MATERIALS

Render is tremendously versatile and can be used to achieve dozens of effects. Smoothed and painted, it can have all the shine of plastic, or if left rough with the lines of the float still showing, it has the appearance of rammed soil. For a weathered stone effect, smooth the render into gentle undulations and coat with earthy coloured paint. The coping also affects the look. Bricks and polished paving stones are crisp and clean, while timber decking creates a seaside feel. For a jungle look, round the render over the top of the wall, creating the illusion that the wall is made from mud. Give it a lick of zingy ginger paint and plant large-leaved palms and grasses behind.

3 Laying concrete blocks is easier than laying bricks, but the principles are exactly the same. Work from the face side of the wall building the ends of the straight sections first and running taut lines between them to give you the level of each course (see page 278 for details). Then build up the curves using a level and matching in with the straight sections. Start by mixing a 6:1 sand and cement mix mortar and lay the blocks onto this, tapping down until the joints are 10mm (½in) deep and the blocks are level. Buttering the end of each block with mortar (see page 279 for details) and pushing it up against the last is the correct way to lay them, but if you struggle doing this, use a pointing trowel to fill the gaps afterwards.

4 On the second course, angle plastic weep holes downwards from the back of the wall. These drainage pipes should be set into the mortar between the blocks every 900mm (3ft). Cut the pipe so that the ends protrude at least 20mm (¾in) beyond the face of the wall to make space for the render. Alternatively lay a drainage pipe along the back of the wall (see page 277 for details).

5 As long as the joints of each course are staggered your pointing doesn't matter. In fact, the rougher it is, the better key it will give the render. For strength though, the wall must be level both across the tops of the blocks and up the face of the wall. Check this by placing a level up against its face as you build.

6 When the wall is complete, leave for two days to dry. Then mix up a render consisting of 3:1:1 sand, cement and lime (make this slightly stiffer than the mortar used in the blockwork). Place a flat board at the foot of the wall to catch any dropped render and working up from the base, smear the render onto the wall using a metal float. Aim to keep the depth of the render roughly 10mm (½in). To create an edge to work to at the top of the wall, hold a length of wood or another float so that

3 *When the straight sections have been laid, butter the ends of the half blocks for the curves and push them up against the last.*

4 *On the second course, create weep holes by setting drainage pipes into the mortar between the blocks every 900mm (3ft).*

5 *As you go along, keep checking that the wall is level across the tops of the blocks and up the face of the wall.*

it overhangs the face of the wall by 10mm (½in). This allows you to scrape the render off the float and ensures that its top is flush with the top of the wall.

7 When the wall is complete, allow to dry for 20 minutes or so, before smoothing over the surface with a plastic float. For a really flat finish, work the float in a circular motion until all of the dips and lines are filled. Then, smooth around the drainage weep holes with a pointing trowel. Alternatively, for an earthy Mediterranean effect, just take off the worst peaks.

8 Allow the render 24 hours to dry before laying the coping stones on top of the wall. These sit on a bed of 6:1 sand and cement mortar. Lay them in a similar way to the blocks, tapping them so that they are level, but make sure to catch any mortar that oozes over the face of the wall with a trowel. Then fill the gaps between them with mortar. Paint the wall and lay gravel to hide the drainage holes. At the back of the wall, paint

bitumastic sealant around the weep holes and line with plastic damp-proof membrane (see page 277), cutting slits for each hole. Back-fill with washed gravel to a depth of 300mm (12in) separating it from the soil with geotextile (this stops fine particles blocking up the drainage holes). Then back-fill with soil to the top of the wall and plant.

Applying render

If you are building a rendered wall next to a border, ensure that the base of the render sits a few centimetres (about an inch) above the soil level. This prevents it from soaking up groundwater, which leads to algae forming on the face of the wall and increases the risk of frost damage. On curved sections of a wall, mark a neat line along the base of the render with a pointing trowel and scrape it away before it dries. On straight walls, attach a length of 10mm (½in) timber batten with screws just above soil level height, then apply the render using the timber as a base. Once dry, the wood can be removed.

6 To ensure that the top of the render is flush with the top of the wall, hold a float so that it overhangs the face of the wall.

7 After the wall is complete, smooth over the surface with a plastic float and use a pointing trowel to smooth around the weep holes.

8 Having left the render to dry, lay the coping stones on top of the wall, tapping them down so they are level.

gabion WALL

Traditionally the materials used in sea defences, stone-filled steel cages suit modern garden designs very well, striking the required balance between the natural and the built environments. They are also easy to build and an economical way to create a sturdy, low wall.

1 | This gabion wall is built over a clinker driveway so the ground was already compact and firm. If you are building a gabion wall at the back of the border, excavate the top 100–150mm (4–6in) of soil and level to create a firm base. Assemble the gabions by winding the helical wire spirals along each edge, leaving one panel open for the lid. Set the gabions in position with their lids opening towards the face side and so that the helical spiral on their corners overlaps. Then, fix the gabions together by pushing locking pins (straight metal rods with a hooked end) down through the overlapping wire spiral on the corners. Half-fill the face of the cages with stone, laying them in neat, tightly fitting courses.

2 | The stone used in this project is green slate, which is relatively expensive. This is why it is only used to face the

MATERIALS

400 × 400 × 1000mm (16 × 16 × 39½in) gabions

1000mm (39½in) and 400mm (16in) helical wire spirals

400mm (16in) locking pins

Green slate

Clinker infill/any aggregate

400mm (16in) bracing ties

TOOLS

Geotextile sheets – if using a granular infill

1 Once you have positioned the gabions and fixed them together, half-fill with stones, laying them neatly and as close together as possible.

2 To cut costs on materials, merely use the stone to face the gabion and shovel unwanted material, such as clinker, into sheets of geotextile.

KNOW YOUR MATERIALS

Gabions can be ordered direct from the manufacturer in any size. They are an ideal solution where you want walls and have a lot of material that you want to get rid of, such as stone or broken concrete. The look is dependent on what the inside of the cages are filled with and even they can be covered in timber. Another variation is to use soil as the infill behind the facing stone and plant saplings out through the mesh to soften the face of the stone. Although the sides of the gabions can be held together with wire ties, it is more convenient to use helical wire spirals. These are stronger, can be quickly wound into position and, unlike wire ties, don't leave any sharp edges.

3 As each gabion is filled, secure the lid using spiral ties and lock the gabions by bending over the ends of the spiral wires.

cages. Hidden behind it is a mixture of clinker, broken bricks and sand inside geotextile sheets, which prevent the finer particles from escaping. Gabions can be filled with any stone or aggregate, as long as it is frost-proof and packed in firmly. When you've half-filled the gabion, brace the front and back of the cage with bracing ties every four meshes to prevent the face of the gabion bowing.

3   Fill the cages, firming the infill as you go. Then fold the geotextile sheet over the top, close the lid and seal by winding the spiral wire, lacing along its front edge and sides. Lock the gabions by bending over the ends of the spiral wires (this also makes their sharp ends safe). Repeat the process and then on the final course, cover the geotextile with a layer of stone so that it is hidden.

Planting

To give a gabion wall a 'green' face, pack soil between the courses of stones and plant drought-tolerant plants, such as sedum. (see pages 362-3 for details on watering.)

fences

planning for fences

Fences have the important function of demarcation, but they don't need to be boring. Not only are there lots of different types of fences, but also many variations in style that each can adopt. Timber is the most common type of garden boundary. It is infinitely versatile, weathers well and looks natural in a garden setting. Whether made from panels or slats of wood, it creates a neat, rhythmical line that complements the softer, less formal shape of borders.

Function and style Timber has been used in gardens for thousands of years, because it is easy to work with, long-lasting and integrates with the garden as it ages. Depending on the type of fence, wood lends itself to large perimeter boundaries or lighter internal divides. Truly adaptable, it can be a defence against trespassers or an enclosure to keep children in, or an inviting front garden picket that beckons visitors with a glimpse of the garden.

The main choice is whether to make fences from scratch, cutting timber posts and planks exactly to your own design, or to buy in simpler panel form. There are advantages to each – a home-made version will be perfectly customised to your garden and taste, whereas panel fences are quicker and simpler to erect.

The style is often dictated by the construction methods, for example whether you are using metal brackets or linking the wood with more rustic interlocking mortice joints. The more craft that goes into the fence, the more beautiful it can be. If you are looking for an opportunity for creativity, go for a picket fence. There are infinite possibilities for the shape of the uprights, from Gothic points to arrowheads, as well as any new design of your own.

Design choices One of the first questions you should ask is whether the fence is to be a physical enclosure, so you can see through it or over it but it stops you in your tracks, or a visual enclosure, creating a total screen from the outside world. For example, a picket fence or a low post and rail offers physical enclosure without blocking views or lowering light levels, unlike a close board fence.

In a countryside setting there are often opportunities for incorporating the surrounding landscape into the

A timber pole divide.

Close board fence.

Living willow fence.

Rustic pole fence.

Climbing plants can really spruce up a fence (top left), their foliage blending the timber with the garden. If it is contrast you're after, paint effects, such as black wood stain with acid green paint (top right) make a zingy colour combination. For decoration (above), an arrow-topped picket fence combined with an ornamental arch creates a façade with style.

Hardwood post and rail fences are charming and long lasting – useful for both perimeter and internal divides.

garden, in which case you want a fence that subtly demarcates your land without detracting from the view. A post and rail is not only see-through but adds charm also. On the other hand, in an exposed area or a rural setting you may want a boundary that makes you feel safe and says 'keep out' while providing seclusion, and the best option for this is a close board fence.

Both fences could work as well in a city or suburban environment, but here there are more opportunities for modern twists with woodstains or claddings. Timber boundaries will always be in vogue because of the way they allow you to ring the changes, whether with a fresh paint or by tying in with decking for a modern, Scandinavian look. Dripping with roses and clematis, and allowed to bleach in the sun, they can look old-fashioned or be planed and painted to give a modern, metallic finish.

Types of fencing Panel – this is popularly sold in 1.8 x 1.8m (6 x 6ft) units that are economical to buy and fairly simple to construct, because they go up in 1.8m (6ft) chunks and are held in the ground by fence posts on either side. The more you pay, the better the timber, construction and the detailing of the panel. Bottom of the range panels

tend to become warped over time and really need to be clothed and hidden by plants. You have a choice of wood or concrete gravel boards and posts.

Hit-and-miss – when viewed straight on, this double-faced fence appears solid, but when looked at from the side, has gaps to allow the breeze to filter through it, making it ideal for a windy, exposed situation.

Post and rail – this is a very simple enclosure, and depending on the wood used and the finish, it can have a modern or country look. It can be charming when the flowerheads of low perennials poke through the gaps.

Close board – the effect is like a well-made panel fence, but in fact, it's constructed from individual planks of timber nailed to a post and rail frame. Because it's made from separate timbers, it's easy to modify, say to avoid the branches of a tree or to follow curved or sloping ground. Like a panel fence it is easily painted and embellished with decorative finials and capping rails. Paling fences are an example of close board fencing.

Picket – these fences have bags of charm because they are architectural enough to pick up details in houses, but open and airy enough to allow plants to grow through. Most often used for front gardens, but perhaps under-used as internal divides, such as around a vegetable patch.

The downside of solid fences is that they block out light, making the conditions on their lea side cold and shady. Where possible, it is much better to use fences with gaps between their spars, such as this hit and miss palisade (top left) or diamond-crossed fencing (top right). In more clement growing conditions, plants will happily fill the gaps and even billow through their sides.

Arrowhead picket.

Hexagon picket.

Chestnut pole palisade.

Wattle hurdle.

post and RAIL

A split chestnut or hardwood post and rail fence creates a rustic-looking divide that harmonises with meadow areas, and cottage and prairie-style gardens. The twisted honey-coloured wood makes a see-through frame for borders in winter that gradually fills with flowering plants through the summer.

MATERIALS

1.8m (6ft) chestnut posts or hardwood logs or sleepers; or treated pine posts

TOOLS

Carpentry tools

Masonry and bricklaying tools

Billhook or axe

Drill

1 | The height of the posts and the length of the rails depend on the location of the boundary. In a large garden cutting down the posts and rails isn't necessary. However, in most gardens it is a good idea to cut down the posts and rails, using a panel saw, into 1.2m (4ft) lengths, to produce a scaled down version. To mark the positions of the rails on the fence posts, mock up the fence flat on the ground, moving the rails up and down until they look right. I made the centre of the rails 160mm (6½in) and 500mm (20in) down from the top of the fence post. Make the joints for the rails about 75mm (3in) long and 25mm (1in) wide, drilling out as much wood as possible before chiselling them square.

2 | Cut the rails to length if necessary and sharpen their ends using a billhook or axe (resting them over a block

1 Make mortice joints in the posts by first drilling out as much wood as possible and removing the rest with a chisel.

2 Once the rails have been cut to length, rest them on a block of timber or a tree stump and use a billhook or an axe to sharpen their ends.

KNOW YOUR MATERIALS
Chestnut excels as post and rail fencing. This is due to the twisted and curved nature of the timber, which creates a boundary with a soft, wavy outline that is ideal for informal styles of garden. Alternatively, buy pre-morticed square 750mm (30in) hardwood posts to create a more formal post and rail fence. Recycled timbers are readily available from demolition yards.

3 Use a sledgehammer to drive the posts into the ground, having hooked the rails between the two posts.

of timber or a tree stump is the easiest way to do this). Overlap inside the fence posts making what's called a 'scarf joint'. This gives the rail a neat finish – especially if you sharpen the opposite side of each end as shown. Also sharpen the ends of the post into points.

3 Use a sledgehammer to drive the first post into the ground, checking by eye that it is upright. Take another post, position it and hook rails between the two. They don't need to be tight, as they will be pushed into the joints as you hammer the second post into the ground. Repeat the process right along the fence run. An option at each end is to attach two rails, angling them down from the fence into the soil to give extra support.

Chestnut posts have a remarkable ability to resist the weather and won't rot in above-ground positions for decades. However, it is wise to give the posts extra protection and the best way of doing this is to dip their bases in wood preservative before hammering them into the ground.

post and PANEL

Painted in gentle, hazy blue, this line of dome-topped panel fencing makes the perfect backdrop to a seaside garden. Its straight, crisp lines echo those of the deck and contrast beautifully with the pebbles and large, tropical palms.

1 Most panels have been treated with a timber preservative as part of their manufacture but because the colours are often so lurid, you'll need to paint them anyway. It is a good idea to do this before you build the fence, as it is easier to get into nooks and crannies on both sides without having to step on your own, or neighbours', borders. It also allows you to catch the drips of paint that run from one side of the fence to the other.

2 Run a taut string along the ground to mark out the front of the fence and level out any undulations in the ground. This is necessary because panel fences, particularly those with domed or concave tops, look best when they are all level. If you are building your fence on a slope and have a slight rise along your fence line, you can raise the height of the fence at the bottom of the slope by fixing an

MATERIALS

Dome-topped fence panels

Paint

Pressure-treated 100mm (4in) wooden post and ball-shaped caps

Fence spikes

1.8m (6ft) gravel boards

380mm (15in) wooden pegs

TOOLS

Masonry and bricklaying tools

Fence post driver

Drill

1 Start by painting the panels before erecting them, so that you can get into all the nooks and crannies with ease.

2 Having marked out the front of the fence and levelled the ground, hammer in the first fence spike, making sure it is upright.

KNOW YOUR MATERIALS

There are hundreds of different styles of panel fence, ranging from larch to bamboo and willow panels held in a timber frame. The rule is the more you pay, the more robust the panels will be, and the more thought and time will have gone into their detailing and design. The panels used in this project are made up of two lines of overlapping boards with a 20mm (¾in) gap between them. The gap is small enough to maintain privacy but still allows air to filter through the fence, reducing turbulence on its lea side and buffeting when wind speeds are high (for further information see page 264). For an alternative look, use square or concave-topped panels.

extra gravel board beneath it, while setting the gravel board into the soil at the top. As well as extra gravel boards you'll need longer fence posts for the down-slope end of the fence. Starting at one end of the run, hammer in the first fence spike, ensuring that it is upright and parallel with the line (see page 273 for extra details).

3 Put the first post into the top of the spike, checking that the post is upright with a spirit level as you tighten the bolts. To find the position of the next post spike, either get someone to prop the panel against the first post, or lay the panel flat on the ground using its base as a guide. Because the width of the panels varies, it is always best to measure the distance between posts with the panel that will go between them. Then hammer the next fence spike into the ground. Repeat steps 1, 2 and 3 until the fence has reached the required length.

4 To save the awkward and time-consuming job of sawing the post tops level after the fence is built, use a straight-edged plank to bridge between the top of each fence spike and check their heights with a spirit level. If they are different, tap them down with a sledgehammer, then insert the fence post and tighten.

5 Gravel boards sit below the fence panels, stopping them from coming into contact with the soil and rotting. They also allow you to pile soil against the base of the fence to fill any hollows and even out the soil level. Because they are in contact with the soil, they will rot first, so should always be fixed separately to the panel to allow easy replacing. Do this by centring each gravel board between the fence spikes and hammering three 380mm (15in) treated wooden pegs into the ground alongside the board. To get the longest life out of your gravel boards use treated pine here too.

6 Using a drill, fix the gravel board to the post with two screws. As you work along the row, check that each board is fixed at the same height with a spirit level or

3 Lay the panel flat on the ground using its base as a guide. Then hammer the next fence spike into the ground.

4 Rest a straight-edged plank between the top of each fence spike and check that they are level. Tap them down if necessary.

5 To fix gravel boards to the bottom of the fence, first hammer a treated wooden peg into the ground beside the fence spike.

by running a taut string line between the two end posts to mark their height.

7 Fix panels in place by resting them on top of the gravel boards and screwing diagonally through their sides into the posts. Use three screws spaced evenly down the side of each panel, pilot drilling their holes first. Then, to protect the tops of the post from the weather, nail fence caps to the tops of the posts.

8 Dig over the border in front of the fence, adding extra soil and compost to conceal the metal spikes before planting.

Disguising fence spikes

Because metal fence spikes don't absorb paint as well as the timber in a fence, they are difficult to disguise. The way round this is to either plant an evergreen shrub or perennial in front of them or to bury them beneath the soil. The burying technique works best when the soil on both sides of the fence is raised, or excavated and back-filled after the fence is built.

Replacing broken fence posts

The weakest part of a panel fence, and the most likely to succumb to rot, is where the fence posts come into contact with the soil. It is at this point that the fence will break during strong winds, causing it to list or fall over.

When fence spikes have been used, a broken post is easily unbolted and replaced, but where posts are concreted in, it is almost impossible to pull the broken stump out from the concrete footing. By far the easiest option is to cut off the post at ground level and use a repair spike (these are similar to the fence spikes used in the above project, but with a shorter point). The spike is driven between the remains of the rotten post and the concrete that surrounds it, and provides a socket to hold the replacement post. Always use treated pine that is recommended for use below ground level to avoid problems with timber posts rotting.

6 Having checked that each gravel board is at the same height, screw the board to the post using a drill.

7 Next fix the painted panels by resting them on top of the gravel boards and screwing diagonally into the posts.

8 Finally, dig over the soil in front of your fence, adding extra soil and compost to hide the metal spikes before planting.

close board FENCING

The close board fence combines elegant, regimented lines with strength and rhythm, created by the repeated overlapping boards and arris rails. It is structurally very strong, and it will take the weight of large climbers and trained fruit trees.

1 | The ends of each arris rail have a notch of wood removed from them that corresponds to a similar notch cut in the posts, creating a half-lap joint. This joint gives the fence extra strength and brings the face of the arris rails in line with the face of the posts, so that the feather-edge boards form one continuous line running the length of the fence. To create the notch in the arris rails, lay them with their widest face down and make a saw cut 50mm (2in) in from the ends and 25mm (¾in) deep. Then, starting from the end of the arris, chisel back to the saw cut, removing the uppermost triangle of wood. Chiselling can be made easier and more accurate by making two or three extra saw cuts in from the end.

2 | To make the notch in the fence posts, first mark in pencil the tops and bottoms of the arris rails. The top rail should be 300mm (12in) from the top of the post, the bottom

MATERIALS

Triangular arris rail

100 × 100mm (4 × 4in) posts and 3m (10ft) long feather-edge boards

75mm (3in) galvanised nails

Concrete

150mm (6in) gravel boards

50mm (2in) nails

Post caps and cover strips

TOOLS

Carpentry tools

Groundwork tools

Masonry and bricklaying tools

1 Once you have made a saw cut in the arris rail, chisel back to the cut removing the uppermost triangle of wood.

2 Having marked the tops and bottoms of the arris rails onto the post and used a circular saw to cut along the lines, chisel out the wood.

KNOW YOUR MATERIALS

A close board fence consists of feather-edge boards nailed to horizontal lengths of timber called arris rails, which in turn are fixed to fence posts. As all of the components fit together like a kit, the height of the fence and the distribution of the fence posts can be tweaked to avoid obstacles such as tree roots and branches, or to enclose difficult spaces. Usually, the posts are set at 3m (10ft) centres because the arris rails are sold in 6m (20ft) lengths, and cutting them in half makes them easy to handle and avoids waste. There are two types of arris rail, triangular (used here) and square with a bevelled top. Of the two, the triangular shape has more graceful lines.

rail 1.6m (5ft 5in) from the top, and the middle rail equidistant between the two. The quickest way to cut out the notches is to lay the posts in line on a flat surface (to level up uneven ground, lay down two lengths of timber first, and sit the posts on these). Use a circular saw, with the blade angled at 45 degrees and set to a depth of 25mm (¾in), to cut along the lines, marking the top and bottom of the arris rails. Ensure that the blade is angled towards the centre of the rail, otherwise the joints will be the wrong shape. Then chisel out between the saw cuts.

3 Dig holes 600mm (24in) deep for the end posts and prop in position holding them firmly with wooden stakes driven into the ground. Then run two string lines along the faces of the posts, one at the top and one at the bottom. Mark the position of intermediate fence posts using an arris rail as a spacing guide and dig out 600mm (24in) holes for these. Place a post in each hole and check that it is wide enough to allow the post to touch the lines, marking the front of the fence and the correct depth.

4 Starting at one end and working on one post at a time, fix the bottom arris rail onto the post with a 75mm (3in) nail to ensure the correct spacing. Move the post so that its face comes up to the string lines. Check that the post is at the correct height and upright using a spirit level. Prop in position and back-fill around the post with concrete. Once all the posts are in place, check them for position and level and adjust if necessary, then leave for at least 24 hours to allow the concrete to set.

5 Use 75mm (3in) nails to fix the remaining arris rails to the posts. Because the concrete won't be fully hardened, support the back of each post with a length of sturdy timber while you hammer, or better still, get someone to hold the post steady for you.

6 The position of the gravel board is 50mm (2in) below the bottom arris rail. Mark this position with a line on each post and nail the gravel boards just below it. Any dips or lumps in the soil can be levelled later on.

3 When you have put the posts in the holes, run a line between their tops and bottoms to check that they are positioned correctly.

4 Once you have fixed the bottom arris rail on to the post and put the post in the correct position, back-fill with concrete.

5 When fixing the rails to the posts, make sure the back of the post is supported by a piece of timber or a volunteer.

7　All timber expands and contracts as the temperature and moisture content of the air fluctuates. To allow for this movement, the feather-edge boards overlap each other by 20mm (¾in). To save measuring this overlap for each board, make a spacer from a length of batten cut to the width of the boards with a nail hammered through it 20mm (¾in) from the end. Rest each feather-edge board on the gravel board, check that it is level and fix in place with 50mm (2in) nails – one in each arris rail. Then, using the spacer, position and fix the following board.

8　Nail post caps on the fence posts and cover strips over the feather-edge boards to protect their end grain from the weather. To make the strips fit snugly around the posts, cut notches that are 10mm (½in) deep and 100mm (4in) long where the posts occur. Place into position and sit on top of the fence and nail onto the thickest part of the feather-edge board and the posts.

Tip

It's always easier to build a fence with two people for setting out posts: one person holding them in position and another checking for line and level.

Design choices

If you want to avoid the work of chiselling joints where the arris rails and fence posts meet, you can simply screw the rails to the face of the posts. You have to use square rather than triangular arris rails and, although this is a quicker method, the finished fence will be wider and not as strong. If, on the other hand, the idea of woodwork sets your pulse racing, building a fence with arris rails morticed into the posts will be right up your street. The method of doing this is similar to building a post and rail fence (see pages 318-9). Chisel holes through the posts at the height of each rail and sharpen the rails so they fit snugly inside. Then nail the feather-edge boards in place. The posts are visible from both sides, making for a very smart and narrow boundary.

6 Once the arris rails are in place, nail a gravel board to each post, leaving a 50mm (2in) gap between the board and the ground.

7 Having nailed the first feather-edge board to the arris rail, use a spacer to position the following board.

8 Finally nail post caps onto the tops of the fence posts and cover strips onto the thickest part of the feather-edge boards.

picket FENCE

A walk through a country town will take you past old cottages fronted by charming picket fences, with climbers spun through the top and flowers poking their heads between the palisade. The look need never be clichéd because picket has such potential for whimsical detail that accentuates the personality of its home and owner.

MATERIALS

14 x 70mm (¾ x 2½in) planed timber for the pickets

Paint

75mm (3in) fence posts

Concrete

Batten braces

Screws

Treated timber

21 x 70mm (⅔ x 2½in) planed timber for the arris rails

Height gauge and spacer

Decorative caps

TOOLS

Jigsaw

Surform/sander/grinder/abrasive paper

Spirit level

Handsaw

Drill

1 Sketch out designs that will go with your house. When you've decided which is the most appropriate, make a template from an off-cut of wood to aid marking out. As well as the shape of the top, consider the size of the gap between posts and decide how far apart the pickets need to be to look their best. If the space is wider than the width of the timber it will look gappy, so modify your design until it looks good with a space somewhere between two-thirds and the full width of the timber.

2 Cut the timber for the pickets to length. This should be the desired height of the fence less 50mm (2in), so the base of the pickets is clear of the soil and less likely to rot. Draw around the template on the end of each picket and cut to shape using a jigsaw. To save time, clamp two pickets at a time to a workbench.

1 When you have chosen a design for your pickets, use a jigsaw to make a template from an off-cut of wood.

2 Having drawn around the template on each picket, clamp two to a workbench and cut to shape.

CHOOSING A DESIGN

It's worth taking time to assess the height for your fence. Too small and it can look twee, above waist-height and its elegance is lost. Between 0.5 and 1m (19½ and 39½in) is ideal, depending on the size of the garden it encloses. As for the tops, take your cue for the shape from the location, such as the house, the greenhouse or shapes of distant roofs. The timber for this fence was cut into tulips, to complement the traditional country cottage it surrounds and as a hint as to the owner's passion for flowers. Think about the shape of the gaps between the timbers too. Here they make wine goblet shapes, a celebratory touch.

3 | Remove the edges of the pickets with a surform or electric sander. This gives the fence a softer look and makes painting easier. The tops can be done with abrasive paper or with a grinder fitted with a sanding disk.

4 | Picket fences are difficult to paint because they have so many crooks and crevices. To save time and trouble, give the sides of the pickets a lick of paint in one go. Do this by bunching them on their edge on a table, painting and then tilting them over to prevent the paint from gathering and gluing them together. Once they are dry, turn over and paint the edge on the other side. The colour of paint should, like the design, match the surroundings. Off-white is traditional because it matches well with the window frames of most houses.

5 | Dig holes for the end and corner fence posts (these need to be at least a third of the height of the fence) and set the posts in concrete, propped in an upright position. To prevent posts from moving during construction, hammer a batten diagonally into the soil beside each post and screw it to the side of the post. Where the fence attaches to a wall, as it does here, screw a length of 50 × 100mm (2 × 4in) treated timber directly to the wall (for gates see below). Dig out holes for the intermediate posts, which should be at a maximum of 1.8m (6ft) apart as the arris timber is fairly light. Screw the lower arris rail in position between the end and corner posts – the height from the ground depends on how tall your fence is and what you think will look best, but somewhere between 50 and 150mm (2 and 6in) is the norm. Lower the intermediate fence posts into their holes using the arris as a positioning guide. Use a spirit level to check they are upright and straight, and then screw the arris to their side and fill the hole with concrete.

6 | Allow the concrete to dry for at least 24 hours and then attach the top arris rail. The height, as for the lower arris rail, depends on how tall your fence is and the shape of

3 To give the fence a softer look, use a surform or an electric sander to remove the rough edges.

4 Next lay the pickets in a bunch together on a table and, to save time, paint their edges in one go rather than individually.

5 Having dug the holes and dropped in the posts, use a spirit level to check that they are upright before filling with concrete.

its top. As a general rule, make the space between the top and bottom similar for traditional pointed top designs and bigger at the top to show off more elaborate designs. Before attaching the pickets, paint both arris rails to save time later. To locate the position of the pickets, cut a height gauge from a piece of timber to sit on the top arris rail and a spacer to judge the gap between them. Check with a level before screwing from the back of the fence (so the screws won't show).

7 Remove the batten braces from the fence posts after 48 hours and, using a hand saw, cut post tops to level. Add decorative caps to protect from the weather. There are many types available, for example one in the shape of a ball or one like an acorn. Choose the one that fits most closely with the design of your pickets.

8 For a neat finish, hide the screw holes with a weatherproof filler before painting the faces and backs of the pickets.

Design tips for including gates

If your picket fence includes a gate, this needs to be at a comfortable height to open, regardless of the height of the picket. The concave design shown here highlights the gate's position and its lazily bowing top gives it a relaxed informal look. Also, a concave top works best where the gap between the gate posts is wider than the height of the fence. However, to create a more formal look, go for a domed top because it is taller and more imposing.

Another clue to the gate's position is its visible posts which have arris rails morticed into their sides (see 'Using timber', pages 280-1). It is a little more work but worth doing as it gives a tidy finish, adds extra detail and allows the gate to be hung in line with the fence.

The fixings you choose depend on the style of the gate. In this case, long black iron hinges (instead of a latch) and a gate spring were used, which gently push it shut behind you. As there is no latch, screw a gate stop made from a thin strip of wood to the inside of the post to prevent the spring closing the gate beyond the line of the fence.

6 Before screwing the pickets onto the arris rails, use a spirit level to check that they are completely straight.

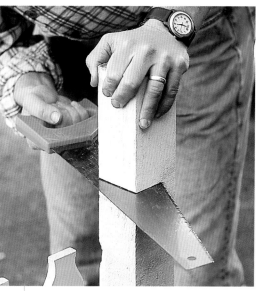

7 Once the pickets are in place, use a hand saw to level off the post tops with the pickets.

8 Finally, paint the faces and backs of the pickets and the arris rails, if they weren't painted at an earlier stage.

trellis, screens and claddings

planning for trellis, screens & claddings

This chapter is devoted to masquerade – hiding the reality of ugly boundaries with dramatic embellishments, while increasing your privacy in the process. Suggestive of outdoor living, the materials are influenced by trends in interior design, which rely on the beauty of individual materials and how well they marry with a natural setting. Their appeal derives as much from the components as the way the light plays through and across their surfaces.

Function and style While the theme of creating privacy and enclosure persists, these trellis, claddings and screens have various functions. Glass gives an open-plan and airy feel to a space, and is particularly suited to small, already-enclosed gardens. It can be used as a detail within a trellis or as the screen itself. The only type of glass to use is toughened and sandblasted as it is opaque, and therefore not a danger to birds, and, of course, very strong. It's a dynamic material that reflects its surroundings and becomes more transparent in rain. At night, in the beam of a spot lamp, it glows and diffuses the light around.

The best trellis has not forgotten its classical heritage, reminiscent of Roman colonnades and medieval cloisters. Sadly, all too often it doesn't live up to its promise due to cheap construction and unimaginative use. But when made well, trellis gives a romantic other-worldliness to an existing wall, and offers exciting opportunities for climbing plants and night-time lighting.

For a more instant transformation you can't beat cladding, such as that made from natural stems like split bamboo. Wired together on rolls, the bamboo can disguise an unappealing fence or enhance a theme, as in a Japanese garden. It is economical and certainly much cheaper than replacing a whole fence. More sophisticated metal claddings, like copper and stainless steel, aren't for such wholesale use. Instead, they can be used as focal points, giving an ordinary boundary an artistic twist.

Temporary screens, like the summer structures that support sweet peas and runner beans, are playful and seasonal. By replacing materials such as bamboo canes with hazel, a plant support screen will last for a good few years. It is also a fantastic way of creating instant

Living willow lattice.

Painted trellis.

Woven willow hurdle.

Heavy timber trellis.

Metal clad walls (above left and right) are surprisingly dynamic. Stainless steel reflects the shapes and colours in the garden that surrounds it, while mild steel turns through every shade of coral and cinnamon as it rusts. Both are modern and uncompromising in effect and are tricky to work with. In complete contrast, bamboo screens (above) are much simpler to construct and change little as they age.

Woven walls have their own character and no two are the same. Hazel hurdles are solid in appearance, and are suitable for perimeter and internal boundaries.

rooms, while waiting for permanent hedges to grow. Long lasting rusted weld mesh screens create an urban feel and introduce spicy colours in an elemental way.

Design choices

Glass and metal should be integrated with the surroundings, and this is best achieved by giving these materials a function, such as masking an unattractive feature or leading the eye to an entrance. Both need an anchor, such as an appropriately modern material at their base or plants that ground them, making them seem like they belong. Metal claddings can be used very subtly, for example to adorn window boxes. This approach works well because it links claddings on walls to other areas of the garden, making the decision to use the material less arbitrary. Similarly, with more traditional screens like timber trellis, linking them to other parts of the garden gives them a context. So, if it's painted, repeat the colour on timberwork elsewhere, such as on fence posts.

Types of trellis, screens and claddings

Glass is expensive because it must be cut to size and toughened before you take delivery. On the positive side, all you have to do is fix it in position, so it's fairly instant. Sandblasted glass has two faces: a smooth side and the side that has been treated. For reflections, have the smooth side outermost or, for a softer finish, display the other side.

You can buy trellis for adding instant height to existing boundaries, for jazzing up walls and fences, and for giving body to freestanding arbours and pergolas. Trellis can be constructed to fit any space without any of the ugly joins that detract from shop-bought panels.

The various types of cladding include bamboo and willow, each endowing a garden with a different character. Bamboo obviously enhances an Oriental theme, but can also look quite jungly, while willow is more suited to a cottage garden.

There are two main choices with stems – to buy either a dead stem that won't re-grow, or a living stem like willow, which will sprout and turn into a living screen. Hazel is more shy to root and bamboo canes, of course, cannot be expected ever to grow!

Metal is available in sheet form or mesh, and the latter is good for giving a modern twist on trellis. Copper and steel is sold by the sheet and can be worked at home with a jigsaw fitted with a metal blade, whereas stainless steel is hard to cut so should be made to order.

Trellis can be a work of art in its own right. The cladding (above left) in the style of a Mondrian painting has stained glass fixed between the bars, adding extra colour and interest. In contrast, the combination of industrial materials in a garden setting, such as stainless steel and corrugated steel sheets (above right), shakes off their municipal associations.

Trellis as balustrade.

Willow in a Japanese-style lattice.

Light, airy, timber trellis.

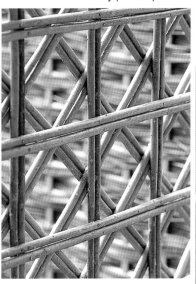

A stem of jasmine twines round the trellis.

glass SCREEN

Using glass in a garden is like bringing the indoors outside. It always looks very modern, whether combined with structural plants like phormiums and palms or with cottage-garden flowers. It's the ideal material for built-up areas, creating privacy without reducing light levels.

1 | This project involves combining ready-made materials from specialist suppliers to make a screen that's unique. Decide on the measurements and number of glass panels and order frames made from 40mm (1½in) boxed steel to hold them from a metal workshop. These should be H-shaped and wide enough to fit the glass and the clamps, plus an extra 3mm (⅛in) to make fixing the glass easier. The legs need to be at least 700mm (27½in) long to provide a deep concrete footing.

Paint the underground section of the frame with rustproof paint before putting the legs in 600mm (24in) holes in the ground and pouring a concrete mix around them. Tamp the concrete to remove any air bubbles with a length of wood and slope its surface with a trowel to shed water away from the metal. Check for level and prop in place with timber while the concrete dries.

MATERIALS

An H-shaped metal frame made from 40mm (1½in) boxed steel – this one is 2.3m (7ft) tall, and just over 1.2m (4ft) wide

Metal paint and rust proofer

Concrete

Eight metal clamps with a brushed finish

Self-tapping screws

Toughened and sandblasted 6mm (¼in) glass – this one is 1.2 x 1.5m (4 x 5ft)

TOOLS

Masonry and bricklaying tools

Drill

Allen keys (to tighten clamps)

1 Having put the legs of the frame in holes, infill with concrete and check for level. Prop in place with timber while the concrete dries.

2 Once the frame is in position, paint the upper part and then attach the metal clamps to it, using self-tapping screws.

KNOW YOUR MATERIALS

Think of a toughened glass screen like you would a car window. If it is well supported and prevented from twisting, it is extremely strong and durable. It is only vulnerable if exceptional pressure is applied to a small area: if, for example, it is deliberately hit hard with a hammer. In the unlikely event of it breaking, it will, like a car window, shatter into tiny pieces that are unlikely to cause serious injury. Always have the glass sandblasted before it is toughened, as this gives it an attractive opaque appearance and makes it visible so birds won't fly into it. Sandblasting gives one side of the glass a matt finish, while the other is glossy and reflective. The choice is yours.

2 After 48 hours, remove the timber supports and paint the upper part of the frame. Then drill evenly spaced holes for metal clamps which are fixed to the frame with self-tapping screws. Self-tapping screws work by cutting their own thread as they are tightened into the metal. They are simple to use as long as the hole they are wound into is just the right size, so either experiment on a metal off-cut with different bits or buy one to match with the screws. The clamps are made of aluminium and hold the glass in place between rubber jaws. To hold a 1.2 x 1.5m (4 x 5ft) sheet of glass you'll need eight clamps, two for the base and three up each side.

3 Lift the glass into position (this is a two-person job), resting its base on rubber stops placed on the bottom clamps. Fit the backs on the clamps and tighten. To prevent rain water getting inside the open tops of the metal frame, plug with rubber stops. And to stop unsightly mud splashes in wet weather, plant evergreens at the base or mulch with gravel.

3 Lift the glass into position, resting its base on rubber stops placed on the bottom clamps. Next fit the backs on the clamps and tighten.

shop-bought TRELLIS

Trellis is more than a support for climbing plants. With a little imagination, it can be transformed into a focal point, which captures the sun and shadows by day and illuminates the garden by night.

1 Painting trellis by hand is a slow and laborious business as the surface area of each panel is vast and because the timber almost always completely absorbs the first coat. It is more efficient to hire a hand-held paint sprayer which will do the job in minutes, without leaving unsightly drips down the timber. Always choose a dry still day, water down the paint by a third, prop the trellis against a plastic sheet to catch any drift and spray evenly across each panel, paying attention to the recesses around the frame. Allow 15 minutes for the paint to dry and apply another coat. When you have finished, fill the container with warm water and spray to clean the nozzle.

2 To make the trellis pillars, screw together the 0.3m (1ft) panels into three-sided boxes, using L-shaped metal brackets to hold their corners together.

MATERIALS

Nine 1.8 x 0.3m (6 x 1ft) diamond trellis panels

Two 1 x 1.8m (3 x 6ft) square panels

Water-soluble paint

Plastic sheeting

Twelve L-shaped metal brackets

Twelve flat metal fixing plates

Rawl plugs

Three low voltage 'uplights'

TOOLS

Hire tools

Spirit level

Drill

1 Having watered down the paint by a third, rest the trellis against the plastic sheeting and use a hand-held sprayer to paint.

2 Make the trellis pillars by screwing together the 0.3m (1ft) panels into three-sided boxes, using L-shaped brackets at the corners.

KNOW YOUR MATERIALS

To look good, trellis needs to be well made with straight spars and evenly proportioned squares. Often, shop-bought trellis falls short of these standards and although it might seem like a bargain, it never lives up to its full potential. The things that separate the good from the bad are timber quality, hole size and design. So, make sure that the finish of the wood is even and not a patchy mix of rough-sawn and smooth timber. Holes bigger than 120mm (5in) are too large and will always look out of scale and, if you're using it structurally, for example for making pillars for lighting, always opt for trellis panels with a framed edge as this increases their strength.

3 Screw flat metal fixing plates to the back of the trellis pillars and screw them to the wall. Use a spirit level to check they are upright.

3 Screw flat metal fixing plates to the back of the trellis pillars and screw to the wall as shown, checking that each pillar is upright with a spirit level. To fix the trellis infills between the pillars, position against the wall and drill through them to mark the plaster/brick work below. Then remove the trellis, and drill and plug the wall before placing the trellis back in position and fixing with screws.

Installing lighting

For lighting, use three low voltage 'uplights' bolted to the floor at the base of each pillar. Low voltage lights consist of a transformer that steps down the voltage from the mains electricity supply to just 12 volts, meaning that even if the wires were accidentally cut, there would be no risk of electrocution. Available as kits, you don't need a professional electrician to install them; simply position the transformer near a power socket indoors and run the wire to the lights along the base of the wall. This way the wires are hidden when the trellis is screwed in place.

custom-made TRELLIS

Custom-made trellis enables you to create an illusion of opulence and grandeur without breaking the bank. By making your own trellis you can tailor it to your garden precisely, transforming run-of-the-mill walls into classical colonnades and arches.

1 The size of the timber trellis depends on its situation. In this project 20 × 8mm (¾ × ¼in) planed batten was used as the finished trellis was situated in a yard only 5m (16ft) square. Anything bigger would have looked coarse. If you are cladding a large expanse of wall that's visible from further away, use a larger timber such as 25 × 20mm (1 × ¾in) batten. Either buy it planed or save money by removing the rough edges yourself with an electric plane. You don't need to buy treated timber, as long as the base of the trellis is above soil level and you paint it with a protective wood stain. The first thing to do when building trellis is to make your uprights by cutting twelve equal lengths of batten about 1.5m (5ft) long.

2 Cut the horizontal spars making them 150mm (6in) long and nail them to the uprights using one of the

MATERIALS

60m (180ft) of planed 20 × 8mm (¾in × ¼in) batten

15mm (⅝in) copper tacks

1.2 × 2.4m (4 × 8ft) sheet of 12mm (½in) marine plywood

Protective wood stain

Rawl plugs

50mm (2in) screws

TOOLS

Carpentry tools

Bricklaying tools

Electric plane

Hammer

Drill with masonry bit

1 Start by making your uprights by cutting twelve equal lengths of batten, approximately 1.5m (5ft) long.

2 Cut the horizontal spars, making them 150mm (6in) long, and nail them to the uprights using a horizontal as a spacing guide.

KNOW YOUR MATERIALS

Combining squares and diamonds gives the trellis a three-dimensional appearance. The square sections look heavier and recessed compared to the diamond panels and for this reason they look best when used as pillars, or as infill between them. Always separate the two patterns with lengths of batten or plinths (as done here) to create the impression that one sits behind or atop the other. Another trick to create a 3-D effect is to sandwich the horizontal and diamond spars between a double frame (see step 2). This means that they are held proud of the wall, which allows shadows to play behind them, thereby producing an illusion of depth.

horizontals as a spacing guide to ensure that the squares are even. When you reach the height you want, cut the tops of the uprights flush with the last horizontal. Then sandwich the horizontals between another upright nailed over their top.

3 On top of the uprights, plinths add extra detail and separate the square from the diamond trellis. To make them, screw two rectangles of 12mm (½in) marine plywood together as shown – the larger rectangle is 240 x 75mm (9½ x 3in) and the smaller rectangle is 200 x 55mm (8 x 2½in). If you use a jigsaw, sand their edges to remove any splinters. Then pilot drill and screw them to the top of the uprights.

4 Each arch is made up of four semicircles of marine plywood – two at the front and two at the back, held together with batten. Each semicircle is 25mm (1in) wide. Mark them out on the marine plywood sheet and cut them out with a jigsaw, making the inside radius of the smaller semicircle 660mm (25in) and the inside of the larger one 750mm (30in). The best way to do this is to hammer a nail into the plywood and tie a length of string to it. Then measure the radius that you want against the string and use it as a guide as you pen round your semicircle. Cut out the first one of each size and draw around them to mark out the rest.

5 When they are all cut, sand down their edges. Assemble them by setting a larger and a smaller semicircle out on a bench, and attaching evenly spaced 70mm (2¾in) lengths of battens between them using copper tacks. Then tack two more semicircles on the top to sandwich the battens in place.

6 The diagonal lattice can be any height. The one in this project is 600mm (24in), but its width must be the same as the distance between the outside spars of the end uprights. To measure this accurately, set out the uprights with the arches on their tops on level ground – as they

3 To make a plinth for the top of the upright, screw two rectangles together and screw them to the upright.

4 Mark out the semicircles on the marine plywood and cut them with a jigsaw. Each arch is made up of four semicircles.

5 Tack battens between the semicircles, then place two more lengths of plywood on top to sandwich the battens in place.

would be on the wall. Once you have your measurements, cut and set out lengths of batten in a rectangle on the ground. Then nail your diagonals to it. Keep the distance between the diagonals even with a spacer and check that the outside rectangle remains square.

7 When both sets of diagonals are in place, turn the panel over so that the rectangular outer edge is uppermost and position the arches side by side onto the top as shown. Check that the gaps between their ends and the outside of the trellis panel are the same, then mark around them with a pen and cut carefully along the lines with a jigsaw. When this job is done, cut away any lengths of diagonals that protrude beyond the outer rectangle with a jigsaw.

8 Make a plinth for the top of the diamond panel out of two rectangles of marine plywood screwed together as in step 3 opposite. As before, make the larger rectangle 25mm (1in) wider than the smaller one. The lengths should be 75mm (3in) and 50mm (2in) longer than the diamond panel, which allows for an overhang. Paint the whole trellis with a protective woodstain – this is best done before fixing it to the wall, and if you have a lot to do, consider hiring a paint sprayer.

Attaching the trellis to the wall is a two-person job. First, hold each piece in position checking that it is true with a spirit level, then drill a hole through it with a masonry bit marking the brickwork below. Remove the trellis and drill into the bricks. Push a rawl plug into the hole, put the trellis back and fix with screws. Finally, screw the plinth onto the top of the diamond panel.

Planting

Plant climbers such as a large flowered clematis and climbing roses at the feet of the columns so that they can scramble up towards the arches. Clematis are good as their growth tends to be 'toppy' without much foliage below 1.5m (5ft), so they'll naturally fill the diamond lattice with flower. Roses, on the other hand, are easy to train and look fabulous when tied around the arches.

6 Once you have worked out the measurements of your rectangle, set it out on the ground and nail your diagonals to it.

7 Next lay the arches onto the diamond panel, mark around them and then cut along the line with a jigsaw.

8 Having fixed your trellis to the wall, using rawl plugs and screws, fasten the plinth to the top of the diamond panel.

split bamboo SCREEN

The crisp lines of a split bamboo screen can disguise all sorts of boundaries, from unattractive concrete posts and panels to boring timber fences. Bamboo screens needn't be restricted to Japanese gardens either, as they can accentuate a tropical theme where large-leaved plants are grown. They work well in city gardens where their strong vertical lines echo those in the surrounding urban jungle.

1 | Broken, loose or rotten posts in the existing fence will need replacing first. For concrete fence posts, use a masonry drill to make and plug three holes in each – one at the top, one at the bottom and one between the two.

2 | Cut a set of uprights from rough sawn timber that are 150mm (6in) lower than the finished height of the screen, and screw to the fence posts. Then measure and cut three rails for each upright and screw in position with L-shaped brackets (to compensate for any leaning posts measure and cut each rail individually). The framework isolates the screen from the fence panels, allowing them to be replaced or removed for access.

3 | Unroll the bamboo and nail to the framework using staples. To ensure that the top is level, sit the unrolled

MATERIALS

2 x 5m (6½ x 16ft) split
bamboo screening

50 x 50mm (2 x 2in) treated
rough sawn timber

10mm (½in) staples

L-shaped brackets

25mm (1in) screws

75mm (3in) screws

(Rawl plugs if the posts
are concrete)

TOOLS

Masonry drill and bits

Screwdriver

Hammer

1 Using a powerful masonry drill, make three holes in the concrete fence posts and rawl plug them.

2 Having fixed rough sawn timber uprights to the posts, cut three rails for each upright and screw them on.

KNOW YOUR MATERIALS

Bamboo screens are manufactured in Vietnam and China and since the late 1990s, new designs have become increasingly available. For an internal divide that looks good from both sides, heavy-duty, whole cane screens, wired and strung between sturdy timber posts, are just the job. Screens with twiggy tops and sideshoots have a thatchy, less formal look. The quality of bamboo screening can vary enormously, so it is worth checking the canes before you buy.

3 *Finally, staple the bamboo onto the framework, making sure it is level by resting its base on a timber plank.*

screen on to a timber plank before fixing with staples. This also keeps the bottom of the screen proud of the soil and helps extend its life.

Keeping up appearances for the neighbours

If you are raising the height of an external boundary with a screen, talk to your neighbours before starting and bear in mind that the back of the screen and the timber work that holds it in place will need to be disguised from their side. Do this, either by fixing trellis along the top of the fence or covering the visible timber work with a strip of screen. This leaves your neighbours with the existing fence topped with a neat screen coping.

Screen quality

Avoid screens that have frayed ends, slack wires or uneven spaces. A good way of judging the quality is to pick up the roll: if it feels light, the chances are that the screen is of an inferior grade and will soon deteriorate in the garden.

hazel SCREEN

This undemanding and economical hazel rod garden screen makes a perfect surround for a cut flower garden, allowing glimpses of the blooms in borders while scented sweet peas clamber up its sides. You could use bamboo as an alternative material.

MATERIALS

Hazel rods

Twine

TOOLS

Staking bar

Spade

Loppers

Secateurs

1 | Push a series of uprights into the soil leaving 0.6m (2ft) spaces between them, choosing the straightest and thickest rods for this job. It's up to you whether the screen is straight, gently curved or serpentine. The base of each rod should be pressed into the soil by at least 200mm (8in). If the ground is too hard to do this by hand, make a hole with a staking bar if you've got one, or open up a slit in the ground with a spade, press the hazel rod into the opening and firm back around it. When all of the uprights are in, link them together with a horizontal hazel rod tied to each one with twine at the height you want the screen.

2 | The diagonals are pushed in next, at an angle of roughly 45 degrees with 300mm (12in) spaces between them. Choose the longest lengths for the middle section

1 Start by pushing a series of uprights at least 200mm (8in) into the soil, using the straightest and thickest rods.

2 Next push the diagonals into the soil, putting the longest lengths into the central section, leaving a 300mm (12in) space between them.

KNOW YOUR MATERIALS
Hazel rods or similar materials such as bamboo have long been used in gardens for plant supports. They are cheap to buy and easy to work with, so they are perfect for building temporary screens that can be dismantled and reassembled as the mood takes you. Each rod has a useful life of four or five years after which time it becomes brittle and will need replacing.

3 *Tie the diagonals to the uprights where they cross. Twist their tops around the horizontals and tie them in.*

of the screen and use shorter, thinner rods for the corners. Because the diagonals at the top right and left of the screen are above soil level, and therefore can't be pushed into the ground, they need to be tied to the uprights with twine.

3   Tie the diagonals to the uprights where they cross. Then twist their tops around the horizontal holding them in place with twine. Alternatively, you can bind them with a few lengths of willow or simply cut them off just above the horizontal rod with loppers. Plant a row of sweet peas at the foot of the screen for scent or use other annual climbers such as nasturtium to beautify your new garden addition.

Alternative materials
For an Oriental theme, use bamboo canes instead of the hazel rods, binding them together with lengths of tarred, black string. String ties can be very ornamental, especially if the same knot is used throughout.

copper CLADDING

Copper has a tremendous dynamism in a garden setting, due to the exotic blue-green patina it develops with time. It adds natural colour without the risk of creating jarring contrasts, as can be the case with paint, and imbues a small space with novelty and luxury.

1 Start by cladding the wall in 12mm (½in) marine plywood to even out any irregularities in the brick or plaster work and to create a smooth surface for gluing the copper. When cladding complicated walls like this alcove, make a template out of cardboard, ensuring it fits the wall perfectly. Lay the template onto the marine plywood, and draw round it and cut with a jigsaw. Fix the marine plywood to the wall by first propping it in position and drilling through every 700mm (27½in) to mark the bricks beneath. Remove it and drill and rawl plug the bricks, then prop it back in place and hold with screws.

2 Use the same cardboard template to mark the copper, using a marker pen to give a clear line. If there are any inaccuracies in the template they'll be visible as gaps around the marine plywood on the wall, so as you mark

MATERIALS

Cardboard

12mm (½in) marine plywood

Rawl plugs

Screws

Copper sheet (available from metalwork suppliers)

Silicone glue or copper tacks

TOOLS

Jigsaw (sheet metal blade)

Drill

Metal file

Rubber mallet

1 Make a template out of stiff cardboard and use it to cut out the marine plywood, which needs to be rawl plugged to the wall.

2 Having used the template to mark the copper, cut the metal with a jigsaw making sure the copper is well supported.

KNOW YOUR MATERIALS

To make your copper appear old and weathered, burnish it in parts with a flame weeder or gas torch from the kitchen, the type chefs use to caramelise crème brûlée. This treatment creates dramatic dark blue clouds against the vivid copper, coloured with rainbow shades, like petrol in a puddle. Stainless steel also makes a good metal cladding. Fix it onto marine plywood in the same way as copper. As you can't cut it yourself, measure up the area first and buy it ready-cut to size. If you prefer the distressed, seaside look of rusted metal, use mild steel sheeting. Because of its weight, bolt directly to the wall.

the copper adjust the line accordingly. Cut the copper with a jigsaw fitted with a sheet metal blade. Copper is surprisingly easy to cut. Keep the blade of the jigsaw close to the side of the bench so that the copper is supported. Once cut, use a metal file to remove burrs from the edge.

3   The copper can be fixed with copper tacks or with silicone glue. Because tacks are more obtrusive it is essential that they are hammered in in symmetrical straight lines or in deliberate swirls to prevent them detracting from the sheet. To do this, mark their positions before hammering home. For a smooth finish, silicone glue is best. This is available from builders' and plumbers' suppliers along with the gun needed to squeeze it from the tube. Apply the glue in lines onto the marine plywood, taking particular care to coat the corners. Then press the copper sheet back onto it, tapping with a rubber mallet to ensure good contact. Prop a length of timber against the copper to hold it in place while the glue dries, which takes between three and four hours.

3 Squeeze silicone glue onto the marine plywood, then press the copper sheet back onto it. Tap it with a rubber mallet to ensure good contact.

rusted MESH

For a modern take on trellis, steel mesh is the ideal alternative. Because it rusts, the orange complements the dark leaves of climbers like ivy, which contrive to give it Gothic good looks. Despite it rusting, it will last for years.

1 The supports for the reinforcement mesh are made from boxed steel sections 25mm (¾in) in diameter. Use a hacksaw to cut the mesh to the height of the screen plus 600mm (24in) for fixing in the ground. Drill holes 600mm (24in) apart through the above ground section. Give the below ground section a coat of rustproof paint.

2 Mark the positions of the posts on the ground and dig a 300mm (12in) hole for each. Then push the posts another 300mm (12in) into the soil at the bottom of each hole, which holds them firm as you pour concrete around their collars. (Use the fence post technique given on page 273 to level up the posts and ensure that they are the same height.) Smooth over the top of the collars with a trowel, so that any water runs away from the posts.

MATERIALS

1.2 x 1.8m (4 x 6ft) reinforcement mesh

2.5m (8ft) lengths of 25mm (1in) boxed steel

Rust proofing paint

Galvanised wire

Concrete

TOOLS

Masonry and bricklaying tools

Hacksaw

Drill

Pliers

1 Use a hacksaw to cut the boxed steel to length and drill holes in the above ground section to support the mesh.

2 Dig holes for the uprights, pour concrete around them and smooth over the top with a trowel.

KNOW YOUR MATERIALS

The primary use for steel reinforcement mesh is for strengthening concrete footings and slabs. It can be bought from builders' suppliers and landscape supply yards; the chances are that it will be delivered in 6 x 2.4m (20 x 8ft) sheets, so it will need to be cut down to your preferred size. Cut with a hacksaw or an angle grinder or hire a bolt cutter to do the job.

For an extra touch of detail, moon gates and arched windows can be cut into the screen and given definition by plaiting wire over the cut ends.

3 Tie the panels to the posts with galvanised wire looped through the holes in the posts, tightening it by twisting with pliers. Plant ivy (*Hedera*) every 300mm (12in) along the base of the screen and, as it grows, train to the metal. When it is established, clip with shears regularly to encourage it to bush out and feed it with a general fertiliser.

Alternative materials

If the rusty look isn't your thing, use stainless steel or aluminium screening with aluminium box section posts. These weather to a steely grey and never rust. Ironwork can be painted, but needs to be rust free and painted with a primer first, otherwise the rust will appear after just a few months. For a more private screen with small diamond-shaped holes use sheets of barbecue mesh, which, as its name suggests, is more commonly used for cooking grills. Because the holes are small, barbecue mesh looks particularly attractive at night when back-lit with golden spotlights.

3 Put the steel mesh in position and tie it to the uprights with galvanised wire. Use pliers to twist and tighten the wire.

living boundaries

planning for living boundaries

This chapter has been included because you cannot talk about boundaries without at least mentioning living ones. A garden is never complete without plants – whether it's flowers growing in a dry stone wall, climbers rambling around a gate or a hedge peeking over the top of a wooden fence, without plants a boundary is stark and cold, and never fully integrated.

Function and style You can't talk about building boundaries without at least touching on the planting, because the two go hand in hand. Plants embellish garden boundaries by imparting a certain dynamism to otherwise static materials. It's a two-way street, of course, because the plants benefit from the microclimate created by the boundary and the support, while the boundary can claim more seasonality as the plants flower, tint in autumn and spring into life early in the year.

Establishing Many people are more afraid of buying plants than they are of DIY, but this is based on the belief that you have to grow the plants. The plants grow themselves! The things to worry about are planting them in the right spot and getting them established. The key is to improve the soil with commercially available compost, well-rotted manure or homemade compost before planting. Then, make sure plants are well watered, particularly in the first summer. If your problem is which plants to choose, check out plants that are thriving in neighbours' gardens and take advice from nearby nurseries or garden centres as they will know which species do well in the local soil.

Design choices Walls – There are three ways in which plants can be combined with walls – as climbers, as cascading plants for the top of retaining walls and as plants growing within walls. For climbers, see information about fences on page 358.

Low retaining walls make ideal falls for cascading plants, benefiting species that don't mind it dry and prefer to mound and tumble, rather than climb. Good subjects include grasses such as the red-leaved *Stipa arundinacea* and *Carex buchanii*; shrubs such as *Cotoneaster dammeri*;

Living willow screen.

Hedge-topped fence.

Pleached lime trees.

Formal hedge.

The look of a living boundary depends on the type of plants used and how they are maintained. Regularly clipped evergreens (top left) become permanently neat surrounds, while training climbers across a trellis fence is an effective means of harnessing nature's inclination to riot. For the ultimate trained boundary, you can't beat fruit trees with their main branches espalliered (wired horizontally) for a sculptural winter framework (above).

The branches of pleached lime trees are grafted and twisted, so that in time they grow together – it is as though they are holding hands.

and perennials such as *Nepeta* 'Walkers Low' and many hardy cranesbill geraniums. Watering in the first year is essential for establishment. If you want plants to grow inside a wall, a soaker hose should be installed during construction and plugged into the water supply regularly.

In ready-built walls, irrigation is often impossible to install. In such cases the best way to green them up is by sowing seed directly into soil-filled gaps. Of course, you can't put just anything in these gaps. You must choose plants that are naturally adapted to these tough conditions, such as alpines or those that happily live on steep gravel beds in the wild. Good choices from seed include *Erigeron karvinskianus*, *Linaria* (alpine toadflax) and thyme. By sowing direct, the plants are less likely to get a shock from the change in conditions than if they are transplanted from a pot. In time, they will begin to set seed and colonise without your intervention. This is also a good technique for establishing plants, such as lady's mantle (*Alchemilla*), at the base of a wall or between the gaps in paving.

Fences – There are two types of climbers – self-clinging and ones that need support, and both can be combined with fences. It's often said that you shouldn't put self-clinging climbers onto a fence, because of their weight, but I don't think there is a worry if it is well-made. Self-clinging climbers, like Virginia creeper (*Parthenocissus quinquefolia*), Boston ivy (*Parthenocissus tricuspidata*) and ivy, can look after themselves, but those with tendrils, such as clematis, require a ladder of wires to help them climb. Using vine eyes to attach wires to the fence posts will allow space behind for climbers to grow and air to circulate. When planting, avoid the rain-shadow of the fence by leaving a space of 450mm (18in) between the base and the planting hole. Tilt the rootball at a 45° angle towards the support to encourage it to climb in the direction you want.

Trellis – Because trellis is more flimsy, prevent the stems growing behind the spars, as they can push it out of shape as they grow. Train the stems onto the support, by tying stems to the front with soft twine.

Hedges – Hedges are cheaper and usually more sympathetic with their surroundings than a new hard structure, but take longer to reach any height. But the two work together well, whether it's a conifer and an iron railing fence in a formal front garden, or a low lavender hedge peeking through a picket. A clever combination is a yew hedge clipped into the back of a closeboard fence, so the internal screen is a green living hedge, while the outside world sees a solid timber boundary.

All living boundaries bring seasonality to a garden, but beech and hornbeam are particularly dynamic – greening up in spring and retaining russet autumn colour right through the worst of the winter. Hornbeam takes training particularly well (above left) and its main branches can be clipped into giant walls, like the beech (above right).

Trellis on a panelled fence.

Laid hedge with ash tree.

Half round posts.

A frost-covered beech hedge.

willow WALL

Earth and willow wands may not seem like a promising combination for a wall, but together they make a long-lasting and strong boundary. If the wall is planted with wildflowers and grasses, its sides will flower and colour with the changing seasons.

1 Mark the footprint of the wall on the ground with paint, spacing the two sides of the wall 60mm (24in) apart and connecting their ends with a gentle curve. For strength, make the sides serpentine. Then, use loppers to cut the base of the thicker willow into 1m (3ft) lengths to make the uprights, measuring at least 25mm (¾in) in diameter at their thinnest end. Push the uprights into the ground, 250–300mm (10–12in) apart, and angling the tops of the two sides together to give the sides an A-shaped profile. Having an uneven number of uprights makes weaving easier so add an extra one, adjusting the spacing of its neighbours to fit. When you're happy with their position, hammer them firm with a wooden mallet or beetle.

2 Using single lengths of the thinner willow, weave in and out of the uprights about halfway up their sides. As you

MATERIALS

Bundles of willow or similar material 25–50mm (1–2in) for the uprights and bundles of graded willow 10–12mm (½in) in diameter for the sides

Soaker hose/micro irrigation pipe

Topsoil

Turf

TOOLS

Carpentry tools

Loppers and secateurs

Mallet or beetle

1 Having cut the lengths for the uprights, push them into the ground, spacing them 250–300mm (10–12in) apart.

2 Weave single lengths of willow in and out of the uprights halfway up their sides, and tuck the end of each length inside the wall.

KNOW YOUR MATERIALS

Willow is a fabulous building material and is ideal for creating garden boundaries. As well as being wonderfully malleable and very easy to work with, it is also surprisingly strong. Willow may be available from specialist growers. Brightly coloured willows such as the orange *Salix alba* 'Britzensis' and the black *Salix daphnoides* are available, both adding striking detail to new structures. If you prefer, you could use a combination of different types of willow instead of a single variety in order to create a truly unique boundary. If you are unable to source a supply of willow, you could use bamboo as an alternative material – the finished result would look just as good.

reach the end of each length, tuck it inside of the wall and introduce another willow length, matching the thick end of one to the thin end of the other until you've gone right around the structure twice. If you have an odd number of uprights, the second layer of willow will alternate with the first and each upright will be firmly bound inside and out. Check your weave against the photo and working round the wall, push the willow down until it is in contact with the ground.

3 The first two layers of willow rods hold the uprights steady and once they are in position, the remainder can be woven in by the handful. Take up to four or five lengths at a time and tap them down so that their thick ends are together, and weave in and out of the uprights. As before, introduce another handful when the first comes to its end, tucking any whippy bits inside the wall. Work around the wall, building up the sides in a continuous weave, and making sure that each course alternates with the one below.

4 To use the willow efficiently, spread the rods in each handful out flat so that they have the widest spread. Don't worry about any small gaps, as these will be filled by grasses and flowers once the wall is established. When the sides of the wall reach half their finished height, fill between them with soil, firming it into the corners with the soles of your feet (it's much easier to do this as you go along rather than after the sides are complete).

5 Weave up to the finished height of between 700mm (27½in) and 900mm (36in), filling with soil and firming as you go and taking care to maintain the wall's A-shaped profile. (If the sides do start to splay, tie across the wall with nylon rope or thick string to hold them together.) Then, cut the tops of the uprights level with loppers and trim off any straggly tops or protruding ends using a pair of secateurs.

6 Cut the micro irrigation pipe to the length of the wall, tie a knot in one end and attach a hosepipe adaptor to the

3 Take four or five lengths at a time and weave them through the uprights, ensuring that each course alternates with the one below.

4 Once the sides of the wall have reached half their height, fill between them with soil, firming it in with the soles of your feet.

5 Having woven up to the finished height and filled it with soil, tidy up the wall by cutting off protruding ends with secateurs.

other. Lay the pipe on top of the wall and feed the end with the hose adaptor through the side in an inconspicuous place.

7 Next cover the hose with more soil, doming it up by 100–150mm (4–6in) over the height of the sides to fill any gaps if the soil inside the wall settles. Then lay turf along the top of the wall or plant with a mixture of primroses (*Primula vulgaris*), lady's mantle (*Alchemilla*) and cranesbill geraniums (*Geranium* spp.).

8 To fill the pockets between each layer of willow, sow a mixture of wildflower seeds such as ox eye daisies and foxgloves. In autumn, plant bluebells and daffodils to flower the following spring. Alternatively use a mixture of herbaceous plants – in this project variegated hosta and a lemon balm (*Melissa*) sprouted from the sides after smuggling themselves in to the wall as roots mixed with the topsoil fill. They look very good and, surprisingly, are thriving in their new lofty position.

Using and caring for willow

A willow wall works both as an internal divide and around a perimeter and it looks good in any location whether urban or rural. In a country setting its soft flowery sides blend perfectly with its surroundings, adding bags of cottage garden charm; while in a contemporary garden, mixed in with synthetic materials, such as glass and metal, the naturalness and country craft of the wall become more apparent.

Willow has a dogged ability to survive even after the harshest treatment. So much so, that the cut branches will happily sprout new leaves even after being hammered into the ground. This tenacity makes willow ideal for soil-filled walls as the stems quickly re-grow, binding the sides together with their roots. To prevent it from taking over and squeezing out the wild flowers, prune back the fresh stems that appear through the summer with shears. Also, connect a hose to the irrigation pipe in periods of drought, leaving it on for an hour at a time to ensure all the soil inside the wall gets a good soak.

6 Lay micro irrigation pipe the length of the wall, tying up one end and feeding the end with a hose pipe adaptor discreetly through the side.

7 Having covered the hose pipe with soil, doming it up above the height of the sides, lay turf along the top.

8 Finally, fill the pockets between each layer of willow rods with a mixture of wildflower seeds, such as foxgloves (Digitalis).

window in HEDGE

A circular window will instantly give hedges character, colour and charm. In gardens made sombre by shady tall hedges, a window in the living boundary will instantly brighten up the appearance of the hedging and lift the shadow it casts.

1 | The window frame is supported in the hedge on an H-shaped timber mount, which consists of two uprights cut at 100mm (4in) above the height you want the centre of the window and a crosspiece that is cut to the width of the window frame. Mark the position of the crosspiece by laying the uprights on level ground and setting the window between them with its centre 100mm (4in) below their tops. Fix the crosspiece below the window using L-shaped brackets and wood screws.

2 | The feet of the mount are held in the hedge with fence spikes, which can be hammered into the line of the hedge without causing excessive root disturbance. Make sure that the fence spikes are spaced to the same width as the mount (if the trunks of the hedge plants correspond with the spikes, position the spikes

MATERIALS

75mm (3in) fence spikes

75mm (3in) posts

Gable end/circular window

100mm (4in) screws

Four L-shaped brackets

Dark wood stain for posts

Glass paint or stained glass (optional)

TOOLS

Masonry and bricklaying tools

Cross cutting saw

Drill and pilot bit

Fence spike driver

1 Make an H-shaped mount for the window using 75mm (3in) fence posts fixed together with L-shaped brackets.

2 Hammer the two fence spikes the width of the mount apart into the line of the hedge.

The most economical way to buy a circular window is from a salvage yard. The condition can be variable, so check over the frame to make sure that the woodwork is sound. Don't worry if the glass is broken as this is cheaper and easier to replace than damaged spars or a rotten timber. Clean up the glass and replace any cracked sections, and then give the frame a coat of wood preserver to protect it from the weather.

3 Secure the window onto the crosspiece by pilot drilling angled holes through the window frame into the uprights.

just in front of the trees) and use a fence spike driver to protect their tops as you hammer. In hedges with dense foliage, it is easier to construct the mount in situ by tapping the uprights into the fence spikes and then attaching the crosspiece in the hedge. To help disguise the timber so that it does not detract from the natural look of the finished window, paint with a black or dark brown wood stain.

3 Rest the window on the crosspiece and secure by pilot drilling angled holes through the face of the window frame into the uprights and fixing with 100mm (4in) screws. Tie branches that block the window back with string and hide the mount by pulling foliage in front of it. Any branches that obscure the glass and are too big to tie back, prune with loppers. After installing the window, the hedge will need a few months to grow around it completely. To encourage this process, water and feed during the growing season, clipping when necessary.

entrances

planning for entrances

Opening a gate onto a garden should be a meditative and romantic experience, as you exchange the hurly-burly of outside life for peace and tranquillity. It's an invitation to the most pleasurable of activities: gardening. Although a gate's function is essentially about providing access, it also welcomes, frames the view of the garden beyond and engenders a sense of exploration.

Function and style Access might be the primary reason for designing an entrance in a boundary, but it is not always its most important function. You can place entrances even where they are not needed to separate different areas and thereby create a feeling of space. A cleverly placed gate can lead you on a whole new axis, imparting a sense of direction and mystery to your garden. It can also make areas seem more secluded and secret, enabling you to develop completely separate themes, even in fairly small spaces.

A door can bring a feeling of quality, especially if it's heavy and decorated with ironwork. Whether open or closed, it's a full stop between a front and back garden. Of course, in the broadest sense of the word, an entrance needn't even be a physical doorway, but simply the thinning of a path. Traditional Japanese gardens employ the tactic of creating low arches that not only slow the pace but also make the visitor stoop to enter the next room, demanding your full attention. It's a great device for children's gardens too, for example by using a low door that only they can get through, like a shortcut to Alice's Wonderland. At the opposite end of the scale, extremely large doors can make you feel positively Lilliputian, although the use of outsize doors originates from castle entrances as a device to say, 'we are powerful, don't mess with us!'

Design choices As with all boundaries, first decide whether you want it to be see-through or to act as a screen, hiding the garden beyond. See-through entrances such as ironwork gates and picket, are diverting to the eye and create a picture, while still defending the garden on the other side. They must be used with care, however,

A gate within a door.

Heavy iron studs.

Plain picket gate.

Arrowhead/French gothic picket.

A gate such as the bar and brace (top left), is the obvious way to demarcate an entrance, but there are other techniques, too. A choice of bamboo screening (top right) can signal a change of pace or theme, while tall brick piers (above) make for a dramatic and imposing entrance, even when the access is open.

A rusty gate placed among the flowery borders of a cottage garden is suggestive of a boundary long overgrown and smothered in blooms.

as you don't want them overlooking a patio or seating area, where you want privacy. More enclosing are solid gates, but even these can have peepholes or windows built in to lighten their heavy feel.

The type of gate you choose should be dictated by the adjacent boundary. Brick and stone walls suit heavy, decorated wooden or wrought-iron doors, because the quality of the materials complements their surround. They are old materials and designs that have been used since time immemorial. You can get this look even with a fence by bolstering the density of the boundary with trellis and classic roses and ivy to give the whole structure more weight.

To make an entrance as dramatic as possible, you need to embellish the surrounds. Traditional treatments include abundant planting, particularly scented flowers which bombard your senses as you slow to open the gate. Good plants include winter-flowering *Viburnum farreri* and sweet box (*Sarcococca*) and swags of summer roses and jasmine (*Jasminum*) which can be trained into a fragrant frame for the doorway.

If you're making a gate in a timber fence, it's appropriate to make it in a similar wood and pick out details in the boundary. To prevent the gate from being camouflaged it must be distinguished in some way. For example, in a picket fence make the posts either side slightly larger and prominent with finials and give it a convex or curved top.

You can also use paint effects to highlight the entrance. The right stain can give even cheap pine the look of weathered oak. Hinges, latches, doorsprings and bolts – collectively known as door furniture – all offer opportunity for embellishment and detail. You needn't just go for the basic type, there are many different finishes and the shapes range from elaborate fleur-de-lys designs and beaten ironwork to stainless steel. The size of furniture you choose may be in scale with the doorway or outsize to give the illusion of salvage. The furniture relates to how you want the gate to work. You don't want the best side stuck against the wall if it is going to spend most of its life ajar. Also give some consideration to the direction it's going to open – which side should you have the hinges on, so it opens in the most convenient direction.

The materials you use in the gate can take their influence from the surrounding landscape. This works very well in woodland gardens where branches from the trees are used in the construction.

A see-through gate allows glimpses of the garden beyond and, as such, the materials used in its manufacture must link with those visible through its louvres. For example, behind a modern metal gate (above left) you would expect to find metal planters, water features or steel grid paving, linking the view to what is in the garden. What lies behind a solid gate is a secret, unless it is propped ajar (above right) as an invitation to enter.

Beech arch.

Cottage-garden gate.

Vine-covered gate.

Flowery tunnel.

timber DOOR

An imposing wooden door decorated with ornamental studs and hinges is the most grand and aristocratic of garden entrances. When closed, the robust façade creates an air of impregnability, suggesting that whatever is on the other side must be worth seeing. The click of the latch and the pleasing swing as the weighty door arcs open, tempts you through to discover the secret garden beyond.

MATERIALS

Seven oak planks from cut down railway sleepers (or timber) 22mm (⅞in) thick, 240mm (9½in) wide and at least the height of the door

Thirty-two 40mm (1½in) brass screws

Ninety-six 40mm (1½in) decorative nails

Twelve 75mm (3in) decorative nails

Five large decorative iron hinges

Fleur-de-lys butterfly latch

TOOLS

Carpentry tools

Plane

Sander

Hammer

Router

Circular saw

1 | Cut the planks to the height you want the door and then cut them to width using a circular saw fitted with a 'fence' (a guide bar that ensures that cuts are straight). How wide the planks are depends on the width of the door, and a little maths is necessary to get this right as they aren't of equal width. When put together, all four have to be 3–4mm (⅛in) smaller than the width of the opening, but the two central planks need to be 20mm (¾in) narrower than the edge planks. This ensures that the cover strips (see step 3) that are fixed over the joints between the planks are evenly spaced. To get this right, cut a strip of timber that's the width of the opening and mark the position of each plank and cover strip to ensure that their spacing is correct. If you are using reclaimed timber, save the soundest planks for the ledges (see step 2) and check for

I Using a circular saw, cut the planks to the required width. Remove any lumps and bumps with a plane.

2 Evenly space five ledges to the back of the door and secure them to the planks with brass screws.

KNOW YOUR MATERIALS

The oak planks used for this door were once tar-covered railway sleepers, bolted to tracks and pummelled by passing trains. Despite this ignominious past, the oak (which was used before pine became ubiquitous) looks as good as if it was cut for the purpose. The only tell-tale sign is the odd bolt-hole where the rails were once secured to the sleepers. Cut-down sleepers are available from salvage yards. Always buy decorative nails and door furniture that have been coated with rustproof paint. This stops corrosion and prevents tannins in the oak reacting with the iron, which would cause grey stains to appear on the face of the door.

straightness. Use a plane where necessary to remove any lumps and bumps.

2 The ledges, which are fixed to the back of the door, hold the door together. Their length is the same width as the door and they can be any width, although to look more in scale, they should be 20–30mm (¾–1in) thinner than the planks used for the face of the door and have their edges rounded with a sander.

To create an ancient heavy look, evenly space five ledges on the back of the door leaving a slightly larger gap between the bottom of the door and the first ledge. Secure them with two brass screws in each plank (always pilot drill and countersink the holes first). Although the brass looks bright, it won't take long before it weathers down to the colour of oak.

3 The cover strips are made by cutting a plank down into 45mm (1¾in) strips with a circular saw. You need three to cover the joints on the face of the door and enough to make a surround for the door's edge. Clamp each strip to a work bench and, using a router, cut a C-shaped bevel along both edges of the three central cover strips. Then bevel one side of the two longest edging strips leaving the top and bottom strip as they are.

4 Lay the top strip in position on the face of the door and check that it is square, then fix with evenly spaced 40mm (1½in) decorative nails (in this project four were used). Always drill a pilot hole for the nails first, otherwise the wood will split.

5 Cut the central cover strips to length (they should be the height of the door minus the width of the top and bottom strips). Support the door on timber battens and butt the cover strips against the top edge strip and fix with 75mm (3in) decorative nails driven through the gaps and through the ledges. Flip the door over and bend the centimetre (half inch) of nail that protrudes through the door with a hammer.

3 Clamp each cover strip to a work bench and use a router to cut a C-shaped bevel along both edges of the three central strips.

4 Put the top edge strip in position and check that is it square before fixing to the planks with evenly spaced decorative nails.

5 Having cut the central cover strips to length, butt them against the top edge strip and fix with decorative nails.

As the nails are hammered over, the cover strips are pulled tightly into the door. Then flip the door back over and fit the edge strips with their bevelled corner facing towards the centre of the door and finally the strip along the bottom of the door. Pilot drill all nail holes before hammering.

6 Make a cardboard template to locate the positions of the decorative nails between the cover strips and over the ledges. Pilot drill holes through the template before hammering home the 40mm (1½in) nails.

7 On old doors, the hinges are always set beneath the ledges. To enhance the olde worlde look use five, one screwed beneath each ledge. Another design option is to use two sizes of hinges with three 300mm (12in) hinges in the middle and two 450mm (18in) hinges at the top and bottom of the door. Doing this gives the door a brawny appearance much the same as the hinges of a treasure chest.

8 Position the door in the opening and prop it on wooden wedges while you screw the hinges to the frame. Any sides that stick can be sanded down once the door is hung. Finally, fit the butterfly latch to the door and the catch on the frame.

Alternative materials and designs

The feel and appearance of oak is hard to match but if you want to save money, you can get pretty close to it with pine. If you use pine, once the door has been built give it a coat of oak-effect wood stain to darken it down and to protect it from the weather.

No matter what timber you use, if it is to look in keeping, an 'antique' door must be set into an appropriate opening, like the brick piers used here. If you have only fences, it would work if you disguised the edges with ivy or heavy trellis. Alternatively, cut an opening in a hedge.

When hammering nails home, support the underside of the door with a brick to soak up the vibration.

6 Make a cardboard template to position decorative nails between the cover strips and over the ledges.

7 Set large decorative iron hinges, coated in rustproof paint to prevent corrosion, beneath each ledge.

8 Position the door in the opening and prop it up on wooden wedges while you screw the hinges to the frame.

rustic GATE

Touching the bark of trees never fails to send a tingle through my fingers, and that's part of the appeal of this birch gate. The natural materials and homespun, yeoman style perfectly capture the spirit of the garden with its silver birch and the clouds of wild herbs that surround it. Where an off-the-peg gate could easily jar in such a natural setting, its pale pickets look as if they have swung in the dappled shade for years.

1 Gates are susceptible to wear and tear, and because of this it is important to have a sturdy frame. To make the frame, cut two lengths 50 x 50mm (2 x 2in) timber to the width of the opening less 5mm (⅕in) to allow the gate to open. Cut another two lengths to make the uprights (in this project they were 750mm/30in) and cut half-lap joints in the ends of the timber by sawing and chiselling halfway through the timbers where they meet (for details see page 280) and screw together. As an alternative to half-lap joints you can use L-shaped metal brackets to hold the corners together.

2 Make the X-shaped brace for the centre of the gate by laying two lengths of 50 x 50mm (2 x 2in) timber diagonally across the frame and marking where they meet the inside edge. Cut at this point and check that each length fits snugly into the frame. Join them

MATERIALS

5m (16ft) of 50 x 50mm (2 x 2in) rough sawn treated timber

50mm (2in) screws

Birch poles or similar branches in diameters of 20–50mm (¾–2in)

L-shaped metal brackets (optional)

Hinges and latch

TOOLS

Wood saw

Drill and pilot bit

Chisel and mallet

Garden loppers

1 Having worked out the measurements of the frame, cut the timber to the required lengths and screw the pieces together.

2 Next make the X-shaped brace for the centre of the gate. Cut two lengths of timber and mark where they meet the inside edge.

KNOW YOUR MATERIALS

Of course, birch isn't the only timber suitable for a rustic garden gate; any wood that looks appropriate in the setting will work. Hazel, beech, sycamore and even conifer branches (with leaves removed) are all in keeping, more so if they are prunings from trees that grow in your own garden. If you want to create the effect of white birch bark, there are wood stains available in silver birch colours, which protect the timber too. Birch is a very soft wood, but you can overcome its susceptibility to rot by keeping it out of contact with the soil and giving it the occasional coat of linseed oil or wood preservative.

3 Work out the spacing of the birch lengths and screw them in place. Use a saw or garden loppers to cut off the top.

together by marking where they cross and saw halfway through the timber at this point. Remove the timber between the cuts with a chisel. As an easier alternative, it is perfectly acceptable, although less attractive, to use just one brace. Ensure that it runs diagonally up from the hinge side of the gate to give maximum support to the frame.

3 Lay the lengths of birch onto the frame and when you're happy with their spacing, pilot drill and screw in place. It's a good idea to prop the gate in position as a visual aid when you are deciding the most appropriate height for the tops before marking and cutting the birch to length. In this project the tops were cut with a domed top that arched above the frame by 75–150mm (3–6in) to highlight the position of the gate, but a staggered top would look just as good. You can use a saw or garden loppers to do this. Fit hinges and a latch to the frame and hang in position.

index

Credits and supplier information

The publisher and photographer would like to thank the following for permission to take photographs of their gardens and water features for Part 1 of this book:

Susan and Alastair Alexander: p127 (designer: Mark Braniff)

Sue and Alastair Brown: p65 (designer: Kate Dix at Plum Garden Designs)

Mr and Mrs Chambers, Kiftsgate Court, Gloucestershire (National Garden Scheme): pp8-9; p30 far left; 31 below (designer: Simon Allison)

Ian Clien: p123

Fairhaven Garden Trust, Norfolk (open to the public): p53 below

Monique and David Gregson, 2Fish Gallery, Diss, Norfolk: p21; p54; p76

Ian Griffiths: p35

The Hannah Pechar Sculpture Garden: p30 far right (landscape designer: Antony Paul); p33 below far left (landscape designer: Antony Paul); p53 above right (landscape designer: Antony Paul); p74 far left ((landscape designer: Antony Paul); p77 above left (landscape designer: Antony Paul); p98 (Swaylines, designer: Andrew Ewing); p99 above right (Water Sculpture, designer: Ben Barnell); p99 below centre left (designer:Tzubai); p119 below (Pebble, designer: Jean Lowe)

Catherine Heatherington (designer): p79

Catherine Horwood (NGS): p121

Chris Knows: p118 far left

Elizabeth Mactyrue-Brown, Hertfordshire: p75 below (designer: Richard Key)

Johann and Gail Meeke: p113

Mickfield Water Garden Centre, Mickfield, near Stowmarket, Suffolk (for allowing us to take various photographs of water plants, fish and other products)

Rousham, Oxfordshire (open to the public): p52 far right

RHS Chelsea Flower Show 2001: p23 centre left, p33 above left and p55 above left (A Real Japanese Garden, The Daily Telegraph); p30 centre right; p31 above right (Laurent-Perrier/Harpers and Queen, designer: Tom Stuart-Smith); p32, p53 above left and p97 above right (London Borough of Barnet Skills Training Centre, designer: Frank Gardener); p33 above right (Blue Circle Garden, designers: Carole Vincent and Jill Mellor); p33 below centre left (Brinsbury College); p33 below centre right and below far right; p52 far left (designer: Brian Alabaster); p55 below far right; p74 centre left; p75 above right and p77 below centre left (The Curc Garden, designer: Andy Sturgeon); p77 above right (City Space, designer: Mark Antony Walker); p77 below centre right (designer: Simon Percival); p96 far left, centre left and far right; p96 centre right and p119 above left (designers: Stoltzman and Thomas); p97 above left; p99 above left; p118 far right

RHS Hampton Court Flower Show 2001: p10; p11 below left; p11 below right (Cherry Burton Garden Design); p12 below left and above right; p13 (The Tree of Knowledge, Richmond Adult Community College); p20; pp28-30 (Eastern Promise Dorset Water Lily Company); p47 (A Swimming Pool, Anglo Aquarium Plant Company, designer: David Lloyd Morgan); pp50-2 and p77 below far left (P&O Cruises Tropical experience, designer: Jane Mooney); p52 centre left (Vivid Space Design); p52 centre right (The Paradise Garden, designer: Elizabeth Apedaile); p55 above right, below far left, below centre left and below centre right; pp72-3 (An English Garden Designer in France, designer: P Dyer); p74 centre right and far right; p75 above left (Urban Chic, Mitsubishi); pp94-5, p99 below centre right and p119 above right (2001 A Garden Odyssey, Farrscape Design); p97 below; p99 below far left and below far right; pp116-7 (The Princess and the Frog, Shani Lawrence Garden Designs); p118 centre left and centre right

Shaun and Pauline Stringer: p57, p125

Writtle College: p22 below left; p23 below left and above right; p39; p46; p61; p69; p83; p87; p91; p101; p105; p109

Yarnton Nurseries, Oxon: p22 above right

The publisher and the stylist would like to thank the following for their kind assistance in supplying materials and decorative items:

The authors recommend the use of OASE pumps, filters and liners when building any garden water feature. For information on the availability of OASE products contact: OASE (UK) Ltd. 01264 333 225, www.oase-pumpen.com

Brian Duffy, Duffy Glass, glass cube p104

CED Ltd, 01708 867 237, sales@ced.ltd.uk: York stone copings p34; porphyry paving p38; slate chippings and marble cobbles p42; various sandstone rocks and beach pebbles p68; slate paddle stones p86; slate coping stones p100; grotto rock p108

Clifton Nurseries, 5A Clifton Villas, Little Venice, London W9 2PH, 020 7289 6851, e-mail@clifton.co.uk, www.clifton.co.uk: ferns, ivy, bamboo and topiary p69, p83, p101

Elephant, 020 7637 7930

Cvo Firevault, www.cvofirevault.co.uk

Gardens & Beyond, wooden loungers pp57, p65 and p123

Granite connection, 01773 533 090, sales@graniteconnection.co.uk: granite bowl (granite connection) p82; granite wheels (granite connection) p90

Green Door, Helen Dewolfe, contemporary basin p112

Habitat, 0844 499 4686, www.habitat.net: glass jug and glasses on table p113

The Holding Company, 020 8445 2888, www.theholdingcompany.co.uk

Ironage Developments Ltd, wet and dry pool p38; copper sheeting p56; steel sides p60; stainless steel p64; steel chute p78; steel rill p82

Jungle Giants, 01584 856 200, bamboo@junglegiants.co.uk: bamboo cascade p86

The Lacquer Chest, 75 Kensington Church Street, London W8 4BG, 020 7937 1306: metal table and chair p101

Lassco, www.lassco.co.uk: Medusa fountain head p100

Lloyd Christie, 020 8332 2229, info@lloydchristie.com, www.lloydchristie.com: metal lounger p39

The Old Bake House, pebble cascade p120; spherical fountain p122; ceramic pool p124

The Pier, lantern p57; urn p101

Rawlinson Garden Products Ltd, 01829 261 121, www.rowgar.co.uk: softwood sleepers p58

S.B Evans & Son, 020 7729 6635, evans@thecitygardenpottery.co.uk: tiered cascade p126

Tropical Surrounds, bamboo, willow and heather screening

The publisher and photographer would like to thank the following for permission to take photographs of their gardens for Part 2 of this book:
(NGS: indicates a garden is open under the National Garden Scheme.)

The Belfry Hotel, Thame, p237

Sue and Jeff Brown, Adderbury, (designers: Jonathan and Amanda Ford) p136; p137 top left, bottom middle; p196 far left; p232 middle right; p235 top left

Mr and Mrs Coote, Headington, pp162-3; p164 middle right; p235 bottom far left

Mr and Mrs Evans, Bath, pp194-5; pp208-9; pp230-1

Jeff and Emma Follas Decorative Landscaping, Fakenham, p167 top right; p233 bottom; p249

Amanda Foster, London, pp130-1; p210 far right

Capel Manor, Enfield, 08456 122 122, p167 bottom middle right and far right; p175 (Gardening Which Gardens); p199 bottom middle right; p235 bottom middle right

Honor Gibbs, EDA Design Associates, Long Credon, p223

Heale House and Plant Centre, Middle Woodford (open to the public) p210 middle right; p212; p213 bottom middle right

Mr and Mrs Hollingbery, Alresford (NGS), p132; p211 top right; p213 bottom middle left

Mr and Mrs Huntingdon, Sudborough (NGS), p165 bottom; p197 bottom

Claire and Nigel Jinks, Thurlaston, p205, p253

Mr and Mrs Key, Fawler, p241

Mrs Rani Lall, Oxford, (NGS), p166; p199 top right; p213 top left; p233 top left

Mr and Mrs Morrison, Turweston, p191

Fiona and John Owens, Chalford, p211 top left

Tony Poulton, Worcester (NGS), p213 bottom far right

RHS Chelsea Flower Show, p137 top right; p164 far left, far right; p165 top left (designer: Stephen Woodhams); p167 bottom far left; p199 bottom middle left; p213 top right

RHS Hampton Court Flower Show, p137 bottom right; p164 middle left; p165 top right (designers: Isabelle Van Groeningen and Gabriella Pape, You magazine); p167 top left (designer: World of Water); p196 middle left, middle right and far right; p73 top left (designer: Charlotte Ashburner, The Millennium Revolution) and top right; p199 top left (designer: You magazine), bottom far left and far right; p210 far left, middle left, middle left and far right; p235 bottom middle left

Mr and Mrs Royle, Balscote (NGS), p211 bottom

Mr and Mrs Sharp, Haddenham, p227, p136

Mr and Mrs Sidaway, Twickenham (NGS), p233 top right; p235 top right

Benjamin Smith Landscape Architect, Litchborough (NGS), 01327 830 144, p234

Diana Yakeley, Yakely Associates, London (NGS), p219

Yarnton Nurseries, Yarnton, p138 bottom right

York Gate, Adel Nr Leeds (open to the public); Gardeners' Royal Benevolent Society, Leatherhead, 01372 373 962, p183

The publisher and photographer would like to thank the following for permission to take photographs of their gardens for Part 3 of this book:
(NGS: indicates a garden is open under the National Garden Scheme.)

Broadlands Garden, Dorset p262

The Burystead Courtyard Garden, Sutton, Cambs p332-3

Cambridge University Botanic Garden p254-5, p356 bottom left, p357 top right, p359 bottom 3rd from left

Capel Manor Gardens, Enfield p264 bottom left

John Drake, Fen Ditton, Cambs p356 bottom 3rd from left, p358 top

Bob and Sue Foulser, Cerne Abbas, Dorset p369 bottom

Marlas Greiger, Howell, Michigan, USA p370

Hookwood farmhouse, West Horsley, Surrey p263 top right, p366-7, p371 bottom left

Robinson College, Cambridge p260-1, p265 top centre, p356 bottom right, p357 bottom

Trinity College, Cambridge p359 top right, p359 bottom right

The Walnuts, Kings Cliffe, Northants p265 bottom right, p293 top left, p293 top right

The publisher would like to thank the following for the use of their photography on the chapter openers:

Ian Hofstetter, p6 (top left)

Tony Lyon, p7, 258 (top left) 259

Howard Rice, p258 (bottom left, right)

Lorna Rose, p6 (right)

Mark Winwood, p259 (top left)

Murdoch Books Picture Library, p128 (left)

Sue Stubbs, p6 (bottom left),

Juliette Wade, p128 (right), 129

Author biographies

Chris Maton and Mark Edwards

The authors, Chris Maton and Mark Edwards, once ran a landscape design and construction company together in London, working in many sectors of the landscape industry. Their innovative designs were featured in many lifestyle and garden magazines. They won a gold medal at the widely acclaimed Chelsea Flower Show and regularly designed show gardens for clients at the Hampton Court Flower Show. They have since parted ways and established separate companies; Chris Maton opened Olivebay and Edwards established Musa Works with his wife, Clare. Both Maton and Edwards are experienced lecturers in their field and have also worked as presenters for television.

Chris Maton can be contacted at Olivebay, www.olivebay.co.uk, 0208 275 7878 or gardens@olivebay.co.uk.

Mark Edwards can be contacted at Musa Works, www.musaworks.com, 01277 235 400 or enquiries@musaworks.com.

Richard Key

Author of several successful garden design and practical construction books, Richard Key is an experienced landscape designer who also lectures in landscape construction and design. He has won medals at the Chelsea and Hampton Court Flower shows and designed two feature gardens for the BBC Gardens by Design series. He also runs his own landscape practice, Richard Key Landscape and Garden Design. Richard was elected a Fellow of the Society of Garden Designers in 2001, he was also previously the Vice Chairman and Treasurer.

The author can be contacted at Richard Key Landscape and Garden Design, www.richardkey.co.uk, 01844 261 481 or 07710 159004.

Toby Buckland

Toby Buckland is a horticulturalist and garden designer with a wealth of literary experience. He writes for the Daily Express and is a regular contributor to Carol Vorderman's Better Homes and Gardens programme, BBC's Garden Magic and Granada Breeze's Cook's Gardens. He is also well-known as the presenter for the BBC's Gardeners' World from 2008-10. In 2008 Toby won the RHS and Best in Show for his Ethical Garden at Gardeners' World Live. In 2009 he won the Environmental Award from the Garden Media Guild, and in 2011 he launched Toby Buckland Nurseries, an online plant nursery.

The author can be contacted at Toby Buckland Nurseries, www.tobybuckland.com, 01626 867013 or info@tobybuckland.com.

Published in 2012 by Murdoch Books Pty Limited
First published in 2001.

Murdoch Books Australia
Pier 8/9
23 Hickson Road
Millers Point NSW 2000
Phone: +61 (0) 2 8220 2000
Fax: +61 (0) 2 8220 2558
www.murdochbooks.com.au
info@murdochbooks.com.au

Murdoch Books UK Limited
Erico House, 6th Floor
93–99 Upper Richmond Road
Putney, London SW15 2TG
Phone: +44 (0) 20 8785 5995
Fax: +44 (0) 20 8785 5985
www.murdochbooks.co.uk
info@murdochbooks.co.uk

For Corporate Orders & Custom Publishing contact Noel Hammond,
National Business Development Manager Murdoch Books Australia

Publisher: Paul Mitchell
Project Editor: Kit Carstairs
Editors: Claire Musters, Alastair Laing, Selena Mumford and Dawn Henderson
Photographers: Juliette Wade and Howard Rice
Stylist: Stephanie Bateman
Illustrator: Nicola Gregory
Production: Alex Gonzalez

Text © Murdoch Books 2012
The moral right of the author has been asserted.
Design © Murdoch Books Pty Limited 2012
Cover photography credits go to Howard Rice (front right and back middle),
Lorna Rose (front left and back right) and Juliette Wade (front middle and back left)

All rights reserved. No part of this publication may be reproduced, stored in a retrieval
system or transmitted in any form or by any means, electronic, mechanical, photocopying,
recording or otherwise, without the prior written permission of the publisher.

National Library of Australia Cataloguing-in-Publication entry
Chris Maton ... [et al.].
Garden DIY ISBN 9781742667911 (hbk.)
Includes index.
Gardening—Amateurs' manuals.
Other Authors/Contributors: Maton, Chris.
635

A catalogue record for this book is available from the British Library.

Printed by Hang Tai Printing Company Ltd.

Readers of this book must ensure that any work or project undertaken complies with local
legislative and approval requirements relevant to their particular circumstances. Furthermore,
this work is necessarily of a general nature and cannot be a substitute for appropriate
professional advice.